A
DICTIONARY
OF
SYMPTOMS

A DICTIONARY OF SYMPTOMS

A medical dictionary to help sufferers,
by easier self-diagnosis, to eliminate
groundless fears and know when to
consult their doctor

by
Dr. JOAN GOMEZ
Edited and with an Introduction by
Dr. MARVIN J. GERSH

STEIN AND DAY/Publishers/New York

ACKNOWLEDGMENTS

I am most grateful to those leaders in the various fields of medicine who have so carefully and kindly assisted and collaborated with me by their suggestions, corrections and encouragement:

A. G. Amias, F.R.C.S., M.R.C.O.G., Consulting Obstetrician and Gynecologist to St. George's Hospital.

K. M. Citron, M.D., M.R.C.P., Asst. Physician to Brompton Hospital.

R. G. Counihan, M.B., B.CH., B.A.O., D.R.C.O.G., General Practitioner.

A. W. Frankland, D.M., Physician to Clinic for Allergic Disorders, St. Mary's Hospital; Director: Allergy Dept., Wright-Fleming Inst. of Microbiology, St. Mary's Hospital.

P. R. French, F.R.C.S., Orthopedic Surgeon to St. George's Hospital.

Trevor Howell, F.R.C.P.E., Physician to Geriatric Research Unit, St. John's Hospital.

M. I. A. Hunter, M.D., F.R.C.P., Physician to Cardiological Dept., St. George's Hospital, Dean of the Medical School, St. George's Hospital.

R. L. Moody, M.B., D.P.M., Physician i/c Dept. of Child Psychiatry, St. George's Hospital.

J. N. O'Reilly, D.M., M.R.C.P., Pediatrician to Queen Elizabeth Hospital, St. Helier Hospital, and S.S. John and Elizabeth Hospital.

B. H. Pickard, F.R.C.S., Ear, Nose, and Throat Surgeon to St. George's Hospital, Atkinson Morley Hospital, and Moorfield's Eye Hospital.

E. W. Prosser Thomas, M.D., Dermatologist to St. Helier Hospital.

B. W. Wells, T.D., M.S., F.R.C.S., Surgeon, Nelson Hospital.

My thanks are due, too, to my publisher and printer for their unfailing courtesy and consideration; and, of course, to my dear husband who has spared time from his own busy practice and research commitments to help me; and to our children, without whom none of it would have been worthwhile.

INTRODUCTION

AMONG THE afflictions of human nature that help to keep a doctor's practice from being perfect, probably the most widely spread malady is the one that impels patients to corner the doctor for consultation in the midst of a cocktail party. Ducking this kind of encounter is something at which every physician learns to become more or less adroit. But just as troublesome to a doctor can be a patient's self-diagnosis, made through careful attention to what diseases, new or old, are being examined in the current issues of popular magazines, and what symptoms, acute or chronic, are described in various home-remedy guides.

(Even before such popularized medicine came along, of course, there were doctors who took umbrage at the self-informed patient. There is a story about Dr. Oliver Wendell Holmes coming upon a patient of his one day in the library. Noting that the man was absorbed in a medical text, Dr. Holmes tapped him on the shoulder, leaned over and whispered, "Prithee, sir, be careful—thou may some day die of a misprint.")

A Dictionary of Symptoms, by Dr. Joan Gomez, is something different at last: a book that will be a boon to the patient without being a bane to the doctor. Dr. Gomez, an Englishwoman with a busy general practice in suburban London, and the mother of ten children who range in age from three to 19, has written a pithy medical source book in a no-nonsense style that bears the imprint of her long personal experience.

What will the reader, who thinks he's got something wrong with him but isn't sure *what,* find within these pages? Any number of answers to what could be wrong—what could be causing practically any symptom he has or has conjured up. Dr. Gomez' book gives a clinician's appraisal of the possibilities.

Unless you're a hypochondriac anyway, the idea of reading about various illnesses that could have befallen you may seem frightening. But in my own medical experience I have never found a patient who was not in some sense relieved by realistic possibilities—no matter how grave—after having lived through the anxiety of not knowing. It is better to face any demon directly than to imagine his form and shape in the shadows.

In my student days I proceeded to imagine for myself a series of diseases encountered successively in one course after another: I first suffered from gallstones, went on to a duodenal ulcer, suspected emphysema, and graduated with a sophisticated, if less menacing, case of lupus erythematsous. For those of you not fortunate enough to be medical students but who do enjoy your own feelings of morbidity, Dr. Gomez' book might be subtitled, "The Intelligent Layman's Guide to Selective Hypochondriasis."

The book won't turn you into a hypochondriac, but if you are one already, it will make you a more *interesting* one. How much more attentive your listeners will be when you say, "I've got chronic rhinorrhea," rather than losing your audience with, "My nose runs all the time."

The general two-culture problem of science and the layman pointed up by C. P. Snow is nowhere more apparent than in the crisis of confidence, the general disenchantment, that the public has been feeling for the medical profession. *A Dictionary of Symptoms* may help bridge the abyss between doctors and their patients by enabling you, as the potential patient, to cross over and have a look at what goes on in your doctor's head when you confront him with a symptom. From what you tell him, he has to make a differential diagnosis; often, the wider his knowledge, the greater number of possibilities he must take into account. (That's what all those tests are about.)

An informed person can be of real help to a physician. I remember one instance of caring for a child who had been running a high fever for two weeks. Every test to try finding the source of this fever was unrevealing. But the mother suddenly remembered that the child had had fleeting pains in his legs and asked me if it could be rheumatic fever. It was her suggestion that started me in the right direction: the boy turned out to have, not rheumatic fever, but rheumatoid arthritis—an enormously difficult problem to diagnose unless obvious joint symptoms are present.

In yet another sense, *A Dictionary of Symptoms* can be a help to both you and your physician. Once upon a time, a doctor could satisfy his patient by saying, for example, "You have chest trouble," or "The trouble is in your head." The modern patient wants and needs to know more, but an overworked physician may not sufficiently explain the nature of the illness. Dr. Gomez does—in explanations that are short, to the point, and easy to understand.

A Dictionary of Symptoms can also be fun. I myself like to browse through ordinary dictionaries, picking up a new word now and then that will add spice to my conversation. How about picking up "ephelis ab igne"—more commonly called "Granny's tartan"? You'll find that bit of medical esoterica readily under the skin section. The book is sensibly set up in such a way that you'll have no trouble finding the possible sources of your symptoms or gaining some knowledge of the maladies that can afflict any one particular area: the back, say, or the abdomen.

I am confident that Dr. Joan Gomez' admirable work, complete in its coverage from birth pangs to the pains of old age, is a book for all seasons.

Briarcliff, New York   MARVIN J. GERSH, M.D.
1968

CONTENTS

PART II. ANALYSIS OF SYMPTOMS

Special Sections

ABOUT THIS BOOK

Its purpose

To give to the ordinary, intelligent man or woman a basis of knowledge and understanding of the functioning of his body; to outline what is not always realized to be normal; to enable him to discover easily and quickly, from his own sensations and observation of himself, the probable cause of any symptom, abnormality or irregularity in his health; to suggest what action he should take; to allay unnecessary anxiety; to indicate clearly those times when advice should be sought, particularly when early treatment is valuable although the symptoms appear trivial; to answer some of the simple questions one may feel reluctant to ask a busy doctor; and to help the reader to cooperate fully with his family doctor for the benefit of them both.

How to use it

The book is divided into two parts:

PART I: TABLE OF SYMPTOMS

These are arranged alphabetically within sections for each part of the body, with page references to the detailed accounts in Part II. There are also sections devoted to conditions particularly affecting babies, older children, adolescents, men, and women.

Sections of the list of symptoms:

Head and Neck	Lower extremities
Skin	Back
Chest	Whole body
Abdomen	Childhood
Ano-rectal region	Growing up
Urinary system	Men only
Upper extremities	Women only

The General Section comprises those symptoms which cannot readily be assigned to one area of the body.

PART II: ANALYSIS OF SYMPTOMS

Divided into sections under the same headings as Part I, and including a glossary of medical terms and an index.

The symptom or irregularity causing concern should first be found in the Table of Symptoms, and then looked up by the page references to Part II. The references to pain in the chest, for in-

stance, listed under Chest in the Table of Symptoms, are to pages
121 to 123 in Part II. In many cases more than one symptom will
be present: looking up each one increases the accuracy of assessment of the probable cause.

The questions this book aims to help you answer

What condition is likely to be the cause of what I have noticed?
Should I call the doctor?
Need I see the doctor at all at present?
Ought I go to bed, rest, or stay indoors?
What is the treatment likely to be? What can I do for myself?
Is this likely to be an infectious condition?
How long is it likely to last?
What can I do to avoid this trouble in the future?

Wherever possible, the brief answers are coded in brackets be-
side the heading of each symptom or disorder; the key is printed on
page 14, at the end of Part I. In many cases the significance of a
symptom varies according to whether it is of recent onset, or has
been present over a long period. The discussion of such symptoms
begins with their separation into Acute: present for less than two
weeks; and Chronic: present for more than six weeks. This is also
recorded in the coding. Symptoms present for intermediate periods
must be considered as under both heads.

Index

Further information about many symptoms or disorders may be
found in other sections by referring to the Index at the back of
the book.

Glossary

Although technical language has been avoided as much as possible, there is appended a list of some of the terms which may not
be fully understood by the non-medical reader.

Completeness has been attempted in outline, but common and
important conditions, such as sore throat and high blood pressure,
and broad subjects like adolescence, have been allotted more space
than the rare diseases.

It has been my endeavor to produce something of service to you
when a health problem arises, whether you are a man or a woman,
just growing up or fifty plus, or a parent worried about your child.

J. G.

Part I—Table of Symptoms

SYMPTOMS OF THE HEAD AND NECK

Symptoms of the Head

Ache, headache, 16–22, 326–7
Baldness, 28–30
Big head, 20–21
Bleeding from scalp, 24–25
Concussion, 25–26
Cradle cap, 314
Dandruff, 27
Dizziness, 22–23
Fainting, 23–24
Falling, 23, 285
Falling hair, 28–30
Flaking of the scalp, 28
Giddiness, 22–23
Gray hair, 31
Hangover, 19
Injury, 24–26
Itching, 28
Lice, 28
Lump on head, 26–27
Sick headache, 17
White hair, 31

Symptoms of the Face
(See also Sections on Skin, Eyes, Nose, and Mouth)

Aching in cheek bones, 47–48, 327
Acne, 33–34, 100–1
Altered color, 32–33
Blackheads, 34, 100–1
Blemishes, 34, 100–1
Blushing, 33
Cauliflower nose, 33
Chapping of lip, 39
Clenched teeth, 37
Cold sore, 38
Cracked lips, 39
Flushing, 33
Habit spasm, 36, 345
High color, 32
Hot flushes, 34
Ingrowing hair, 35
Lockjaw, 37
Lump on face, 35
Oiliness, 100
Pain, 37
Pallor, 32, 33
Paralysis, 38
Red face, 32, 33
Red nose, 33
Sore dry lips, 39
Sore on lip, 39
Spots, 34, 35
Swelling, 35
Tics, 36
Twitching, 35–36
Weakness, 38
White patches on lips, 39
Yellow complexion, 33

Symptoms of the Nose

Allergy, 46–47, 270–2
Bleeding, 41–42
Catarrh, 44–45
Cold, 43–44, 322–4, 336
Deformity, 40–41
Discharge, 43–44
Hay fever, 46
Odd shape, 40–41
Red nose, 33, 36
Runny nose, 43–44
Sneezing, 42–43
Snoring, 42, 317

Symptoms of the Mouth

Bad breath, 52–53
Bad taste, 53
Black tongue, 55
Bluish tongue, 55

Symptoms of the Mouth (cont.)

Symptoms of the Eye

Symptoms of the Ear

Symptoms of the Throat and Neck

SYMPTOMS OF THE SKIN
(See also Sections on Face, Head, Nose, Eyes, Legs and Feet)

SYMPTOMS OF THE SKIN (cont.)

SYMPTOMS OF THE CHEST

SYMPTOMS OF THE ABDOMEN

Gas, see Flatulence.
Heartburn, 169
Hiccup, 168–9
Indigestion, 171–2
Internal parasites, 195
Jaundice, 177
Loss of weight, 165, 279–80, 342–3
Lump in groin, 187
Nausea, 166–7
Pain in abdomen, 165–6, 181–5
Pain in stomach, 165–6

Rupture, 172, 186–7
Sickness, see Vomiting.
Stomach ache, 165–6, 181–5
Swelling, 185
Tenderness, 181, see Diarrhea, Dysentery.
Unpleasant breath, 52, 165
Vomiting, 166–7
Vomiting blood, 167–8
Wind, see Flatulence.

SYMPTOMS OF THE ANO-RECTAL REGION
(See also Abdominal Section)

Abnormal stools, 187–94, 196–7
Abscess, 201
Ache, 198–203
Alternating diarrhea and constipation, 190
Bad-smelling stool, 197
Black stool, 197
Bleeding, 197
Constipation, 196
Cyst, 201
Diarrhea, 196
Discharge, 199–203
Floating stool, 197
Hard stool, 196

Itching, 93–94
Liquid stool, 196
Lump, 199–202
Pain, 196, 202–3
Pain on passing a stool, 202
Pain on sitting down, 203
Pale stool, 197
Pencil stool, 196
Piles, 198–9
Protrusion, 198
Red stool, 197
Swelling, 199–201
White stool, 197
Worms, 202

SYMPTOMS OF THE URINARY SYSTEM
(See also Men Only Section)

Urinary Effects:
Abnormal odor, 210
Bed-wetting, 346–7
Blood in urine, 210–11
Blue urine, 210
Brown or black urine, 210
Changes in the stream, 209
Cloudy urine, 212
Diminished quantity, 208
Dribbling, 209
Escape of urine during laughter, 210
Foaming urine, 210
Frequent passing of urine, 206–7
Gravel, 213

Green urine, 210
Inability to pass urine, 207–8
Increased amount, 206–7
Milky urine, 210
Pain on passing urine, 208–9
Pale urine, 210
Pink urine, 210
Pus in urine, 212–13
Red urine, 210
Rising at night to pass urine, 207
Smoky urine, 211
Stoppage of flow, 209
Weak stream, 209
Yellow or orange urine, 210

SYMPTOMS OF THE URINARY SYSTEM (cont.)

SYMPTOMS OF THE UPPER EXTREMITIES
(See also Skin Section)

SYMPTOMS OF THE LOWER EXTREMITIES

Symptoms of Hip and Thigh

Symptoms of Knee and Leg

Symptoms of Feet and Ankles
(See also Skin Section)

SYMPTOMS OF THE BACK

SYMPTOMS OF THE BACK (cont.)

SYMPTOMS AFFECTING THE WHOLE BODY

SYMPTOMS OF CHILDHOOD

Part I—The First Year

Part II—Ages 1–13

Part II—Ages 1–13 (cont.)

SYMPTOMS OF GROWING UP

SYMPTOMS OF MEN ONLY
(See also Sections on Urinary System and Growing Up)

SYMPTOMS OF WOMEN ONLY
(See also Sections on Urinary System and Growing Up)

KEY TO SYMBOLS:

A: Acute, lasting less than two weeks.
Ch: Chronic, lasting more than six weeks.
A Ch: Either, or acute may be followed by chronic condition.

Doctor
U: Urgent call to doctor, or get to hospital by ambulance.
S: See your doctor.
SU: See your doctor; urgent.
48: Wait 48 hours. Then, if not better, call or visit doctor.
N: Not necessary to consult doctor unless other symptoms arise.

Treatment
B: Bed rest.
I: Stay indoors, not necessarily in bed.
O: Off work but not in bed.
C: Contagious or infectious. Consider other people.
R: Take more rest.
W: No need to curtail normal activity.
An: Analgesic such as aspirin advisable.

Probable Duration of Condition
1/7: Less than a day.
1: Up to a week.
2: Up to two weeks.
6: Up to six weeks.
6/12: Six months or more.
X: Care required indefinitely.

Part II—Analysis of Symptoms

HEAD AND NECK SECTION

The Head

The head consists essentially of a bony framework, the skull, for the owner's most valuable possession, his brain. The whole purpose of the rest of the body is to protect and serve the head, containing as it does the human computer, the part through which mind and character function, and the communications center, giving and receiving impressions both internally, to and from other parts of the body, and externally.

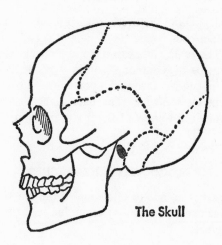

The Skull

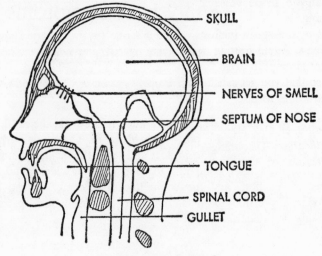

Section through Head

HEADACHE

Called "the silent cry of the overburdened mind," it is the commonest of all human complaints.

Mechanism: The brain, although it can appreciate pain from other parts, is incapable of registering pain in itself. If its coverings are anesthetised, it can be operated upon while the patient is conscious, without his feeling it. The pain of headache comes from the inner or outer coverings of the brain, or from its small blood vessels.

BLOOD VESSEL HEADACHES

The commonest type, due to dilatation of the blood vessels of the brain or its membranes, and frequently due to, or precipitated by, emotional factors.

Simple   [A: N, W or R, 1/7]
Dilatation of the brain arteries, a reflex effect of unpleasant mental activity, such as fear, resentment, anxiety. Comparable with the

well-known blood vessel dilatation caused entirely by emotion—blushing.

Treatment: Aspirin ineffective in this type. Try fresh approach to problems. Avoid fretting over details. Avoid purposeless worrying. Do not attempt to drive yourself on "off days." Modify your standards so that you get satisfaction from what you *can* have, and what you are *able* to do.

Migraine or Sick Headache [A: S, B, An, X, 1/7]

Identification: Throbbing, commonly one side only (migraine is a contraction of Greek *hemicrania:* halfhead), accompanied by nausea, vomiting, and visual disturbances, such as flashes, distortions, or black spots, and occasionally speech difficulties. Often preceded by an odd out-of-sorts feeling the day before.

Often starts in childhood and diminishes in middle age. It has a hereditary link, and is commoner in women, in the intelligent, and the ambitious. See Allergy.

Treatment: Lie down in a darkened room. Effective drugs are available for treatment of acute attacks, and to lessen their frequency in the future.

Outlook: Recurrence likely every few months or, without treatment, as often as twice a week or more.

Histamine Headache   [A: S, An, X]

A variant of migraine, affecting mainly middle-aged men. Typically, comes on at night, accompanied by watery eye and runny nose, and is relieved by sitting or getting up.

Treatment: As for migraine.

OTHER BLOOD VESSEL HEADACHES

Part of a Febrile Illness   [A: B, An]

Such conditions as measles or influenza, anything that causes a fever, usually produces a headache. If you suspect this, take your temperature, and have the infection treated.

High Blood Pressure Headaches   [S,R]

Identification: Dull ache at back of head, may be throbbing, sense

of fullness, often getting better at about noon. Dizziness sometimes accompanies it. *Not common:* far more frequent is a simple headache due to anxiety about the blood pressure.
Treatment: Visit doctor's office for check of blood pressure.

Arteriosclerotic Headaches   [N, R, X]
Identification: Age 60 plus. Unpredictable in time, type, site and duration. Often brought on by awkwardly twisting neck.
Treatment: Short rest. Deliberate calm. There is, in fact, no need to worry.

In Diabetes   [S, R, 1/7]
Headache occurs when blood sugar is too low, and particularly with certain insulins.
Treatment: Take a sugary drink or snack.

TENSION HEADACHE

[A Ch: 48, R, An, 1/7-6]
This type accounts for one third of all headaches. The pain is caused by prolonged contraction of the muscles of the neck and scalp, and is comparable with pain in an overused muscle during running.
Causes: Fear or anxiety creating emotional tension; postural tension, as in a student huddled too long over his books, or a driver staring too long at the road. Occasionally follows a blow on the head.
Identification: Not severe, not throbbing, not accompanied by nausea. Frequently starts at the back of the head and may spread to encircle the whole of it, or concentrate in one part. Tenderness of scalp, forehead, or neck to pressure.
Prevention: Learn a lesson in sensible living and keep within your limits.
Treatment: As of simple blood vessel headache (above) except that it is in this type of headache that aspirin is most effective. Hot packs, heat lamp or massage of neck and scalp also help.

Party Headache: Hangover Headache   [A: N, R, An, 1/7]
Usually a tension headache. Alcohol causes dilatation of the blood vessels, those within the skull as well as those which cause a flushed face, and a headache coming on at a party may be due to that effect.

This action of the alcohol, however, wears off in an hour or two, and even during a party the mental tension caused by the excitement, and the physical tension from the noise, smoke and bright lights are likelier causes of headache.

The "morning after" which only affects some, while others start their day clear-eyed and clear-headed, is dependent upon psychological make-up. One person after drinking or staying up late may have a feeling of guilt or anxiety lest he will "suffer for it," or work less efficiently, or there may be tension-bearing encounters with other people in the morning.

Treatment: As for tension headaches. The rationale of the "hair of the dog," which can be helpful, is that a small dose of alcohol reduces tension.

HEADACHES NOT DUE TO TENSION OR BLOOD VESSEL DILATATION

Less than 3% of all headaches.

Eyestrain Headache   [Ch: S]
Identification: Redness, soreness of eyes. Rarely due to errors of refraction requiring spectacles. Student's headache is likelier to be a postural tension type.
Obtain ophthalmologist's opinion (not optician's).

Glaucoma Headache   [A Ch: SU, R, X]
Rare; only in those over 35.
Hereditary link: others in the family have probably had it.
Identification: Pain starting in eye, and spreading. Eyeball hard to touch. Mistiness of vision and rainbow rings round distant objects may occur. Pain can be excruciating in acute attacks, but if the condition is chronic, the pain is a dull ache over the eye.
Treatment: Most important that a doctor should be consulted without delay.

Sinus Headache [A: S, B, An, F, 2] [Ch: S, R, An, X, 2]
This, too, is less common than is generally supposed.
Cause: Inflammation of the sinuses, the air spaces in the bone above and below the eye, which communicate with the nose.
Identification: Usually comes with a severe cold. The nose is clogged, sometimes with a discharge of much yellow, or blood-streaked pus; sometimes it is stuffy, but dry, when the entrances to the sinuses are blocked.

Characteristically at its worst at midday. Pain increased by stooping and by changes of pressure, ascending or descending by elevator or airplane. Tenderness of face bones over affected sinus. Eyes ache; uncomfortable to move them.
Treatment: Temperature raised or pain severe or recurrent, or other symptoms: antibiotics through doctor. Hot flannel or hot water bottle on face, inhalations are helpful as well as the usual analgesics.

Temperature normal: analgesics, fresh air.
Long term: Doctor's treatment of sinus infection.
Prevention: Avoidance of hot, dry, and stuffy atmospheres. Frequent doses of fresh air.
See also Sinusitis.

Brain Tumor Headache [S]
Including abscesses, clots from injury. Very rare, but amenable to surgical treatment.
Identification: Headache has no distinguishing characteristics, but it may wake the patient at night. May be accompanied by irritability, changes in personality, hallucinations.
Treatment: Go to doctor for check: it will probably turn out to be a reassurance.

Mountain Sickness
Headache, lassitude, irritability at high altitudes, due to oxygen lack. Come down, or rest every fifteen paces if you *must* go on.

Paget's Disease, "Big Head" [Ch: S]
A combination of absorption of old bone and production of too

much new bone, which occasionally occurs, particularly in elderly men.

Identification: Larger hat required, because of increase in size of skull bones; leg bones become enlarged and somewhat bowed; headache often, occasionally other bones ache. Deafness is sometimes the first sign.

Treatment: None special at present available, but the disorder gets worse only very slowly and does not endanger life at any time.

OTHER CAUSES OF HEADACHE

Likely to be distinguished by other symptoms more directly referable to the underlying condition:

Cerebral hemorrhage	Menstrual period
Cerebral thrombosis	Quinine, and some patients on iron
Ear disease	Tobacco
Dental disease	Carbon monoxide, carbon dioxide,
Travel sickness	coal gas, acetone
Epilepsy	Poor ventilation
Sunstroke	Kidney disease
Neuralgia	

CONDITIONS NOT NOW CONSIDERED TO BE CAUSES OF HEADACHE

Constipation; dietary indiscretion; astigmatism; barometric pressure. That there is some association is common knowledge, however.

Constipation: All the evidence indicates that the headache of constipation is not due to the sluggish emptying of the gut, but either to the laxatives taken, or to anxiety about the uncomfortable, unemptied colon, or possibly the feeling of guilt, rooted in infancy, at "missing a day." Constipation often arises in circumstances themselves strange or stressful, like the first few days away on vacation.

Relief of the constipation relieves or coincides with the relief of anxiety or tension.

Dietary indiscretion: Too much, too highly seasoned, bad or unsuitable food can have no direct effect on the head, but depression and headache are common in nervous dyspepsia, anxiety, etc., as in constipation, above, or as part of gastritis or of any illness. See Party Headache above.

Astigmatism: Eyestrain from faults in refraction, astigmatic or other, is not so much a cause of headache as is the tension of posture that accompanies study or other concentrated use of the eyes.

Barometric pressure: This in itself has no effect in producing headache, but variations may bring to the notice blocked and infected ears or sinuses. See Sinus headache.

Mountain sickness (or other altitude sickness) is due to oxygen lack.

DIZZINESS: GIDDINESS

Medical term: Vertigo.

A faint or unsteady feeling is often referred to as giddiness or dizziness, but true vertigo implies disorientation in space, or a sensation of movement often rotatory, either of objects which are actually stationary, or of the individual himself. In severe cases, he may sway, stagger, or even fall.

It is a disturbance of the balancing mechanism, either direct or through a temporarily inadequate supply of blood to the brain.

Identification of Causes

Sudden paroxysms, accompanied by ringing in the ears and deafness, and perhaps also nausea and vomiting, and pallor: Ménière's disease.

Coming on after lying down or prolonged stooping, especially in those over fifty, or in convalescents. Delayed readjustment of circulatory arrangements for the upright position, so that the brain is temporarily short of blood.

Treatment: Immediate: Sit down and bend forward, or lie flat on floor if possible. Get up slowly. *Long term:* If such episodes are severe or frequent, see doctor for check of blood vessels, heart, brain, blood, etc.

Associated with headache, or odd sensation in head: High blood pressure; Migraine; Epilepsy.

Associated with ear disease.

In the elderly: "Hardening" of the arteries makes them less efficient, rather like rusted pipes, and this commonly produces a decrease in the blood supply to the brain and certain special nerves, which may temporarily become inadequate. See Arteriosclerosis.

FAINTING

Medical term: Syncope.

Feeling faint can include having to lie down, palpitation, sweating, nausea, blackout, giddiness.

A faint is a transient loss of consciousness. The patient falls down.

Simple Faint

Identification: Attack preceded by the symptoms of feeling faint. Face ashy pale, breathing rapid, pulse feeble. Unconscious.

After a few minutes consciousness gradually returns.

Cause: Lack of blood supplying the brain.

In a young person: Fall of blood pressure due to emotional upset; sickening for an acute infection; overheated, ill-ventilated rooms; prolonged standing especially when much of the blood is in the skin, as on parade in hot weather; pain; exhaustion; pregnancy, particularly at the time when one first feels the baby move; anemia; and actual loss of blood.

In the elderly: Probably most often due to momentary tightening of an already narrowed artery. See Arteriosclerosis.

NOTE: HEART DISEASE IS VERY SELDOM THE CAUSE OF FAINTING.

Treatment: Immediate: Place the person lying flat, or sitting with the head bent low if there is insufficient space. Smelling salts and cold water on the face may help.

Later: Seek underlying cause, likely to be trivial in a young person, but in an elderly person a medical check is desirable.

Minor Epileptic Attack

May be mistaken for simple faint.

Identification: Not preceded by warning symptoms affecting faint. Recovery as sudden as onset, and more rapid than from a simple faint. See Epilepsy.

Lack of Sugar in the Blood   [A: U]
Identification: Preceded by much sweating. Occurs in diabetics taking insulin, or after prolonged muscular exertion without food.
Treatment: Sugary drink if able to swallow. See Diabetes. See Coma and Fits in General Section.

HEAD INJURY

"No head injury is so trivial that it can be ignored, or so serious as to be despaired of"—as true today as in the days of Hippocrates, 400 years before Christ.

The particular structure and function of the head makes the symptoms of head injury differ from those of other parts of the body.

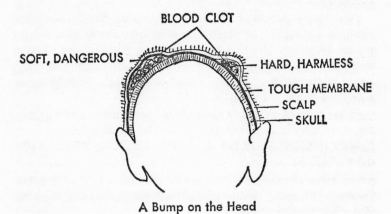

A Bump on the Head

Bleeding from the Scalp
The scalp is attached to the underlying, inelastic skull with very little tissue between, and because of this a blow on the head, even with a blunt instrument, can cause the scalp to split as though

cleanly cut. The edges of the wound tend to be pulled apart by the muscular tension of the scalp. This combined with the excellent blood supply to the scalp makes the bleeding profuse.

It also leads to rapid healing and unlikelihood of infection occurring in scalp wounds. Apparently severe injuries of the scalp heal surprisingly well.

Treatment: Control bleeding by firm bandage until help is available, or bleeding stops. In any case keep up pressure for five minutes.

Have patient sitting up, but supported.

Depending on severity of bleeding, get patient by emergency ambulance to hospital, or call or visit doctor for examination of wound, stitching if necessary, and assessment of possible deeper injury.

Outlook: Very good. Healing likely to be rapid and trouble free. Hair will not grow in the actual scar.

Lump on Head Following a Blow   [A: if severe: S, An, 2]
Firm, Small, Tender Swelling at Site of Injury. Skin, if visible, discolored.

This is a simple bruise, but owing to the inelasticity of the tissue the fluid and blood which leak out form this characteristically limited swelling.

Treatment: Cool compress may be soothing. Aspirin if head aches. If the blow was hard or there is drowsiness, nausea, or confusion, a doctor's advice is necessary.

Outlook: Lump will disappear spontaneously.

Large, Soft Swelling   [A: U, B, 2]
Not necessarily confined to area of injury. This is deeper and maybe more serious, as a fracture of the skull could be present.

Treatment: Hospital, or doctor at home in the first instance, because of the possibility of fracture.

Outlook: The swelling itself will disappear in a week or two, and leave no after effects.

Concussion   [A: U, B, R, 6]
When a boxer is knocked out, for instance, there is a period when

the blood vessels of the brain contract, so that the brain cells receive an inadequate supply of blood, and cannot function properly. Sometimes there is actual bruising of the brain and multiple tiny hemorrhages in its tissue.

Identification: Pale, clammy skin; shallow breathing; fast weak pulse; may vomit or pass water.

Disturbance of consciousness may be so slight as to be a momentary dizziness, or so severe that unconsciousness continues for weeks.

Treatment: Quiet, dark room, head low until consciousness returns, then raised on two pillows. No stimulants. Bed for two weeks at least. Avoidance of brain strain, particularly in those who usually do brain work.

After effects: Usually none, except that memory of the injury is absent, and sometimes greater memory loss. Headache may persist, and occasionally irritability, and lack of concentration for some weeks.

"Punch-Drunk" [Ch]

A term implying permanent damage to the brain and impairment of its working, due to repeated bruising that leads to degeneration of the brain cells. It occurs most frequently in boxers.

LUMP ON THE HEAD

Tender: see Head injury.
Painless:
Warts.
Sebaceous cyst (Wen).
Dermoid cyst.

Wen [Ch: S, W. 1]

Medical name: Sebaceous cyst.

Identification: Hard knob or knobs anywhere on head, actually *in* the skin. Can enlarge to hen's egg size. Scalp over is bald, because of pressure. Due to blockage of the gland which lubricates the hair, damming back the secretion, which becomes solid. Can become infected, and then smells very unpleasant.

Treatment: By doctor, removal by freezing, cutting out, or tying round the base, using a local anesthetic when necessary.
After effects: None likely; no recurrence likely.

Dermoid Cysts [Ch: N, X, 2]
Uncommon, developmental cysts occurring at the junctions of the skull bones or root of nose, or corner of eyebrow, attached not to skin but to underlying bone. May not be large enough to be noticeable until child is ten or more years old. Harmless and enlarge very slowly.
Treatment: Surgical.

DANDRUFF

The commonest of all skin disorders affecting everyone to some extent.
Identification: Loose flakes falling out from scalp when hair brushed, and lying on the shoulders like coarse powder.

Two types: Dry scales, and yellowish greasy-looking scales, sometimes called seborrhoea because it was thought, mistakenly, that the greasy appearance was due to sebum, the hair lubricant. It is, in fact, a soaking of the scales with serum, the fluid that oozes from wounds, etc.

Irritation of scalp if scales accumulate. May be redness of scalp along hair margin.
Cause: The flakes are discarded particles of the horny layer of the skin, produced in excess.
Treatment: Shampoo hair daily for two weeks with hexachlorophene shampoo. Apply daily, indefinitely, lotion containing selenium, resorcin, sulphur, or salicylic acid.

Consult doctor if no improvement in two weeks.
Outlook: Almost complete cure in two weeks, but recurrence likely without continual vigilance and care.
Prevention: Regular, frequent shampooing. Scrupulous hygiene of brush and comb; no borrowing or lending.

OTHER SCALP SIGNS

Scaling of Scalp
Causes: Dandruff (above); Psoriasis, see Skin Section.

Itching, Irritation of Scalp (See also Skin Section)
With flaking of skin: dandruff; psoriasis.
With grayish bald patches: ringworm. Usually children.
With gray lumps on hair (often children): lice (pediculosis capitis).

Lice [Ch: S, C, 2]
The grayish-white lumps on the hair are nits, the eggs of the head louse.
Treatment: A specific lotion put on and left without washing for ten days is a common and effective method.

BALDNESS: LOSS OF HAIR

Medical term: Alopecia.
Normally, there are more than a thousand hairs per square inch of scalp. Each individual hair lasts from two to five years, allowing for a natural hair loss of around eighty hairs a day. Each hair follicle rests temporarily, after it has shed a hair, so that on the scalp there are ninety per cent of the follicles normally active, and ten per cent resting, the reverse of the condition over the rest of the body.

Baldness of some degree is extremely common, affecting over forty per cent of all men and eight per cent of women. There are several types, which can be differentiated.

Examine the scalp by standing under a bright light in front of a mirror.

Identification of Type of Hair Loss
Total loss of hair: Alopecia totalis, a variety of alopecia areata (below).
General thinning: Following acute feverish illness like influenza; after childbirth; accompanying debilitating illnesses, such as anemia, tuberculosis, diabetes mellitus. This type recovers as the general health picks up.

Thinning, becoming complete loss on front of head: Common baldness.

Patchy: Edges of patches clear cut, skin shiny, hairs around the borders alopecia areata.

Skin scaly, hair stumps ⅛ in. long, dull, broken, bent, usually in a child under four years: ringworm.

Indefinite edge to patches, hairs broken but of normal texture: Hair pulling and twisting—a nervous habit occurring in children and young girls.

There are other causes of patchy baldness or thinning, for which a skin specialist's advice should be sought (*not that of a hairdresser,* whose business is to sell commercial products).

Common Baldness [Ch: N, W]

Hardly a disease since it is a normal accompaniment of aging; but in many men it occurs prematurely, even beginning in the twenties.
Causes: Hereditary tendency; a man may assess the future of his hair by photographs of his father and grandfather. This is by far the most important factor.

Male sex hormones stimulate the secretion of scalp oil, and this is usually associated with loss of hair. Baldness of the head and increase in hair on face and body are therefore an indication of virility and occur at the time when there is the highest level of male hormone in the blood. Plentiful scalp hair is as characteristic of the eunuch as absence of beard.

The comparatively few women who suffer from thinning hair of this type do so after the menopause, when female hormone production has ebbed.

Dandruff and seborrheic dermatitis are thought by some to contribute to balding, but there are many people who have dandruff all their lives and die with a full head of hair.
Treatment: None effective, although more than a million dollars a year are expended on it. An American Medical Association Committee declared:

"If the general health of a man is satisfactory, and loss of hair is progressive . . . medical science does not know of any device, substance, or method which will regenerate hair."

Dandruff should be treated for its own sake.

Outlook: A slowly progressive condition requiring resignation—or a toupé.

Current research: At the New York University Bellevue Medical Center, hormone injections into the scalp are being tried. Tufts of hair lasting a few months are produced at each injection site: many hundreds, several times a year, would be required to restore anything like normal appearance.

Alopecia Areata   [Ch: W 6 — 6/12]
Identification: Above.

Far less common than common baldness.

Cause: Unknown, but it sometimes follows a shock or fright. Rare in anyone over forty-five.

Treatment: None has apparent effect. A vacation benefits general health and psychology. Spontaneous recovery usual. Occasionally lasts years, rarely permanent.

Outlook: Recovery usually complete, but hair on former bald patches may remain white. Recurrence common.

Ringworm of the Scalp   [Ch: S, O, C, 6/12]
Medical name: Tinea tonsurans.
Identification: Above.

Due to a fungus, and acquired by direct contact with caps or combs used by infected persons. Infectious, and therefore should be dealt with as soon as possible. Diagnosis must be made by a doctor.

A good head of healthy hair can be expected within six months. Untreated, the condition goes on until puberty but with thorough treatment no recurrence will occur except through re-infection. No permanent effect on the hair or scalp.

Treatment: Griseofulvin tablets two or three times a day according to age, and through doctor. Hair must be clipped or shaved in affected patches, the scalp washed twice a week. After four weeks on this regime, normal healthy hair will be growing. *This is cut off,* for a second time, and the cure considered complete. The short hair has then to catch up with the rest.

Treatment must be repeated from the beginning, should a new patch appear or occur in another area.

WHITENING, GRAYING OF HAIR

[Ch: N, W]

Medical name: Canities.

Coloring matter is built into the hair deep in the scalp, and its production falls off and finally ceases with age.

Causes of Premature Graying

Heredity.

Red or auburn hair usually loses its brilliant pigments early. Neutral shades of brown continue longest.

Patches of white hair may follow alopecia areata. Accounts for the hair "turning white overnight" are probably exaggerations, but physical or mental stress may accelerate the process.

Treatment: None effective.

The Face

Examine your own face in a threefold mirror, and you will observe that the two sides are not identical. The ancients believed that one side reflected the soul, the other the will.

It has a special interest for us as the mirror of health and humor.

Asymmetry

UNUSUAL COLOR OF FACE

Pallor

May be normal, healthy, and of the type much admired in a Victorian miss. Pallor arising in a formerly rosier face may be significant.

Including the inside of the lower lid: anemia.

Grayish pallor
Puffy and waxen } types of kidney trouble.

Café-au-lait complexion (sallow) could be disease of valves of heart.

Muddy pallor: constipation.

Lemony pallor: pernicious anemia, or mepacrine; some internal disorders.

Yellow-white, papery: old age, natural and normal.

Ashen, in shock, feeling faint, or internal bleeding.

Toxic effects of infection.

It is important to consult your doctor as some conditions creating pallor may be serious.

High Color

This, too, can be consistent with first class health, or sunburn, but it may also have other significance, for instance:

Generally ruddy, in high blood pressure.

Purplish red, in some blood disorders.

Cheeks and lips red, the rest creamy: mitral disease of the heart.

Bronzing: glandular trouble (Addison's disease).

Bronzing in butterfly shape: chloasma, a brownish pigmentation in pregnancy. Sometimes occurs with use of birth control pills.

Rashes and skin diseases: See under Skins, Infectious fevers, Flushing.

A doctor's advice is necessary to be sure of the cause and appropriate action.

Mauve, Blue, or Purple Complexion

Unless you are very cold, this is certainly abnormal.

In a child: congenital heart disease ("blue baby" growing up).

Face only affected: Scars in lung, from healed tubercle or pleurisy; emphysema (a lung complaint); methemoglobinemia, probably from a sulpha drug, a change in the red pigment of the blood.

Face *and* extremities: Heart difficulty, obstruction to veins returning blood to heart.

All blueness should be investigated by a doctor.

Yellow
See Jaundice; see Lemony pallor, above.

FLUSHING

Flushing and blushing are sudden temporary reddenings of the face caused by dilatation of the blood vessels in the skin.

Blushing is due entirely to emotional factors, notably shyness or shame, a manifestation of the unconscious part of the personality. Flushing is only occasionally due to emotion alone; it lasts longer.

Both are commoner in the female sex.

Causes of Flushing
Acne rosacea.
Hot flushes.
Indigestion.
Alcohol.
Pregnancy.
Diabetes, with either too much or too little insulin.
Epilepsy, before an attack.
Fever.

Acne Rosacea   [Ch: N, 6]
Identification: Flushing, mainly involving nose and cheeks, coming on after meals, hot drinks, coming into a hot room out of the cold, and excitement. The flush in time becomes permanent, with small dilated blood vessels visible, and enlargement in the affected area, of the skin glands. This can be very marked, and produce *cauliflower nose* or *potato nose*.
Conditions often associated: Dyspeptic pain, wind or constipation,

scurfy scalp. Pustules on face. Especial fondness for tea or alcohol.

This complaint, commoner in women (except for the cauliflower nose), arises after thirty, is cosmetically distressing, and may give a false impression of alcoholic over-indulgence when too many cups of tea may be to blame.

Treatment: Are the teeth efficient? Avoid the precipitating factors, and drink cool coffee, milk or fruit drinks. Calamine lotion soothes and disguises. If no improvement in a week or so, consult doctor. Cauliflower nose can be treated surgically.

Outlook: Slowly progressive, ugly, unless treated. Not dangerous.

Hot Flushes   [A Ch: W, 6/12—2 years]
See also Menopause in Women's Section.

Part of the constitutional upset which sometimes accompanies the menopause, the epoch of glandular change in a woman's life when the periods are ceasing, any time between thirty-five and fifty-five years.

Identification: Burning of face, perspiration, followed by cold stage. Change of rhythm of menstruation, emotional disturbance.

A normal, though annoying, phenomenon. If distressed by it, see doctor who may prescribe tablets or injections. This disorder eventually goes away completely, whether treated or not.

BLEMISHES, SPOTS, RASHES ON THE FACE

The skin of the face is particularly noticeable and the most exposed to sun, wind, and weather. Warts, moles, blood warts, keratoses are all common on the face, and also skin cancer.
See Skin Section.

Rashes of illnesses such as measles, smallpox, typhoid are often noticed first on the face.

Acne, the ugly pustular plague of adolescence, attacks the face.
Infected spots are also common.

Blackheads occur in most people, but a noticeable number is the beginning of acne. Soap and water washing and the avoidance of face creams, since the skin is already too greasy, are wise preventive measures. See Acne.

Ingrowing hairs can occur only on the beard or armpit area of an adult who shaves. The short-cut hair "loses its way" and pokes under the skin instead of out, and this is recognizable when you have considered the possibility. Changing to an electric razor, or possibly vice versa, may prevent future trouble.

Impetigo, common in children, is an infection of the skin of the face consisting of spots and crusting.

SWELLING OF THE FACE

Causes
Both sides:

Mumps: usually one side swells twenty-four hours earlier than the other.

Eye inflammations.

Hives: other areas may be affected.

Acne rosacea, with flushing.

Paget's disease, enlargement of lower jawbone and forehead in the elderly.

One side only:

Insect bites, boils, carbuncles.

Infected teeth, gumboil.

Enlarged glands in front of ear: various causes.

Cysts, soft
Tumors, solid $\left.\right\}$ simple, or pre-cancerous

Limbs and trunk also affected:

Toxemia of pregnancy, latter half.

Kidney trouble, puffiness worse in the mornings.

Whooping cough.

Heart trouble, though in this the dependent parts are most affected.

See also Swelling of eyelids.

TWITCHING OF THE FACE

Unintended movements, and unusual nervous twitches of the face. See Twitching in Children's Section.

Tic [Ch: N or S, X, 2]

Identification: Irregular and frequently defensive movements, e.g. blinking or grimacing, often involving both sides. These are not serious, and are the outward sign of nervousness. *Habit spasm:* a facial trick such as sniffing, acquired during a cold, if perpetuated, is a form of tic common in children.

Treatment: Attention to general health, and any worries. Do not criticize someone with a tic, irritating though it can be.

Outlook: One tic, if cured, is often replaced by another, and tics arising in those over forty are likely to be permanent. They do no harm.

Facial Spasm [A Ch: SU]

Identification: Always one-sided, usually intermittent; the muscles are weak on that side.

This condition indicates trouble involving a facial nerve. It is important to identify the cause, which may be harmless, but could be serious.

Tic Douloureux [A: S, I, An, X]

Medical term: Trigeminal neuralgia.

A painful disease that strikes without warning, usually at fifty years or older, either sex. Its cause is a mystery, but *there is absolutely nothing neurotic about this trouble.*

Identification: One side only: bouts of lancing pain in temple, jaw, teeth or ear, triggered off by the smallest stimuli—shaving, jarring, a cold draft, eating very hot or cold food—twitching of the face on the affected side; sometimes flushing; sometimes watering of one eye, one nostril, or mouth.

Treatment: During attack drink through a straw, stay indoors, use analgesics. The pain does not usually last long, but comes back.

See doctor for more adequate medication, or surgical treatment if necessary. The latter can be very effective.

Outlook: Waves of attacks are interspersed with remissions perhaps of years, for years.

No danger to life.

CLENCHED TEETH

Medical term: Trismus.

Lockjaw [A: U, B, 6]
Medical term: Tetanus.
A dangerous disease caused by bacillus tetani, normally present in cultivated soil, getting into the body through a wound.
Identification: Injury, especially deep, eight-twelve days before; painful spasms of jaw muscles and at back of neck; mouth cannot be opened. Other muscles involved later. Rise of temperature; sweating.
Prevention: Anti-tetanus immunization is now given routinely to children, along with their anti-diphtheria and whooping cough injections. Immunity can also be given by injection shortly after a penetrating wound has occurred.

Inflammation Affecting Jaw Muscles [A]
Dental abscess ⎫
Mumps   ⎬ all obvious.
Tonsillitis, quinsy ⎭

Hysterical Spasm of Jaw
In nervous subjects who have heard of lockjaw! There are no other symptoms, usually.

PAIN IN THE FACE

Causes
Tic douloureux.
Shingles.
Migraine, sick headache.
Sinusitis.
Dental decay, gumboil.
Bell's palsy.
Tumors pressing on nerve.
Lockjaw.
See also: Pain in the eye, Headache, Earache.

WEAKNESS OR PARALYSIS OF FACE

Bell's Palsy   [A Ch: S, R, 6—6/12]

This common disease is possibly due to a virus and frequently comes on after exposure to cold.

Identification: Stiffness and loss of power of face: inability to close eyes, raise eyebrows, whistle. Smile lopsided. There may be slight pain.

Doctor will give treatment. Recovery slow but usually complete.

Poliomyelitis   [A: S, B, C, 2—6/12]

May affect the face. There will be fever, headache, and pain.

Ear Trouble

Especially mastoid.

Associated with Impending or Recent Stroke

In older people.

There are various rarer causes of facial paralysis or weakness, and a doctor should be consulted in any unexplained case.

See also Drooping eyelid.

CRACKS OR SORES ON THE LIPS

Cold Sore   [A: N, W, 2]

Medical name: Herpes simplex.

Identification: A slightly swollen, painful, red patch on lip or border of nostrils, appears overnight. Minute blisters arise on this patch; they turn yellow, crust, and come off as a scab.

Cause: A virus normally present in most people's saliva. Precipitating causes include: lowered resistance during a cold or feverish illness, sun glare (a glacier sore is a variety of herpes simplex), excitement (actresses on a first night), and onset of a menstrual period.

This disease is as old as the Egyptians; even mummies show the traces!

Treatment: Keep the part clean and dry, with calamine or talcum powder.

Unless infected, no scarring.

Prevention: No method known.

Sore, Dry Lips   [A Ch]

With papery peeling: occur in gastric disturbances, feverish illnesses, and the nervous trick of biting and licking the lips. Use a chap stick.

Cracks in the Corners or Center of Lower Lip   [A Ch: N, 2]

Can be simply due to over-exposure to sun or cold wind. *Chapping* arises similarly. Use chap stick.

If associated with sore eyes and scaling skin around the nose, cracks may be due to Vitamin B lack. Take extra liver, yeast, egg, greens, cheese.

Perlèche. In children only, symmetrical, gray, moist patches starting at the corners; a fungus infection needing doctor's treatment.   [S, 2]

Persistent Sore, Crack, Ulcer, or Lump on Lip   [Ch: SU]

If present for more than two weeks:

Could be precancerous, and needs to be investigated. Cancer of the lip has a wonderfully high rate of cure, so do not hesitate to get advice promptly.

Warts and simple growths can also occur on the lips.

WHITE PATCHES ON LIPS

[Ch: SU]

Medical term: Leucoplakia.

Milky, slightly thickened surface on part of lips, mouth or tongue. Can be precancerous, and its appearance means that advice should be sought and smoking, if any, stopped and oral hygiene attended to.

The Nose

The outer part of the nose is the most prominent feature of the face, a popularly supposed guide to character. But the nose, like an iceberg, has nine-tenths hidden to the one-tenth visible: large air chambers and passage ways, and a quarter-sized area of extraordinary delicacy which has remarkable powers of assessing innumerable flavors from the mouth, myriad scents from outside.

DEFORMITY: ODD SHAPES OF THE NOSE

Noses vary greatly, and may be irregular in form naturally or because of injury.

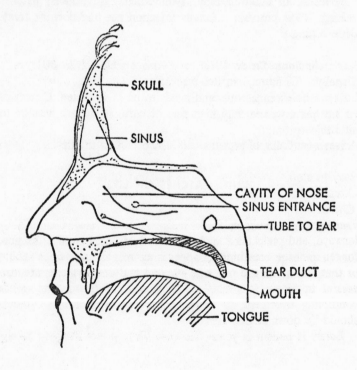

External Deformity

Of no importance except cosmetically. Plastic surgery can remodel the nose.

Internal Deformity [Ch: S]

The septum, or wall between the two nostrils, may be crooked (deviated). It may obstruct the breathing or, by blocking the entrance to a sinus, cause infection.

Treatment: Simple operation. Hospitalization seven to ten days.

NOSE BLEEDING

Medical term: Epistaxis.

The nasal septum has a particularly lavish blood supply, being the meeting place of five arteries; small wonder that nose bleeding is a common symptom. There are two forms usually met with:

Spontaneous nose bleed (sometimes called adolescent).

High blood pressure nose bleed (sometimes called secondary).

Differentiation

Spontaneous type	*High blood pressure type*
Usually: Children, especially boys; adolescents, especially girls at period times; and young adults.	Middle age, forty plus.
Arises near front of septum.	Arises far back, or high up in nose.
Easy to stop.	Difficult to stop.
Often recurs.	May recur.

Treatment: Immediate: Have patient sit up, head bent slightly forward, and press his finger against the bleeding side of the nose for ten minutes, breathing through his mouth. He must not swallow, or that will move and break newly forming clot. If this is not successful in fifteen to twenty minutes, call the doctor, meanwhile continuing treatment. If much blood has been lost the patient should lie down rather than sit.

Later: If patient is young the nose bleed is not likely to be significant of other trouble. Nose bleeding coming on in someone over forty needs immediate investigation by doctor.

Recurrent nose bleeds in a young person may be due to an abnormality of the blood vessels inside the nose, which can be dealt with by cautery.

Other Causes of Nose Bleed, Less Common

Injury, tumor of nose, some heart troubles, blood disorders such as anemia, fevers including influenza and smallpox, and weak blood vessels in old age, without high blood pressure.

SNORING

Inelegant and embarrassing. Can bring on dry throat and respiratory infection when cold air, unwarmed and unfiltered by nose, enters throat.

Causes [Ch]

Deep sleep, especially lying on the back.

Adenoids, especially in children.

Polyps: allergic swellings of the lining of the nose. Can be removed simply, but may recur.

Deformity of nose.

Difficulty in closing mouth.

Habit, perhaps acquired during an infection.

Temporary Causes [A]

Infections of the nose with a discharge which may block the nose.

Treatment: Physical cause if present. Sleep on the side. Strap a ping-pong ball to the small of the back.

SNEEZING

Medical term: Sternutation.

A minor explosion, brought on usually by irritation of the lining of the nose, but sometimes by glaring sunlight on the eye.

Causes

Common cold.

Allergic rhinitis, including hay fever.

Asthma, in some allergic cases.

Insect or object up the nose.

Irritating inhalants: powders and particles of sawdust, soap powders, gases.

Harmless in itself—even a pleasure—but it may bring on nose bleeding, spasm of pain in certain types of backache, etc.

RUNNING NOSE

Causes

Common cold.

Hay fever.

Allergic rhinitis.

Sinusitis.

Early stages of infectious fevers, especially measles.

Something up the nose, especially in children.

Chronic Catarrh. See below.

COMMON COLD

[A: N, R, An, 1–2]

A virus infection of the lining of the nose and its air passages predisposing to invasion by bacteria, some 300 times as large as the virus. Colds are spread from person to person by droplets in the breath and are no respecters of age or sex.

Colds are under intense research study, and at least nine strains of cold-producing virus have been isolated. It is the large number of organisms responsible for colds that has, so far, made the production of an efficient vaccine impracticable.

Identification: Clear nasal discharge, becoming in a day or two thick and often yellow (stage of bacterial invasion); slight sore throat often preceding the runny nose; headache usual; sometimes slight fever; sneezing.

Duration: One–three days uncomplicated. Seven–fourteen days with the usual bacterial as well as the virus attack.

Additional troubles such as sinusitis, tonsillitis, bronchitis may prolong the illness, or it may, if inadequately treated, run on into a chronic condition.

Treatment: There is none, as yet.

The corner stone of management is rest, keeping one's reserves to cope with the infection. This means cutting out avoidable physical exertion and inessential social activities—a person with a cold is far from an asset at any function. Extra drinks of tea, coffee, fruit juices, etc., help the dry throat and loss of fluid through the nose.

Aspirin, two 5 gr. tablets with water, may be useful when there is headache and throat discomfort, but have no effect on the progress of the illness.

Value of Traditional and Other Remedies

Penicillin, sulpha drugs: No effect on cold virus, but may help to keep down bacterial invaders.

"Cold cures" containing quinine, acetanilide, phenacetin: No effect on infectious process, may relieve headache.

Hot drinks, hot baths, whisky, etc.: Induce sweating, possibly comforting.

Prevention: One cold does not give more than a few days' immunity, so when possible, avoid people with heavy infection.

Chilling and fatigue, by themselves, do not cause colds.

Adults normally have three to four colds a year; if you have more than this, consult your doctor, as you may have a sinus or other infection, or an allergic condition, that needs dealing with.

The cold is one of our commonest nuisances, but perhaps the slackening of pace which a cold enforces is a safety-valve in the stressful life of Western civilization.

CATARRH: NASAL CATARRH, CHRONIC CATARRH

[Ch: N or S, 6]

One of the vague, complaining terms the doctor hears most frequently, applied to anything like a head cold that does not clear up. Some physicians do not recognize catarrh as an entity, preferring to think in terms of allergic rhinitis and sinusitis only; others, however, do consider that there exists a chronic state of stuffy or discharging nose, depending largely on constitution and habits of living.

They postulate two common types:

VAGOTONIC TYPE: the majority

Do not like Exercise;

Fresh air;

Excitement; yet without stimulation they become sluggish.

Do like   Food, a little too much;

Artificial warmth: hot baths, warm rooms, many clothes.

Nose blocked always, sometimes running profusely; drips slide down back of throat from nose; headaches. Lining of nose wet, pale, soft.

SYMPATHETICOTONIC TYPE: the minority

On the ball, on their toes, eager, keyed-up.

Nose blocked, but not so runny; lining reddish.

Factors Worsening Catarrh in Both Types

Nasal drops and sprays: Tempting for a catarrhal subject to turn to them for the temporary relief they afford. But they are habit forming and harmful to the nose, making the lining more and more chronically congested and thickened.

Smoking, by its irritating effect.

Alcohol, because it causes congestion.

Anxiety: worries over home, work, children, money. . . .

Treatment: Revolutionize your way of living to include fresh air and exercise in plenty, and no more than is necessary of food, clothing, heating—and worry. Moderation with tobacco, alcohol, and late nights.

If a month of this does not put you right, visit your doctor, who may have tricks up his sleeve for obstinate catarrh.

Other Causes of Catarrh

Allergy.

Deformity of nose.

Sinusitis. Not as common as supposed.

Children with catarrh   [Ch: S]

In their case the sinuses *are* commonly at fault, and adenoids, tonsils, and allergy account for the rest. See Children's Section.

HAY FEVER

[A Ch: S, R, X, 6]

See Allergy.

May be mistaken for "summer cold," but there is no infection. Hay fever is an allergy, that is, a condition in which the person has become sensitized to one or more pollen proteins (often grass or trees) and reacts with nasal symptoms. There is often a family tendency, so heredity plays a part.

Identification: Profuse, watery, nasal discharge; violent sneezing; blocked nose; red, watery eyes; lining of nose pale and thick in cases of long-standing.

Comes on in the pollen season, disappears after it, and is milder when it is raining and the pollen is kept down.

Treatment: Avoid the countryside on hot, windy days in the season. Sun glasses may help sore runny eyes in the glare. *Antihistamine tablets* control symptoms but enhance drowsiness, which can be dangerous if, for instance, you are driving. Your doctor may also prescribe *steroid* drugs, highly effective but may have side effects if used continuously. Drops and sprays give temporary relief—and lasting harm to the nasal lining.

Age range: Hay fever can start any time after four years and diminishes from forty.

Prevention: Desensitization. If the allergen responsible for your particular hay fever can be identified (by skin test), your doctor may be able to arrange a course of injections of minute amounts of the culprit, which will reverse the process of having become sensitive. The course must start early in the year to be completed in time for the hay fever season.

Avoid causative agents.

ALLERGIC RHINITIS

[Ch: S, W, X, 6]

See Allergy.

An allergy similar to hay fever but not restricted to any particular season, since it is due to sensitivity not to pollens but to such substances as house dust, wool, molds and feathers, animal hair, bacteria, or certain foods and drugs.

Symptoms are similar to those of hay fever.

Treatment: see Hay fever. Clear your bedroom of dust-harboring rugs, and choose glazed, unfluffy material for your curtains.

Replace feather pillows with plastic or rubber foam.

SINUSITIS

The sinuses are hollow, air-filled spaces in the cheek bones and bones behind the eyebrows, which give resonance to the voice and added protection to eye and brain. They communicate with the nose, from which infection can readily reach them, but any infected material cannot easily drain out, as from a runny nose, because the exits are small and easily blocked.

The cheekbone (maxillary) sinuses are most often affected.

ACUTE SINUSITIS   [A: S, B, An, 2–6]
Usually with or following a cold, influenza, or measles.

Identification: Pain in face, often throbbing, made worse by stooping or jarring; nasal discharge; blocked nose; fever usually; headache often.

Treatment: Bed rest and analgesics, plus hot water bottle to face. Menthol inhalations, preceded by ephedrine nasal drops, help make the sinus entrance clear.

From doctor: Antibiotics usually advisable; occasionally, when the infection has subsided, surgical drainage of the sinuses is required.

Duration: Two–three weeks before back to normal in a moderately severe case, but the condition can become chronic (see below), and recurrence is common.

Prevention: Check for predisposing causes:

Deformity of nasal septum.

Allergic conditions making nasal lining swollen.

Do not neglect colds.

Avoid humid climates, hot, dry rooms, diving, which may force
   in water, and infection.

Take daily: Cool, fresh air.

CHRONIC SINUSITIS   [Ch: S, 6]

Identification: Blocked, discharging nostril on one side; unpleasant breath; huskiness or nasal voice; sometimes dull headache or pain or pricking in face.

Treatment: Open air vacation. Sinus washouts as advised by doctor.

Check on predisposing causes.

Preventive measures as for acute sinusitis.

The Mouth

The mouth contains the tongue, organ of speech and taste, distinguishing among bitter, sweet, salty, and sour, and thirty-two reasons for dental hygiene. The salivary glands pour their magic juice into the mouth so that while we are still chewing, digestion begins; keep a piece of bread in the mouth, and it will begin to taste sweet as it is converted into sugar. Absorption of some nutriments, or drugs, such as nitroglycerine tablets for angina, can also occur in the mouth, before swallowing.

The ear, via the Eustachian tube, the nose, and the throat all communicate through the mouth.

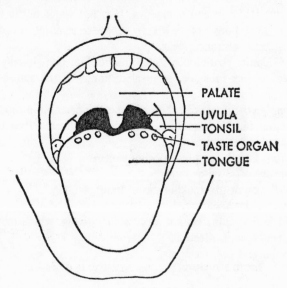

PALATE
UVULA
TONSIL
TASTE ORGAN
TONGUE

THE TEETH

Discolored Teeth

Decay, cavities: Darkly indented lines especially in the crevices. Dentist.

Tobacco: Brown staining, from smoking or chewing. See Tongue also.

Exposed inner layer of dentine: Yellowish discoloration in worn down edges of teeth. A sign of long service and good use. No treatment necessary.

Stain: Strong tea, black coffee, iron medicines.

Tetracycline: Taken by mother during pregnancy, or by children in formative years, may produce dark bands in the enamel of the front teeth.

Cracked or Broken Teeth

Due to injury or decay. Even if the tooth is painless, treatment is essential, because jags of tooth frequently set up chronic irritation, with serious consequences to tongue or cheek or tooth. Dentist.

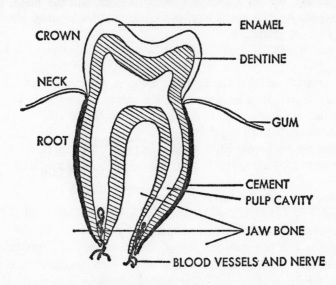

Tooth structure: section through a molar

Toothache

Causes

Dental decay, causing inflammation of tooth pulp or the membrane round the teeth. Commonest in the formative years but can occur at any time, a concomitant of the eating habits of our civilization, particularly the soft, highly refined, starchy and sweet foods.

Treatment: Dentist. Meanwhile pain may be eased by aspirin or hot water bottle to jaw.

Prevention: Regular tooth cleaning, last thing at night (no night cap after) and after each meal. Healthy eating habits: hard food, no over indulgence in sweets and confections; plenty of fruit, particularly at the end of each meal.

Check-up by dentist every six months.

Extra milk and Vitamin D in pregnancy, for nursing mothers, and for children.

Exposed dentine: Outer layer of enamel absent for any reason. Excruciating pain on eating hot, cold, or sweet food.

Treatment: Dentist. Not serious.

Filling too near pulp: Also much affected by heat and cold.

Treatment: Dentist. Care over temperature of food and drink.

Dead tooth: Pain not severe, but tooth tender on biting. Dentist may advise extraction.

Impacted wisdom tooth: May not be visible. Diagnosis by X-ray. Dentist.

Abscess (Gumboil): small, flabby lump in gum, and intermittent ache, or pain may be severe and throbbing, with swelling of jaw and face and sometimes fever. A nasty taste in the mouth.

Treatment: Dentist, urgently.

Apparent toothache: From trouble in parts which share the same nerves as the teeth: ear infection; sinusitis; trigeminal neuralgia.

Difficulties with Dentures

Learning to tolerate them: There may have to be weeks of eating cautiously by the wearer and many adjustments by dentist, but patience and perseverance pay off. Most wearers of dentures are completely unaware of them most of the time, and find after the first month or two their appreciation of flavor is perfect. It is essential to wear them night as well as day to feel them a natural part of the mouth.

Ulcers and dentures: Occur most often when spicy foods are eaten, and particularly when you have a cold. A few days eating on the unaffected side of the mouth is usually sufficient for cure, and perhaps leaving the dentures out for a night.

Slipping dentures: The gums gradually shrink after the teeth are gone, and the dentures become loose. See dentist.

Stains: Occur even more readily on false teeth than natural, but may be cured or prevented by more vigorous use of denture cleansers.

Disturbed sense of taste: Occasionally due to denture pressing on a nerve. Cured when denture removed or adjusted. Otherwise, a matter of getting used to them.

Chattering Teeth

Causes

Cold: Shivering is an automatic muscular exercise which occurs to produce heat when the body is chilled, particularly by a cold dip. When the jaw muscles shiver, the teeth chatter.

High fever: The temperature regulating mechanism is out of order in high fever, so that the person feels alternately very hot and deadly cold, although in fact he is hot all the time. Shivering occurs, and the teeth chatter when the patient thinks he is cold. Particularly noticeable in malaria.

Fear or fury: In these circumstances the muscles, including the teeth chatterers, are quivering because they are alerted for action— fight or flight.

Inflamed Gums, "Pink Toothbrush," Pyorrhea

Medical term: Gingivitis, peridontal disease.

First Stage   [A Ch: S, 2]

Smooth, glossy, slightly swollen and red gum margins, which bleed at the touch of the tooth brush. Tender.

Cause: Food stagnating and causing infection around the teeth. Deposits of tartar predispose.

Treatment: Regular, thorough tooth cleaning. Removal of tartar by dentist. Mouth washes.

Progress: Complete cure without effect on teeth, in two weeks, usually.

Second Stage   [Ch: S, 6]

Occurs only if first stage neglected.

Pockets of pus around teeth; gum receding; teeth loose.

Treatment: Even the skill of a good dentist may not be enough to save the teeth.

Vincent's Infection of the Mouth   [A: S, B, C, 2]

An infectious inflammation of the gums with yellow ulcers, swollen glands in the neck, and fever. Most common in institutions.

Penicillin deals with this magically well, but meticulous mouth care is needed afterwards.

BAD BREATH, HEAVY BREATH, HALITOSIS

Socially unacceptable, and not always very noticeable to the sufferer.

Check these possible causes

Mouth: Lack of hygiene, particularly of regular tooth cleaning, or cleaning underside of plate: by far the commonest cause.

        Dental decay, or gum trouble.

        Tonsillitis, ulcers in the mouth, thrush.

Nose and sinuses: Chronic infection; temporarily, a cold in the head; in children, a foreign body up the nose.

Lungs: Anything from mild bronchitis to cancer; the most unpleasant is bronchiectasis. Tobacco smoking.

Stomach: Indigestion: "Heavy" breath. Garlic, onions, alcohol, some drugs, e.g. paraldehyde. Special diets for slimming, etc. Vomiting from any cause. *Note:* Constipation in itself does not cause bad breath, but the disturbance of intestinal activity caused by laxatives can do so.

Some general illnesses produce a characteristic breath odor, e.g. acidity in anemia; sweetness in acidosis; plainly unpleasant in illnesses with fever.

Treatment: Meticulous hygiene of the mouth helps, whatever the cause, especially after meals. Hydrogen peroxide mouth washes help after vomiting, and in tonsillitis.

Any infections, etc., should, of course, be attended to, and thought given to what is eaten, drunk or smoked.

Chlorophyll tablets have no action, and scented sweets can make the odor more nauseous. Fresh air in the lungs *may* help, so take regular walks.

TASTE AND MOUTH WATERING

Bad Taste in Mouth
Same conditions as produce bad breath, and also some psychological difficulties. Notably, of course, the morning after the night before!
Treatment: As for bad breath.

Abnormalities of Taste
No Taste, or Diminished
   Cold, hay fever.
   Disorder of nose.
   Feverish illness with furred tongue.
   Injury of or pressure on nerves of taste.
Peculiar Taste
   New dentures (temporary).
   Pregnancy (temporary).
   Epilepsy, before attack.
   Hysteria, after shock.
   Disorders, especially septic, of mouth, nose, lung.
   Medicines containing certain metals, valerian, paraldehyde, castor oil, asafetida, creosote, etc.
Bad taste: Above.

Watering of the Mouth
Causes
   Inflammation of the inside of the mouth: Ulcers, thrush.
   Irritation: Jagged tooth, peridontal disease, stump left in, gumboil, badly fitting plate.
   Pregnancy.

Gastric disturbances: Gastritis, ulcer, dyspepsia.

Certain medicines, particularly those containing mercury.

Tic douloureux.

Without physical cause, to do with worry, shock, emotion.

The thought or smell of savory foods!

Parkinson's disease.

Sometimes there appears to be an excessive amount of saliva, but the real trouble is a *difficulty in swallowing,* which makes it overflow.

ABNORMAL COLOR OF TONGUE

Furred or Coated Tongue   [A Ch: N]

Fur is matter that accumulates on the papillae, usually during sleep (babies have no papillae and no furring), and it is normally present at the back of the tongue where the roof of the mouth does not rub it.

You can have a furred tongue and be in perfect health, but usually it occurs in trouble affecting the stomach, though not in the lower digestive organs, and in some feverish illnesses. No treatment is necessary.

Brownish-yellow Tongue   [Ch: S]

Causes:

Tetracycline.

Tobacco: nicotine and tar stain the tongue, which is also likely to be drier than normal, from much smoking.

Pernicious anemia, tongue also sore. Not common.

Age forty to sixty.

Fiery Red Tongue   [A: S]

May be painful. Due to inflammation, glossitis.

Causes

Vitamin B deficiency.

Reaction to certain medicines.

None apparent.

Considered by some to be occasionally precancerous. Consult doctor for treatment.

Bluish Discoloration [N]

A type of birth mark, present since childhood. Slightly raised, may be hairy. Does not hurt or bleed. Can be a nuisance, but not dangerous.

White, Wet, Crusting [SU]

May also occur inside cheek, or on lip: leucoplakia. Caused by chronic irritation from smoking, syphilis, etc. Definitely precancerous: needs prompt medical care.

Black Tongue

Black patch near center. Cause unknown: may be fungal, after antibiotic. Goes away spontaneously. Try raw pineapple, or paint from doctor.

Glossy Tongue [S]

Smooth, slightly red, in elderly people. Natural atrophy of age. Check for dyspepsia.

ULCERS OF TONGUE AND MOUTH

Superficial, not Hard

SIMPLE   [A: N, 1]

Canker sores: tiny blisters bordered with red, which burst to form small painful ulcers. Occur in colds, dyspepsia, or due to irritation from jagged tooth.

Treatment: Mouth washes; dental, if necessary. Unimportant.

THRUSH   [A: S, 2]

White spots, which may peel to leave little ulcers. Breath offensive. Usually infants. Sometimes follows administration of antibiotics.

IN CHICKEN POX, MEASLES, ETC.

Deep, or with Hard, Stiff Surrounding Area [Ch: SU]

Not normally painful to start with. This may be important, as a precursor of cancer, or a sign of syphilis.

The Eye

Each eye is a small, spherical camera with an automatically focusing light filter, the pupil, an accurately centered, adjustable lens, a transparent window self-cleansing by tears, and protective shutters or lids that close whenever necessary without the owner's even having to wish it!

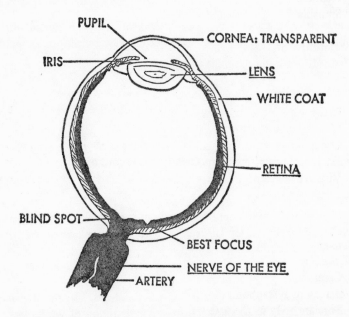

At the back of the eyes are light-sensitive, self-renewing screens that convert the two images seen into electrical impulses in the ocular nerves, which are finally conjured into one composite picture in the brain.

Probably only in man is a single picture seen, and no other animal has the final refinement of continuous, binocular stereoscopic vision. Our next cousins, the apes, can achieve it for short periods only, we believe.

Pain or Soreness in the Eye
Causes

Eyestrain because of bad lighting, and errors of refraction, especially far sightedness.

Inflammation of any part of the eye.

Foreign body in the eye.

Influenza, colds, and certain fevers.

Shingles.

Migraine.

Neuralgia.

Sinusitis.

Intolerance of Light
Medical term: Photophobia.
Causes

As of pain, see above.

Drugs such as quinine, potassium bromide and iodide, arsenic.

Meningitis and some brain diseases.

Occupations involving snow-dazzle, furnace heat, very close work, much bright sunlight, dark work, e.g. mining.

Vitamin deficiency. Lack of riboflavin contained in wheat germ and vegetables.

Blurred or Misty Vision
Causes
In the Eye

Cataract.

Errors of refraction.

Foreign body in the eye.

Glaucoma.

Inflammation of the eye.

Pterygium.

General Conditions

Anemia and certain blood conditions.

Diabetes mellitus.

High blood pressure.

Kidney troubles.

Nerve diseases.
Tobacco and certain drugs.

Contact Lenses

Worn directly on the cornea, the transparent window over the colored part of the eye, instead of spectacles. They are of particular value for those with a high degree of nearsightedness, improving the vision far more than conventional glasses. It takes some persistence to learn the trick of slipping them in and out, and making the eyes become accustomed to their presence. Only an ophthalmologist, especially skilled in the work, should be allowed to fit you, and regular checks of your eyes' condition are essential. Contact lenses should never be left in overnight, and the ophthalmologist's advice about hygiene is important, or the eyes may be damaged.

ERRORS OF REFRACTION

It is extraordinary how nearly perfection is achieved in our complex, duplicated optical arrangements for vision, and not remarkable that minor errors of refraction are common.

The most frequent are:

Nearsightedness (Myopia)

Identification: Distant vision misty, causing difficulty with golf, the theater or the school blackboard, but no discomfort in reading, although the book may be held close. Spectacles should be worn, since this condition tends to worsen, until the normal shrinkage of the tissues after forty corrects the disproportionately large eyeball.

Farsightedness (Hypermetropia)

Identification: Less easily recognized because distant vision is usually good, and near objects can be brought into focus with an effort of accommodation. Headaches and squints may accompany this effort, and the eyes of students or bookkeepers become inflamed. Occasional blurring of the print occurs. Spectacles greatly increase the comfort of close work.

Astigmatism

Since no human eye is absolutely symmetrical, everyone has some degree of astigmatism. Spectacles are needed if there is noticeable distortion of the image seen, or discomfort in viewing.

Hardening of the Lens (Presbyopia)

The lens in the young is elastic, and its degree of curvature can be rapidly modified according to the distance of the object under view —even if the latter is moving. This is accommodation.

In adult life, from the teens onward, the lens gradually becomes hard and stiff, and the power of accommodation for near vision diminishes. At forty-five it is normal for a man to find he is unable to read with the print conveniently close.

At a later stage presbyopia makes road crossing dangerous, since the slowly accommodating eye is inadequate for judging the speed of vehicles. Glasses compensate for the loss of accommodation for reading, but not for assessing road safety.

Treatment of Errors of Refraction: Your eyes should be tested by a doctor or eye specialist, and glasses obtained on his prescription. Serious eye disease could get overlooked if you went only to an optician.

BLACK EYE [A: 2]

The tissues around the eye are baggy and allow leakage into them of an unusual amount of blood and fluid after a blow. This means that a bruise in this area has a striking appearance, disproportionate with the degree of injury.

Treatment: Rest and an ice pack. An injection can be given if appearances matter.

Since the eye is so precious, a doctor should examine it if there is any question of injury to it.

Progress: Colors change from red to deep purple, through green to yellow as the extravasated blood is altered chemically and removed. The whole process may last two weeks.

EYELID TROUBLES

Inflamed Eyelid [A Ch: 48, R, 2]
Medical name: Blepharitis.
An infection of the lid margins, which are sore, red, and crusted.
Common in children.

Contributing Causes

Measles	Rubbing eye, because of error
Scarlet Fever	of refraction.
Dandruff	

Treatment: Bathe eyes three times daily (one teaspoonful of salt
to the pint of warm water). Ointment to prevent lids sticking together and special eye drops, from doctor.

Stye [A: 48, R, 2]
Medical name: Hordoleum.
A pustule at the margin of the lid, often in a hair follicle. Commonly a sign of lowered resistance, or may arise similarly to
blepharitis (above). Often itches in early stages.
Treatment: Do not touch or interfere with the stye. Eat better,
rest more, worry less! Styes tend to recur unless the general health
is good.

Cysts [Ch: S, 1]
Medical name: Chalazion.
Small round lumps may form on the eyelids, usually in young
adults. They are the harmless result of a very mild infective process but, because they are unsightly, should be removed by a simple
operation.

Twitching, Flickering of Eyelids [A Ch: N or S, R]
This can come on apparently out of the blue and continue inter-
mittently for an indefinite time. It is uncomfortable and annoying,
but not of serious significance.

Causes

Fatigue or convalescence, in young people.

Pattern of general muscular weakness in elderly persons, in whom it is very common.

Worry, in both.

Treatment: Extra rest. If no better in a week, doctor may prescribe a sedative.

Sagging Lower Lid   [Ch: N or S, X]

The muscle that holds the eyelid in contact with the eye may become slack and the skin of the eyelid lose its elasticity, especially in outdoor types, past middle life. The exposed eye may be irritated and water, particularly in a cold wind, and the tears overflow uncomfortably over the inefficient lid.

Treatment: Avoid going out in cold, gusty, or dusty weather. Plastic surgery can be very successful.

Drooping Upper Lid   [Ch: S]

This may be congenital or due to an eye disease, such as conjunctivitis, facial paralysis, or severe pain as in migraine; it may indicate a general disease of the nerves, or hysteria.

Diagnosis and treatment can be made only by a doctor.

Swollen Lids   [A Ch: N or S]

May occur with such simple conditions as colds, measles, and crying, but appearing without obvious cause, they may be a pointer to kidney, heart, or gland trouble, or arise as an allergic reaction.

Treatment: Obvious cause: cold pack; otherwise consult doctor for check.

Eyelid Nodules

Medical name: Xanthelasma.

Painless yellowish nodules just under the skin, often concerned with a high fat content in the blood stream, in the senior years. Not serious in themselves and easily removed, but your doctor should know about them.

OTHER ABNORMALITIES

Staring Eyes   [Ch: S]

The eyes stand out, giving the face an astonished look. Unless it is an inherited family characteristic, the likeliest cause is thyroid trouble, but it could possibly be due to a tumor behind the eye.

Consult your doctor.

Shadows or Rings under the Eyes   [N, R]

A purple to gray coloration, without swelling, under the eyes, particularly in children, young people, and women. The tissues are loose here and the skin delicately thin, so if the circulation is sluggish, as may occur in fatigue or convalescence, the blue color of the slowly returning venous blood may show here. It is common in those who have had malaria, but has no special significance.

This condition is only important as Nature's hint to take more rest.

It can occur in babies in their sleep, because that is when their circulation slows down most. It has no other significance.

Watering of the Eyes

Excessive production of the tears which normally perform the vital function of washing the eyes clean is commonly due to irritation:

Dust, sand, or visible speck on the eye.

Inflammation of eyelid, or eye, as conjunctivitis, possibly as part of a cold, measles, etc.

Allergic reaction as in hay fever.

Or the tears may overflow, although normal in quantity because:

The lower lids are sagging.

The duct to nose is blocked.

Treatment: According to cause. Cold makes it worse.

Itching of the Eye

Causes

Pink eye.

Stye.

Less intense:
  Errors of refraction.
  Conjunctivitis.
  Blepharitis: Inflamed lid.

INFLAMED EYE: CONJUNCTIVITIS

Inflammation of the special skin covering the eyeball.
Iden:ification: Gritty feeling in eye, soreness, smarting or pain; redness ("blood shot"); watering; dislike of bright light.

Simple Type   [A: 48, I or W, 1/7–1]
The result of any irritation: smoke, heat, cold, irritating powders, colds, measles, hay fever, and other illnesses.
Treatment: Saline eye-wash (one teaspoon salt per pint of warm water) three times a day.

If no better in one day see doctor for special eye drops and ointment.

"Pink Eye"   [A: S, C, 1]
Symptoms similar but more marked than in simple conjunctivitis. Much itching. It often starts in one eye and affects the other later. Very contagious: occurs in epidemics in schools, or attacks the whole household if one member gets it.
Treatment: Drops, lotion, and ointment from doctor. Scrupulous hygiene of towels, hands, and handkerchiefs is necessary to reduce contagion.

Ophthalmia Neonatorum
A dangerous form of conjunctivitis affecting the newborn. Fortunately it is preventable, and the particular care of new babies' eyes by the obstetrician is to guard against this trouble.

Other Chronic Forms of Conjunctivitis   [Ch: S]
Seen particularly in the ill, undernourished, and neglected; they can cause lasting damage.
Sore eyes should always be seen by a physician.

OTHER CONDITIONS OF THE EYE

Inflammations

Iritis: Inflammation of the colored part of the eye.

Keratitis: Inflammation of the transparent window in front of the pupil.

Glaucoma: Over-distension and distortion of the globe.

All these are painful and serious; they interfere with vision, and in each there is obviously something wrong with the eye.

Expert medical assistance is required.

Bloodshot Eye

Either the general redness of *conjunctivitis,* above, or bleeding under the conjunctiva, making a bright red, flame-shaped area with its apex towards the cornea, known as:

Subconjunctival Hemorrhage [A: S, W, 6]

Occurs after injury, or spontaneously, particularly in the elderly. Painless. Harmless. Sometimes, not always, associated with high blood pressure.

Duration: Three–six weeks, irrespective of treatment.

"Something in the Eye"

Foreign body in the eye.

Grit entering the eye feels uncomfortable, if it is under the lid or on the white of the eye, but sharply painful if it is on the vital transparent cornea, through which you look.

Treatment: If the foreign body cannot be seen, it may be colorless; there may merely be conjunctivitis, simulating the gritty feeling of real grit, or the particle may be stuck to the inside of the upper lid. In the latter case, pulling the upper lid over the lower may dislodge it, or the eyelid may be turned inside outermost over a pencil and examined. An eyewash of normal saline (one teaspoon salt per pint water) may remove an unwanted object.

If foreign body is still there after these gentle methods of removal have been tried, DO NO MORE yourself, but see your doctor.

Cross-Eye, Squint

Medical term: Strabismus.

The lines of vision from the two eyes are not parallel: disastrous from the point of view of appearance, but not necessarily associated with defective sight, although the patient may see double. *Causes:* Hereditary, or an error of refraction much more marked in one eye, especially in the young.

Weakness or paralysis of the muscles which move the eye, as in fatigue, convalescence, and certain illnesses, particularly in old people.

Treatment: By doctor, according to cause.

Color Blindness

In the commonest form red and green cannot be distinguished, and both appear grayish, but sometimes there is only partial loss of color; e.g., some red but not all reds are seen. This condition is usually hereditary, occurring in 3–4% of males but far fewer females.

Rarely it can come on owing to tobacco poisoning.

Treatment: None, but work involving colored signals, as on railways, at sea, or in the air, must be avoided. A boy should not be allowed to set his heart on becoming, say, an airman, if he is color-blind.

Cataract   [Ch: S, W]

Loss of transparency of the glasslike lens of the eye, usually starting at the edge and working towards the center. There is a congenital form, but the commonest cataracts are in people over forty-five, a by-product of aging, sometimes hastened by diabetes, arterial degeneration, parathyroid disorders, and local eye troubles.

Identification: Increasing dimness of vision, particularly for distance; near vision may actually improve temporarily; occasionally two images may be seen by one eye.

Treatment: Operation: 95% successful.

When "ripe," i.e. completely opaque, the lens is removed and spectacles or contact lenses provided to replace its function.

Duration: It takes one–three years for the cataract to develop to the stage when surgery is beneficial. Only a doctor can assess this.

Pterygium   [Ch: S, W, X]

A wedge-shaped, white, opaque growth of tissue over the seeing part of the eye, caused by dust and wind irritation in an outdoor life.

This is not dangerous, never cancerous, but may interfere with the sight.

Treatment: Simple operation.

Prevention: Goggles during dusty outdoor activities.

White Crescents or Rings in the Iris

Medical name: Acrus senilis.

This appearance is a normal concomitant of aging, but it some-times occurs in the forties. The lines are caused by a deposit of fat in the corneal cells. The health of the eye and its sight are not affected, and the significance of arcus is not yet established.

Irregularities of the Pupils   [S U]

Very large, very small, unequal, or oddly shaped pupils are signifi-cant of various disorders and should be seen by a doctor.

Spots, Black Specks, before the Eyes

Moving [N]: Due to catching sight of minute particles in the clear fluid inside the globe of the eye. Typically, they can never be brought into focus. Probably always present, they are only notice-able when one is tired, worried, run-down, or anemic.

Near-sighted people are bothered by them most.

They are of no significance, do not indicate any eye disease.

Fixed [S]: i.e., always in the same position, relative to the ob-ject being viewed.

Probably due to an old scar, but may be significant of other dis-ease, so consult doctor.

Involuntary Jerking of the Eyes   [A: S]

Medical term: Nystagmus.

These rapid repeated jerks occur normally when you look out of a train window, or after spinning round.

If it happens spontaneously, it may indicate some general dis-ease of the nervous system; overstraining the eyes by working in poor light, e.g. compositors, miners; disturbance or disease of the inner ear, e.g. Ménière's disease.

See your doctor.

The Ear

For those under the threat of deafness, the outlook has never been so good as it is today. New and fantastically delicate operating techniques, new and incredibly ingenious electronic aids, have revolutionized the assistance that medicine can give. And progress continues apace in our knowledge of an organ second only to the eye in its marvelous complexity, the ear!

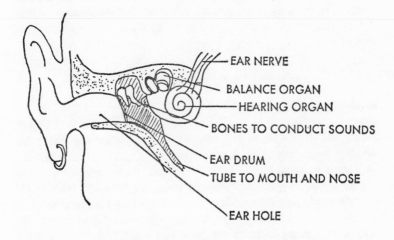

EAR NERVE
BALANCE ORGAN
HEARING ORGAN
BONES TO CONDUCT SOUNDS
EAR DRUM
TUBE TO MOUTH AND NOSE
EAR HOLE

SLIGHT TO MODERATE EARACHE

Inflammation of Lining of Ear Canal   [A Ch: S, W, 1]
Medical name: Otitis externa.

Identification: Irritation, worse on moving jaw, scanty discharge, tenderness on pressure over the tragus, the flap in front of the ear hole.

Treatment: Immediate, at doctor's office: gentle complete clearing out of ear passage. *Long term:* After washing, dry ears gently with a clean towel. Avoid swimming or allowing water into the ears. Do not scratch them—even if they irritate.

Catarrh of the Ear: serous otitis, secretory otitis   [Ch]

Chronic Inflammation of Middle Ear: chronic otitis media   [Ch]

SEVERE, NOT THROBBING, EARACHE

Boil in the Ear Passage   [A: S, O, An, 2–6]
Identification: Pain on a par with toothache, worse on moving jaw, tenderness on pressing tragus in front of ear, deafness. Boil may be visible.
Treatment: Hot water bottle or other local heat helps analgesic. Antibiotic drugs may be prescribed. Attention to general health, since these, as other boils, tend to come when the patient is run-down.

SEVERE, AND THROBBING, EARACHE

Acute Mastoiditis (below).

Acute Inflammation of the Middle Ear   [A: S, B, An, 2]
Medical term: Acute otitis media.
A common, important, painful condition, frequently occurring in children who may scream with the pain; usually starts with a cold in the head, tonsillitis, influenza, or an infectious fever such as measles, whooping cough, or scarlet fever.

The middle ear includes the drum and a chain of movable bones which transmit the vibrations of the drum to the inner ear, the essential part of the organ of hearing. Infection of the middle ear must never be taken lightly.
Identification: Pain as described, fever up to 103°F., often deafness and ringing in the ear, especially in adults. Vomiting may occur in children. Tenderness of bone behind ear, the mastoid process. Discharge may occur, at first mucoid, later thick yellow.
Treatment: Call doctor promptly. He will probably prescribe:
   Antibiotic.

Pain reliever.

Local treatment as necessary.

Drops or inhaler to clear nasal passages, possibly.

Outlook: Most cases resolve satisfactorily, without lasting impairment of hearing, if treatment is begun early and is continued long enough. If treatment is late, inadequate or absent, there may ensue:

Chronic Otitis Media [Ch: S, W, 2]

Symptoms of the acute infection will continue in a modified way, becoming quiescent from time to time, but deafness will increase.

Treatment: By doctor, essential.

Acute Mastoiditis [A: U, B, 6]

Inflammation of the bone behind the ear.

Identification: Patient obviously ill, pain and temperature and deafness increase, creamy discharge, great tenderness over mastoid.

Acute Meningitis [A: U, B]

Irritation or infection of the membranes of the brain.

Both these conditions are very serious and require hospital treatment.

CAUSES OF EARACHE NOT DIRECTLY ASSOCIATED WITH EARS

This is possible because the ear shares its nerve supply with various other parts of the head, and the brain may misinterpret, for instance, toothache as earache. This is known as referred pain. Pain referred to the ear may come from:

Impacted lower molars, especially in boys and girls of eighteen–twenty years.

Faulty jaw joint.

Tonsillitis.

Infected glands in the neck.

Neuralgia of face or tongue.

DISCHARGE AND DEFORMITY

Discharge
Scanty: Otitis externa.
Mucoid or thick and yellow: Otitis media, above.
Profuse and creamy: Mastoiditis.
Bloodstained: Injury by blow on ear, loud bang, poking in some object like a pencil and breaking the drum. Injury of skin of ear passage by poking or scratching. Bleeding from fractured skull.

Deformity
Protruding ears; oddly formed ears: A source of embarrassment well dealt with by the plastic surgeon, ideally between the ages of four and six years.
Cauliflower ears: Caused by bleeding and clot formation under the skin which untreated can cause permanent, shriveled deformity. Plastic surgery greatly improves a developed cauliflower ear.
Ulcers: Usually occur on upper edge of ear. May become cancerous. See doctor.

DEAFNESS

Deafness can be divided into two types, whose differentiation is an important guide to treatment and assessing the probable progress of the condition.

Conductive Deafness
In which there is obstruction to the transmission of the sounds through the outer and middle ear to the actual hearing receiver in the inner ear.
Identification: This deafness is rarely total, because the bones of the skull themselves are still capable of conducting some of the sound. Sufferers can hear quite well if they pull the telephone receiver to their heads; also, because of bone conduction, their own voices sound louder to them than other people's, which makes many of them speak very quietly. These people can be helped by hearing aids.

Types of Conductive Deafness
Wax in ear.
Boils.
Ear drum damage. History of middle ear infection or injury.
Otosclerosis.

Perceptive Deafness

In which there is a fault in the receiving mechanism in the inner ear or in the nerve pathways from it to the brain, or in the brain center itself.

In nerve, or inner ear deafness, in the early stages, other people appear to mumble, because certain high frequency sounds, P's and K's, T's and G's and D's, are not heard, while the rest of the words are. Sufferers are often unable to bear loud sounds, and it is typical of a nerve-deaf person with greatly reduced hearing to complain, "Don't shout, I'm not deaf." Loud sounds are heard at full intensity, though quieter ones may not be perceived at all.

Bone conduction does not help these people, so they hear badly on the telephone, and they are not greatly helped by hearing aids, since greater loudness is accompanied by more distortion of the sounds. Because their own voices sound faint to them, they tend to shout.

Types of Perceptive Deafness
Deafness of old age: Acuity of hearing slowly diminishes in all.
Following an infection such as mumps or measles.
From birth (congenital): either it runs in the family, or the mother had an illness or drug accident during early pregnancy.
Certain drugs, for instance quinine.
Ménière's disease.
Exposure to excessive noise, e.g. boiler makers.

Otosclerosis [Ch: S]

This used to be a tragically incapacitating disease coming on, as it does, in early adulthood, but now it is nearly always curable. It is therefore of vital importance to recognize it and obtain treatment, at whatever age and stage.

The basic difficulty is stickiness and spongy overgrowth of and near the small bones which conduct the sounds from the drum to the cochlea in the inner ear.

Identification: Hereditary link; age 15–30 at onset; females affected twice as often as males; buzzing or ringing in the ear; worse when it is quiet; better able to hear conversation in noisy surroundings (this is merely because the speaker automatically raises his voice). Distortion of sounds, especially noticeable to musicians, precedes actual deafness, but is not so severe as in Ménière's disease.

Treatment: Through doctor, who will refer you to ear specialist. Surgical treatment is very effective when possible, but hearing aids and lip reading may also help.

Outlook: Surgery gives permanent benefit; otherwise the disease progresses, and then becomes static. It is made worse by pregnancy, and may also affect the child.

Notes on Treatment of Deafness
The nerve-deaf, as well as the others, stand today a better-than-ever chance of overcoming their handicap and living a normal life.

New methods of lip reading, language analysis, and auditory training help many, especially children; surgical procedures have made the greatest advance of all: most of the conductive apparatus can be repaired or replaced by the surgeon.

Hearing aids, tiny, transistorized, and inconspicuous, while they cannot replace natural hearing, make what remains of it more useful. *A hearing aid should not be bought without medical advice and a week's trial, at least.*

A difficulty in using a hearing aid is that while the unaided ear automatically censors many irrelevant and unwanted sounds, like other people's conversation at a restaurant, or the background noises in a railway station, the instrument amplifies them all. It is possible, but takes perseverance and time, to learn to ignore and select among the sounds which pour in.

An old-fashioned ear trumpet has this advantage: it may be directed to catch only the voice which its owner wants to hear, or the radio. However, a hearing aid, unlike a trumpet, gives some warning of approaching traffic, a particular hazard to the deaf.

Deafness in Children
Particularly important that this should be recognized and treated as soon as possible. See Children's Section.

Ringing — Buzzing — Hissing in the Ears — Noises in the Head

Medical term: Tinnitus.

Causes

Ear Troubles

Wax or other object in the outer ear.

Inflammation.

Deafness of any type.

Catarrh of the middle ear.

Ménière's disease.

Changes in the ears due to age.

Other causes

Fevers.

Run-down condition: debility, fatigue.

Anemia.

Drugs, e.g. quinine, aspirin.

Very rarely: tumors, can be checked for by doctor.

Exposure to any very loud noise, e.g. soldier on a rifle range.

Heightened consciousness of normal internal sounds, e.g. in a completely silent place.

Psychological.

Impending faint, or epileptic attack.

Treatment of this common complaint is either very simple, e.g. removal of wax, or almost impossible. In the latter case you must learn to ignore what is a harmless, personal, background noise.

Wax in the Ears

Wax is the normal lubrication of the ear and is made by glands in the outer part of the ear passage. In some people an excess is produced, or it may aggregate into a hard lump.

Effects: Deafness, noises in the ear, irritation of the ear passage lining.

Treatment: Do *not* poke any object into the ear.

Warm olive oil, two–three drops, put into the affected ear nightly for a week, will soften hard sticky wax, and it will then probably slip out spontaneously. Syringing of the ear by doctor or nurse may also be necessary.

Objects in the Ear

Beads, peas, etc., may get into the ear, especially in children.

Treatment: Do *not* poke anything whatever into the ear, for the drum may easily be broken.

If the object does not fall out when the head is rested on the affected side, get doctor's skilled assistance.

Insect in the Ear

Treatment: If the creature is alive, drop warm olive oil in the ear, which will cause the intensely irritating movements to stop. Syringing probably necessary.

Do *not* try to get the insect out by poking anything into the ear.

Ménière's Disease   [Ch: S after attack, X]

Associated with increased pressure in the balancing mechanism in the ear. Usually comes on between the ages of forty and sixty, more commonly in men.

Identification: Sudden attack of giddiness, nausea, and usually vomiting. Perceptive type deafness (above), usually in one ear only, with distortion of sounds; noises in the ears.

Treatment: Immediate: Lie on bed till attack passes: *Later:* Doctor will supply medicine to use in attacks, and advice as to regime between attacks. Operation occasionally required.

Duration of attacks: Minutes to hours.

Duration of illness: Progressive over years, with increasing deafness, but finally the attacks cease.

Catarrh of the Ears   [A Ch: S, R, 2]

Medical term: Serous otitis, secretory otitis.

This is not a severe illness, causing little more than discomfort; but unrecognized and untreated, it may lead to permanent deafness. It often occurs in children.

Identification: Deafness, and an unpleasant full feeling in the ear, following a cold.

Treatment: Only a doctor can make a diagnosis and apply the special treatment that may be needed.

MOTION SICKNESS

Travel, car, airplane, sea sickness.

Inside the ear lies the balance organ whose purpose is to help you maintain your balance when walking or climbing. If this organ is overstimulated by movements not in your control, or you are extra sensitive, the messages from it spill over to the vomiting center in the brain and you feel sick. You may also by a similar mechanism sweat, yet feel cold, yawn, and feel depressed.

Women are worst affected, particularly during menstrual periods. Sufferers from high blood pressure, sinusitis, and migraine are especially susceptible.

Treatment: Tablets through your doctor (ask his advice if you are, or might be, pregnant) or pharmacist. Take half an hour before journey.

Other maneuvers: Avoid reading. Avoid twisting the head. Avoid fizzy drinks. Tilt head back and hold it still. Place yourself so that you can see the unmoving horizon. Have windows open if possible.

The Throat and Neck

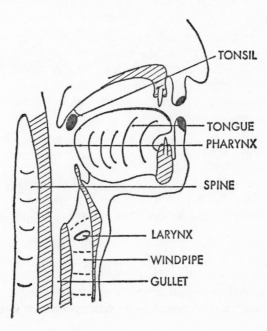

SORE THROAT

One of the commonest and most uncomfortable symptoms, frequently acting as an announcer of another illness.

ACUTE SORE THROAT

Temperature Normal or only Slightly Raised
COMMON COLD
Especially before the nose starts running freely.
DRY THROAT
Often on returning to town after a vacation, or in dry weather in cities.
Identification: Discomfort on swallowing; dry raspy feeling; "tickling." The back of the throat is generally reddened, especially around the edges.
Treatment: Aspirin. Copious hot drinks. Gargles are now thought to spread the infection rather than to subdue it.
FISHBONE SCRATCH   [S or 48, W, 1]
You may hurt your throat by swallowing a fishbone, and feel as though it is stuck. If the feeling persists, go see your doctor. Very often the discomfort continues because of the scratching of the sharp fishbone or other object on its way past, but your doctor will be able to examine your throat properly and make sure. See Fishbone in Throat (below).

Temperature Raised
ACUTE PHARYNGITIS   [A: S, An, 2]
Inflammation of the pharynx, soft palate, and tonsils if present.
Identification: Similar to, but more marked than the beginning of a cold. Back of throat mottled pink and red. Temperature 100°–104°F.

Acute pharyngitis can be an entity on its own, due to the common throat organisms: viruses, streptococci, staphylococci, and the hemophilus influenzae (flu bug).

It may merely be a part of an illness, usually coming on before the rash or other symptoms, for instance: measles (sore eyes probably, and cough); poliomyelitis (severe headache probable); scarlet fever, German measles, chicken pox (rash already present). But sore throats caused by streptococci may lead to rheumatic fever or nephritis. Children with sore throats should be seen by a doctor.

ACUTE TONSILLITIS [A: S, An, 2]

Commonly, but by no means invariably, in children of from four to nine years. See Children's Section.

Identification: An acute pharyngitis (above), but tonsils are swollen and may have yellow spots or ulcers on them. A yellowish membranous patch on one or both tonsils can mean *diphtheria,* particularly in the unimmunized.

Special drugs will be prescribed, as well as measures indicated, for tonsillitis and pharyngitis.

Virus tonsillitis: May not respond to the antibiotics which cure the usual type. Recovery is complete in a week or two, however.

QUINSY [A: U, B, An, 2–6]

An abscess associated with the tonsil.

Identification: Very severe throat pain, sometimes radiating into neck and ears; swallowing almost impossible; difficulty in opening mouth; fever of around 103°F. Swelling and distortion usually of one side only of throat, with much oozing of mucus. Glands in the neck are swollen and tender.

Treatment: Antibiotics and analgesics.

MONONUCLEOSIS [A: S, A, C, 2–6]

An infectious illness, due to a virus, usually affecting children and young adults.

Identification: Sudden fever of 101°–103°F., perhaps mild tonsillitis; headache, painful swollen glands in neck second or third day, followed by other gland enlargement under the arms, etc. Sometimes a rash.

Duration: Variable: two weeks to two months. Glands usually go down in seven days, but may remain for months. Fever may take up to three weeks to settle, and weakness persists for several weeks.

There are not likely to be any after effects ultimately.

Incubation period: Five–twelve days.

How long infectious? No one knows. Keep to yourself until one week after temperature has gone down.

MUMPS   [A: S]

Sore throat, stiff neck, temperature around 102°F., and headache precede the characteristic swelling by four or five days.

ACUTE LARYNGITIS   [A: S, 2]

Hoarseness or loss of voice as well as pain noticed. The causative organisms are often those of acute pharyngitis or tonsillitis. See above.

CHRONIC SORE THROAT

Chronic Pharyngitis

Identification: As acute pharyngitis, but milder and continued. Sometimes the back of the throat has a granular appearance.

Conditions Causing Chronic Pharyngitis

Smoking.

Dust and poor ventilation.

Septic teeth or gums.

Mouth breathing, from nasal obstruction.

Faulty voice production. Chronic laryngitis also present.

Anemia, especially in middle-aged women.

Treatment: Must be directed to the causes.

Chronic Tonsillitis

Usually follows and is caused by attacks of acute tonsillitis.

FISHBONE IN THROAT

If you have swallowed a fishbone, plum stone, or other hard or spiky object, eat one or two mouthfuls of bread (the center part, not crust) and then have a drink.

Most swallowed objects pass through doing no harm, and the digestive juices round off the sharp points of such things as splinters of bone.

If, however, you continue to have a sensation of something stuck in throat or chest, get doctor to check. See Fishbone Scratch (above).

HOARSENESS, LOSS OF VOICE

Sore throat. Above.

Overuse of Normal Voice, or its faulty production
Regularly: "clergyman's throat," also schoolteacher's, stockbroker's. Lessons in voice production needed.

Occasionally: shouting at a match. Restraint needed next time.

Singers: "singer's nodes" are small patches of thickening on the vocal cords, due to strain and misuse of the voice during a cold or other respiratory infection.

Treatment: Removal of nodules. Lessons in speech production.

Chronic Laryngitis
Causes
Infection.
Alcoholism ⎫
Smoking ⎬ restraint needed.
Gout.
Chronic sinusitis.

Acute Laryngitis

Smog or other poisonous gases
Some throats are more sensitive than others.

Swelling of Larynx
Due to general disease, e.g. kidney trouble, allergy, drug sensitivity to, for instance, aspirin or potassium iodide.

Growth on the Cord
Warts, papilloma, or cancer. Because of the latter possibility, *HOARSENESS LASTING MORE THAN TWO WEEKS MUST BE INVESTIGATED.*

ACUTE LARYNGITIS

[A: S, F, An, X, 1–2]
Causes: Cold or influenza, or the infectious fevers. Any age.
Croup in children is a special form.
Identification: Comes on suddenly; huskiness, dry cough, sore to
swallow, may have fever, but not feeling generally ill.
Treatment: SILENCE! Warm, moist atmosphere is comfortable,
from steaming kettle or inhalations.
Duration: One week.
Outlook: Voice may be impaired if overstrain is allowed. The
trouble is likely to recur, so particular care must be taken over
future colds. Removal of the cause and avoidance of over use of
the voice are cornerstones in its cure.

RARE CAUSES OF LOSS OF VOICE

Loss of voice following a shock
  Only a whisper, if anything, can be produced. This is likely to
be a nervous disturbance: Hysterical aphonia.
Loss of voice due to pressure on laryngeal nerve
  This may be due to a swelling or tumor in the neck or chest.

STIFF NECK

Medical term: Torticollis.
  There is only one painless type, and that is congenital. The
ropelike muscle that runs from the mastoid bone behind the ear
to the breastbone is occasionally less well-developed on one side
(usually the right) than the other, and that side of the face is also
smaller.
  All other stiff neck is painful.
  It is always important, and should never be ignored or laughed
at.

ACUTE STIFF NECK

Common Transient Stiff Neck   [A: 48, R, An, 1]

Coming on after exposure to cold, sleeping in a cramped position, unaccustomed exercise like gardening, and often with a cold in the head. Backing the car, with neck twisted and strained, is a common cause.

Treatment: Rest for one–two days. Hot water bottle. Massage. Aspirin. Goes away without trace, often in twenty-four hours.

Because of Inflamed Glands   [A: S]

The glands may be felt as small tender lumps under the jaw or behind the rope-muscle.

Look for the causative trouble in ear, teeth, or throat, and have it fixed.

Injury   [A: 48 or S]

If the neck continues to be stiff and painful after twisting, there may be a crack or sprain in the neck bones or their joints, or a slipped disc in this part of the spine. Only an X-ray and doctor's examination can tell. Without treatment you might have a permanently stiff neck.

SPASMS OF STIFFNESS AND PAIN

[A Ch: N or S]

Medical term: Spasmodic torticollis.

Can be very painful and distressing: the head is pulled to one side. There is, however, nothing physically wrong: this is a form of tic or nervous spasm.

Treatment: Learn to relax. Doctor may help. There is no danger to health in this trouble, which always rights itself during sleep.

CHRONIC STIFF NECK

See doctor in all cases

Arthritis of Neck Joints

Rheumatoid arthritis. After scarlet fever, diphtheria and other infections.

Poker-back

Back becoming stiff and head difficult to raise.

Cancer

Rarely starts in neck.

HEAD RETRACTION

[A: S]

A special kind of stiff neck, in which the head is retracted (pulled back) occurs occasionally in tetanus (lockjaw), meningitis, or in high fever from other illnesses.

SWELLINGS OR LUMPS IN THE NECK

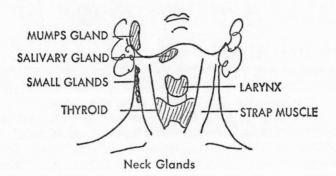

Neck Glands

Enlarged Lymphatic Nodes (Glands)

Feel below angle of jaw and downwards from there.

Infected: from teeth, throat, mouth, or lip. Tender to touch, and possibly even painful without touch. FAR THE COMMONEST.
Tuberculous infection, formerly common in children. Uncommon now.
Secondary to tumors anywhere on the head or chest.
Part of a general illness of lymphatic tissue such as mononucleosis or Hodgkin's disease.
Part of measles, scarlet fever, whooping cough, or chicken pox.

Cysts
Originating from errors of development: always present. Painless. Feel fluid. Not important to health but can be removed if they become awkwardly large.

Lump Immediately below the Jaw
Infected, etc., lymph node: See above. Tender.
Mumps of the salivary gland below the jaw. Painful, and tender.
Blockage of the duct of this gland. Characteristically the swelling increases when food is put in the mouth, especially lemon.

Enlarged Thyroid Gland
This special gland is wrapped around the windpipe; you cannot normally feel it, only if it is enlarged or hard. See discussion of the thyroid gland, below.
Note: Any neck enlargement lasting upwards of a week may be significant, and should be seen by a doctor without delay.

"Lump in the Throat"
A feeling like a ball in the throat, but no visible bulge.

THE THYROID GLAND AND ITS DISORDERS

The thyroid is a butterfly-shaped gland in close proximity to the windpipe, just below the larynx or Adam's apple (Eve's, too!). It is one of the so-called *ductless glands:* it does not pour its product out through a tube, but puts it directly into the bloodstream.

The pea-sized pituitary gland, in the safest part of the skull, is boss of the whole ductless gland system. Under pituitary stimulation the thyroid acts on the body like a car's accelerator, speeding up or permitting to slow down its every activity, including growth.

A child born with a rudimentary thyroid gland is a *cretin,* backward mentally, stunted physically, unless treated with thyroid medication.

Through disease of the thyroid, faulty messages from the pituitary, or shrinking of this gland like other organs, with advancing years, too little thyroxine may be produced. This results in:

Myxedema, or Hypothyroidism   [Ch: S, W, X]
Identification: Sufferer feels cold all the time; gain in weight but not appetite; much sleep but still weary; loss of hair, and what remains is dull; lack of drive; swelling, in later stages, especially of face and eyelids. Slow in every way.
Condition of the gland: Usually small and atrophied and cannot be felt, but sometimes a *simple goiter* (see below) may develop into hypothyroidism. The rare cancer of the thyroid can also lead to diminution of the normal function of the gland.
Treatment: Fortunately cheap, very effective and simple. The missing substance can be taken in tablet form. If you suspect this disorder—see your doctor.

Enlargement of the Thyroid: Goiter
Swelling to be seen and felt in the center of the neck, moving up and down as you swallow. Pressure on the windpipe may cause discomfort and shortness of breath, especially at night, and sometimes cough.

Simple Goiter   [Ch: S, W, X]
Smooth, balloon-like swelling of the whole gland:
>   May be due to shortage of iodine in the diet.
>   Likely in mountainous areas such as Switzerland.
>   Runs in families as well as districts.
>   Puberty ⎱
>   Pregnancy ⎰ temporary, mild, harmless, and self-curing.

Treatment: Iodized salt, for it will help the first and second types of goiter. Quantity sufficient if used in normal amounts in cooking.

Nodular Goiter   [Ch: S, W, X]

Medical name: Adenoma of the thyroid.

A bumpy, grapelike enlargement affecting both sides of the gland.

There may be no other symptoms for years, and then the extra knobs of thyroid tissue may start overproduction of thyroxine, resulting in *secondary thyrotoxicosis*. This is likely at the menopause and is commoner in women than men. Adenomatous enlargement is a benign, or friendly, tumor, so there is no need to worry about cancer. However, it is important that advice should be sought and treatment begun, since at this age the illness may harm the heart if unchecked.

Secondary Thyrotoxicosis

Identification: Loss of weight but wolfish appetite; patient feels heat; hot skin; rapid heart; and signs of sensitization to the alerting hormone, adrenaline. These signs are: nervousness, tremor, staring eyes, sweating, palpitation.

Exophthalmic Goiter   [Ch: S]

Primary thyrotoxicosis, Graves' disease.

Identification: Smooth, all over, moderate enlargement of gland, and symptoms of secondary thyrotoxicosis.

The term exophthalmic means "bulging-eyed." The primary fault in this type of thyrotoxicosis, or overactivity of the thyroid, lies in the pituitary gland, which also has the effect of causing too much fat to be made in the eye socket and pushing the eye forward; this does not occur in the adenomatous type described above. This, added to the staring effect, makes the eyes look like those of a frightened horse, and may even make it difficult to focus on near objects.

This disorder arises most often in women, between puberty and the menopause, but also affects men. It can follow emotional stress, but not necessarily.

Treatment of Thyrotoxicosis: Primary and Secondary

Occasionally primary thyrotoxicosis subsides with such simple measures as rest in bed, sedatives, and removal of any emotional strain. Usually, however, treatment for either type must be specific, either by surgical removal of part of the gland, radioactive iodine, or other medicine, and it usually works very well. Of course, your doctor will know which to advise for you and must supervise.

Solitary Lump in the Thyroid   [Ch: SU]
Possibly a rare non-benign growth, requiring prompt investigation and treatment.

DIFFICULTY IN SWALLOWING

See also in Chest Section: Difficulty in Swallowing
There are several ways in which this symptom may arise.

Something Blocking the Way   [Ch: SU]
Usually there is discomfort but no pain when this is first noticed. There is a feeling of obstruction in the neck or chest, and the initial difficulty is with the solid foods like meat, bread, and vegetables.

This condition must be investigated properly and promptly, so that the blockage, whether it is inside the gullet or something pressing on it from outside, can be relieved. The cause may be simple or serious.

See also Swelling in the Neck.

Nervous Causes without Physical Obstruction
"Lump in the Throat"   [A: 48, W]
Also a feeling of constriction, it is something we have all experienced at times of mental stress. It can be a symptom of anxiety, especially in adolescents and menopausals. The sufferer does not realize the cause of his or her difficulty in swallowing but never loses weight with it! The doctor can help—unless the symptom passes when the patient is calmer.
Alcoholism may affect the nerves controlling swallowing.
Paralysis of the palate: May occur after diphtheria. A mild attack may pass unrecognized except as a sore throat. The food tends to come up into the nose.
Rare paralyses of swallowing apparatus. Your doctor can disentangle the possibilities.

Too Painful to Swallow
Sore throat; inflamed mouth or tongue; laryngitis, and most causes of hoarseness.
Injury: Usually this cause is self-evident, but occasionally a toothbrush bristle can become lodged at the back of the throat unbeknown and cause much swallowing difficulty.

Anemia
Especially in women, between thirty-five and sixty. Uncommon.

DIFFICULTY IN BREATHING

May be felt in the neck or throat, but the majority of the underlying causes are to be found elsewhere. See Chest Section.

COUGH

An abrupt intake of air, followed by a forcible effort at breathing out, with the glottis closed, until the air pressure in the lungs is raised and the doorway of the glottis explodes open. The air shoots out, carrying with it anything that was blocking the bronchial tubes.

Cough is a protective reflex, aimed at ridding the body of mucus, debris, or irritants in the breathing apparatus.

Cough, in some circumstances, serves no good purpose, as in the dry, unproductive bark of, say, laryngitis or tonsillitis.

Coughing something up usually means trouble in the lungs themselves, but not invariably, for matter from the nose or sinuses may slide down the back of the throat, set up an irritation, and be coughed up as sputum.

HOW TO IDENTIFY YOUR COUGH

Unproductive Cough: i.e. nothing is coughed up
Children rarely cough up anything, because they swallow the mucus. This is not harmful.

Short, dry, cough brought on by going into the cold. Due to congestion of the back of the throat, as in colds and simple sore throat, tonsillitis, or smoker's cough.

Similar but coming on after talking: inflammation of the larynx.

Night cough, often due to chronic congestion of the back of the throat, or to an extra long uvula—the little fleshy part dangling from the arch between the tonsils.

Repeated nervous cough: a form of habit spasm.

Long, barking, showy cough: a symptom of hysteria.

Short suppressed cough, with pain in the side, is likely to be due to pleurisy.

Brassy cough, also likened to the sound of a gander, may mean pressure on the bronchi from some swelling in the chest, such as an aneurism, a tumor, or enlarged glands.

    Heart troubles: "heart cough," one type.

    Dental troubles, ear troubles, possibly.

Silent ineffectual cough: paralysis of the vocal cord, a matter for the doctor.

Cough with Very Little Expectoration, and in Paroxysms

Whooping cough, characteristic whoop at end. May cause vomiting.

Like whooping cough but no whoop, in middle-aged, may be emphysema.

Coming on in a warm atmosphere: Consider tuberculosis.

Early morning, often due to irritation of larynx or windpipe. A little sticky mucus may be brought up. Face purple with effort for tiny result. Cough of early tuberculosis may also favor this time.

Asthma attack, often at night.

Cardiac asthma: heart trouble.

Productive Cough: Some matter is coughed up

Recurrent, wheezy cough: Bronchitis.

Asthma is often associated with chronic bronchitis, and in that case there is a typical difficulty in breathing out. Heart troubles.

Paroxysms, with pus in the matter brought up: Bronchiectasis. Tuberculosis. Abscess bursting into a bronchial tube.

Irritating cough, most marked on going to bed and getting up. Infection of nose and perhaps sinuses, with mucus running down the back of the throat, postnasal drip. Early tuberculosis.

Hawking cough: catarrhal throat, especially in cigarette smokers; chronic nasal catarrh; chronic sinusitis.

TREATMENT OF COUGH

Obviously, discovering the cause of the cough and eradicating that is of the first importance, and a productive cough may be doing a useful service by clearing the respiratory tract of harmful or obstructing matter.

However, a dry cough serves no such purpose and does harm by disturbing the sufferer's sleep, and other people. If it is merely that the back of the throat is hypersensitive (e.g. after flu), simple drinks, or sweets, medicated or otherwise, may palliate.

A cough syrup containing a cough-center sedative may help if simple measures are ineffective.

When a dry cough at the beginning of an illness becomes productive, it is much more comfortable; inhalations, a warm steamy atmosphere, and expectorant mixtures may be ordered by the doctor to assist this development.

Never ignore a cough.

Sputum

The material which is coughed up, or expectorated, comes *usually* from the bronchi or lungs, and is considered in detail in the section on the chest.

Influenza [A: 48, B, An, 2]

A highly infectious feverish illness from antiquity, caused by a variety of viruses. Commoner in winter: all ages. Spread by droplets from respiratory passages of victims.

Incubation: 12–48 hours. Probably infective only for the first two days.

Identification: Sudden onset usually: always a raised temperature. Any or all of these: bouts of shivering; pains all over, especially the head and back; cold symptoms; hoarseness; cough; loss of appetite; pain behind the eyes; dizziness; nausea and vomiting—although intestinal flu is probably a separate entity.

Treatment: Analgesics. Antibiotics ineffective except against other invading organisms. Influenza varies greatly in severity and duration: influenzal pneumonia can be a serious complication.

SKIN SECTION

How important is your skin?

It is your armor, composed of millions upon millions of overlapping scales, self-repairing if it is wounded.

It is your raincoat. Whoever heard of anyone's brain or muscles getting soaked when it rained?

It is your overcoat, lined with an insulating layer of fat which gets thin with age, so that grandfathers feel the cold.

It is better fitting than stretch nylon, lasting seventy years plus, and only after decades do the elastic fibers become somewhat slack.

It has a warning system of nerve endings to tell you of heat, cold, pain—or a caress—including its exact location.

It manufactures Vitamin D, can form antibodies against disease, and rids the body of certain poisons.

It is your private climate control. As a cooling system it works like a car radiator: hot blood from the internal organs circulates through the skin at a rate of 50–80 gallons per hour and loses

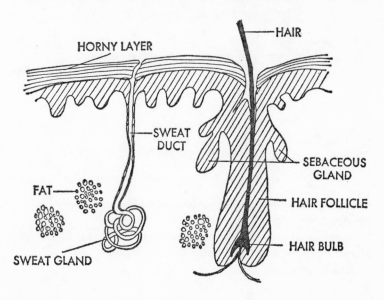

HORNY LAYER

HAIR

SWEAT DUCT

SEBACEOUS GLAND

FAT

HAIR FOLLICLE

HAIR BULB

SWEAT GLAND

heat. Sweat is also poured on to the surface as required, for cooling by evaporation.

When conditions are chill, the blood vessels contract: the skin becomes a blanket. Even the gooseflesh pimples of cold are an attempt to emulate the animals who bush out their fur to increase its insulating effect.

Your skin matters, so look to it. Exposed as it is to the outside world, there is a variety of causative agents for skin troubles, and at least three hundred common skin complaints. All of them, of course, are in plain view.

ITCHING

This curious intermingling of the sensations of pain and touch can be so slight as to be a pleasure, or so severe as to make sleep impossible, suicide contemplatable. It usually comes—and goes—in paroxysms.

Formication: A sensation as though insects are crawling in or on the skin is a form of itching—notably present in cocaine addicts.

ITCHING FOR NO VISIBLE REASON

External Causes

Soaps, bath salts, and detergents to the sensitive.

Scratchy clothing, wool, flannel, nylon, and certain dyes affect some.

Chemicals and dusts. What is your work?

Internal Causes

Natural, though not Invariably Present

Pregnancy ⎱
Menopause ⎰ they pass.

Old age—this does not! (Senile pruritus)

Special Sensitivity

Eating shellfish, strawberries, eggs, milk, pork, and onions. Easy to prevent when you know what to avoid.

Serum injections.

Drugs—are you taking any medicine? Penicillin and aspirin cause allergy most commonly.

Disorders of Parts Other Than the Skin

Diabetes mellitus: irritation from too much sugar in the blood.

Hodgkin's disease.

Internal parasites such as tapeworms. Have you ever been abroad?

Liver disease: the yellow skin of jaundice is the giveaway, but may be absent.

Kidney troubles.

Leukemia.

Neurotic or nervous itch. Have you any anxieties? They may be coming out through your skin.

Persistence of an itch after the cause has gone: common, but rights itself ultimately.

ITCHING SECONDARY TO VISIBLE SKIN DISORDERS

Usually *acute* skin troubles cause itching, and slowly evolving ones do not. There is always itching with:

Hives.

Eczema.

Acute specific fevers with a rash, such as chicken pox, measles, German measles, scarlet fever.

Dermatitis.

LOCAL CONDITIONS PRODUCING LOCALIZED ITCHING

Discharges from nose, ears, mouth, vagina, or rectum. (Localized dermatitis may develop.)

Parasites—such as scabies, fleas, lice.

Bites and stings.

Itching around the Rectum May Be Due to:

Threadworms.

Piles.

Fissure.

Diarrhea or constipation.

Lack of cleanliness.

Eczema.

Acute or chronic anxiety, though not a local condition, very often causes itching in this area.

Occupational Itches, Usually on the Hands

Grocer's itch, from sugar.

Carpenter's itch, from satinwood.

Gardener's itch.

Mites from hens, cows, cats, and rabbits.

Chilblains.

Fungus or other troubles between the toes.

Note: Itching is noticeably absent in syphilitic skin troubles, and always slight in psoriasis. It is much more troublesome in nervous and highstrung persons.

Treatment of itching: Hydrocortisone and other steroid ointments obtained through your doctor. Sedatives may be necessary in the acute phase. *Try not to scratch.*

SPECIAL CAUSES OF ITCHING

Bites and Stings

Sensitivity to bites and stings is extremely variable, but fair-skinned and red-haired people often fare worst.

Bees [A: N]

Remove sting and poison sac by fingernail, taking care not to squeeze out more poison. Antihistamine ointment or baking soda paste.

Wasps, Hornets, Ants [A: N]

Antihistamine ointments. Hot applications are helpful for severe stings, and occasionally treatment as for shock is needed if the victim collapses. If a severe reaction occurs with a sting, such as hives or breathing troubles, see your doctor at once. You may prevent a more serious reaction next time.

Mosquitoes, Gnats, and Midges [A: N]

Prevention: Partial—by smearing the skin with dimethylphthallate or aromatic oil. Preparations from the pharmacist.

Treatment: Irritation allayed by cooling lotion (menthol), antihistamine cream, or bathing with saline. Watch for sepsis; if present, hot soaks, and see doctor.

Fleas [A: N]

Bite has typical red dot in its center. Flea powders with DDT prevent and disinfest. Treat bites as for those of mosquitoes.

Harvest Bugs [A: N]

Bright red, 0.3 mm. long. July to September. Irritation delayed a few hours but lasts 36 hours. Treat as for mosquitoes.

Lice [Ch: S, C, 2]

Head louse, body louse, and crab louse, which inhabits the hairs of the sex area. All a dirty gray, and live on the blood of their host.

Irritation leads to scratching, scratching to infection of the skin and pustular spots.

Treatment: Follow doctor's instructions to the letter. Step up hygiene afterward.

Scabies: "The Itch" [A Ch: S, C, 2]

Contagious. Caused by a mite.

Identification: Intense itching; burrows, where the female acarus lives and lays her eggs, in the skin of wrist, hand (especially between the fingers), buttocks, and armpits; rash also.

Treatment: Benzyl benzoate application. Clothes and bed clothes, as well as patient need disinfestation.

"The itch" is no respecter of person or position, but is not acquired without quite prolonged contact.

Pinworms [A Ch: S, C, 2]

Infection via water or vegetables, and reinfection from scratching near rectum, and getting pinworm eggs under the fingernails. Mainly children, but adults by no means immune.

Identification: Itching around rectum, disturbing sleep; irritability; mucus and white, threadlike worms in the motions.

Treatment: Avoid scratching. Use one-piece sleeping suit, or nightgown tied below feet. Keep fingernails short, and wash them carefully before meals. Medicine from doctor for whole family; repeat after a week.

Duration: Clear in two weeks if treated, and without reinfection.

Senile Pruritus [Ch: N or S]

Identification: Itching in the elderly, often brought on by exposure to cold; you do not have to be senile! Skin dry, thin and shiny, or scaling. It may develop patchy darkening, and small dilated blood vessels may appear.

Treatment: As for itching in general. Do not use soap; instead, sponge skin with emulsifying ointment, such as mineral oil, in warm water.

OTHER SKIN SENSATIONS

Tingling
Burning } skin sensations occurring in eczema, dermatitis,
Prickling cold sores, and cold.

Pain: Felt in shingles, boils, and carbuncles.

Anesthesia: Inability to feel pain.

Hyperesthesia: Undue sensitivity to any contact.

Paresthesia: Unusual sensations from usual stimuli, e.g. pins and needles from plain touch.

All these arise in troubles involving the nerves themselves, for instance, shingles, an injury to or pressure on a nerve to the thigh from a slipping disc in the spine, or rare nerve disorders.

INJURIES OF THE SKIN

Bruise

Identification: Pain, tenderness, swelling and discoloration of the skin, going through stages of red, purple, blue, green, and yellow. Usually follows a blow or sprain.

Mechanism: Blood leaking from damaged vessels and lying loose in the tissues, until the blood pigment is gradually converted into (yellow) bilirubin and absorbed.

If the leak of blood occurs deep in the tissues, it may be days before the bruise "comes out," i.e., shows on the skin, and it may appear at some distance from the hurt place, because of the blood tracking down in the tissues.

Treatment: Cold compress. Hot bath may relieve the ache of extensive bruising. Massage may slightly assist absorption. There are tablets which hasten the disappearance of a bruise, obtainable from the doctor—or injections, if appearances are worth it.

Apparent bruising or bruising with little or no injury can be caused by various blood disorders, general illnesses, jaundice, and certain drugs; it needs medical investigation.

"Black Eye." See Head Section

Blister

For blisters that are part of a skin disorder or eruption, see above. A blister due to injury is a collection of serum under the horny layer of the skin. It is caused by friction, as in marching or rowing, burns (see below), and crushing.

Treatment: Large blisters should be opened with a sterilized needle (made red hot in a flame), dressed with antiseptic cream and bandage.

If on the feet, check fit of shoes, presence of nails, etc., and darns or projecting seams in the socks or stockings.

Blood blisters

Arise in the same way as the clear type, but more easily become infected. They often result from a nip in a car door, or as a manifestation of bone damage in a severe injury.

Burns

If the skin is red and blistered but not broken, a cold tea compress, or tannic acid, or antibiotic cream and a bandage is adequate treatment. If the skin surface is damaged, apply a clean dry dressing, have the person rest quietly, and obtain medical help.

Scalds

These are burns caused by hot liquids and need similar treatment. Scalds can never be as severe as the severest burns but are particularly painful.

Electric and Chemical Burns

These are similar to ordinary burns but heal more slowly. Chemicals should, of course, be neutralized if possible.

ERUPTIONS AND VISIBLE ABNORMALITIES OF THE SKIN

What are they like?

Dry

Weals, i.e., swollen, pink or white areas, or white with red edges.
General redness, or rash. Spots.
Scales.

Wet: Weeping, or blistered.

Pustules.

Ulcers.

Warts, lumps, and excrescences.

Abnormal pigment.

Disorders of hair and scalp: See Head Section.

Disorders of fingers, toes, and *nails.* See Upper and Lower Extremities.

Hives   [A: S, 1]

Medical name: Urticaria.

Identification: Weals with unendurable itching come up suddenly and last a few hours. This is the *acute* type.

Chronic type: Constantly recurring attacks. Very large swellings constitute *angioneurotic edema*—dangerous if the air passages are involved.

Causation: Hives is a manifestation of special sensitivity, or *allergy,* one of our most mysterious and interesting bodily phenomena. Skins susceptible to allergic reactions can often be written on by scratching with a fingernail or pencil, the lines standing out as weals (dermatographia).

Immediate causes of hives include:

Stings by nettle, jellyfish, insects.

Certain foods (itching very noticeable).

Certain drugs, or serum injections. Aspirin and penicillin common offenders.

Poisoning effects of bad food, especially shellfish, pork, onions, milk, and eggs, are also common causes. Sepsis in the body.

Emotional causes, for instance, having to meet an important stranger. A case of the skin speaking for the mind.

Treatment: See Allergy. Your doctor will be able to help—perhaps dramatically.

General Redness or Rash
Eruptive fevers [A]—chicken pox, measles, etc. There will be other signs: raised temperature, headache, feeling ill.
Roseola [A] may resemble measles.

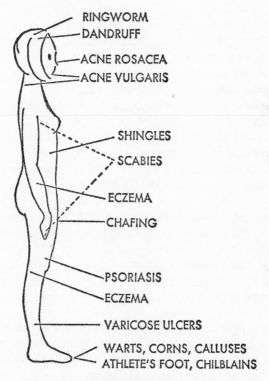

RINGWORM
DANDRUFF
ACNE ROSACEA
ACNE VULGARIS

SHINGLES
SCABIES
ECZEMA
CHAFING

PSORIASIS
ECZEMA
VARICOSE ULCERS
WARTS, CORNS, CALLUSES
ATHLETE'S FOOT, CHILBLAINS

Sites of Common Skin Disorders

Erythema scarlatiniforme [A] looks like scarlet fever. Both of these are basically sensitivity reactions and not serious. Your doctor will disentangle them from the real fevers.
Small children wearing wool clothing [A: Ch] when too warm.

The rash, usually confined to the chest area, is due to wool irritation.

Rashes with Raised Spots (Papules)

Acne Vulgaris [Ch]—the plague of adolescence.

Scabies [A Ch]

Eczema [A Ch] and other conditions can sometimes be papular.

Acne Vulgaris [Ch: S or N; A: X]

Adolescent "spots" are important because of their danger not to life but to the happiness and self-confidence of a young person. This common condition probably accounts for more adolescent and parental despondency than any other.

Identification: Spots: a mixture of blackheads, whiteheads, red or purplish spots from pinhead to pea size, standing out slightly, pustules, scars and pits. They are mainly on the face, back of neck, back, and chest, but sometimes also armpits and buttocks. The impulse, especially among girls, to pick and squeeze them produces sores, crusts, and little bleeding places together with the spots.

The complexion is often muddy and oily, the skin thickened. Lank, oily hair, with dandruff, may accompany the skin trouble and contribute to depression.

Sex: Boys and girls equally affected.

Age: From puberty, which in these days of early maturing may be as young as ten or eleven, until the early twenties, occasionally thirty.

Treatment: Worthwhile, although cure is not possible, and the trouble usually disappears spontaneously—ultimately. Some improvement in the condition can be achieved, and scarring prevented, and much improvement in morale.

Washing: Four or five times a day, with soap and water or special detergent. Dry with a rough towel.

Applications: Sulphur pastes or lotions which cause peeling. Proprietary preparations which help to disguise the blemishes. Removal of individual blackheads with extractor. Not to be overdone, or done at all if there is inflammation.

Sunlight or artificial ultraviolet light, to cause peeling. A dry, sunny climate is ideal, humidity as in India or West Africa is harmful.
Antibiotics continued for three months are useful in resistant or severe pustular cases. Very expensive.
Hormones: Effective in a few selected cases.
Avoid: Chocolate, excessive use of milk or milk products, fur or woolly clothing next to the skin, iodide or bromide medicines, tar and oil products.
Causes and mechanism: When a child is changing into an adult (adolescence), under the influence of substances in the blood called hormones, the sebum glands become active, and the horny layer of the skin is stimulated to more vigorous growth. Excessive amounts of sebum, skin lubricant, may be produced, and to make matters worse, the overgrowth of the top layer of the skin may dam back the material, producing a little lump on the skin round the plug of sebum, which may become black due to oxidation, not dirt. This spot is a blackhead. If it is squeezed, a worm of sebum is extruded.

The red, purple, or pustular spots of acne are due to an inflammatory reaction of the skin against the unnaturally retained plug, and there is usually no infection involved.

All older children, and adults from time to time, particularly women during their periods, have a few acne spots on occasion, but they are usually evanescent. There is a familial tendency to severer acne.

Keeping the sufferer busy with school activities and other interests, plus a sympathetic but sensible attitude on the part of his family, will help ward off depression and prevent his picking at the spots.
Outlook: Acne always gets better; usually there is only one bad year of it, and it is very unusual after 24 or 25.

Localized Redness or Rash

Acne Rosacea: Red Nose [Ch]

Lupus Erythematosus: Butterfly Sore [Ch: S, U]
Identification: Irregularly rounded bright red skin sores on the

cheeks, often joining up over the nose to form a butterfly-shaped area. Sunlight makes the condition worse.

Important to see a doctor, as the skin trouble may be part of a general disease.

Dry Eczema   [A Ch]
Identification: Red, dry, rough, slightly scaling area of skin, often on face. Burning and itching. See Eczema.

Dermatitis   [A Ch]
Inflammation of the skin due to such irritants as hair and fur dyes, detergents, plants, and chemicals.

Bedsores   [Ch: N]
These start as redness over pressure points, in bedfast patients, and will ulcerate unless treated at this stage.
Treatment: Cleanliness, dryness, and relief of pressure by frequent changing of position (two-hourly). A foam rubber doughnut may help, and talcum powder on the skin after washing. Similar sore places can occur with splints or plasters that do not fit well.

Pellagra   [Ch: S, 6]
A deficiency disease in which intake of the vitamin niacin is inadequate. It can occur in affluent societies in those whose diets are almost all fats and carbohydrates (buttered toast), or who take alcohol instead of eating, or have digestive disorders which prevent proper use of the food, or are on isoniazid for treatment of tuberculosis.
Identification: Redness like sunburn, burning and itching, on parts that are exposed or rubbed; weakness; loss of appetite; sometimes diarrhea; depression.
Treatment: Reorganize eating habits for a diet rich in protein and lower in carbohydrates, with liver, lean meat, and tomatoes in abundance. *Nicotinamide tablets,* also.

Intertrigo: Chafing   [A Ch: 48, 1]
Identification: Redness where two skin surfaces are in contact, as

below the breasts in some women, in the groins, behind the ears. Infants and fat people particularly.

Prevention and treatment: Wash, dry, and powder regularly. Clears up in a week with care, but neglected, it may become infected and weeping. Anti-bacterial ointments may be useful, but must be used with care, or they may aggravate the condition.

CONDITIONS BROUGHT ON BY COLD OR HEAT

Chilblains [A Ch: N, 2–6, X]

Identification: Dusky red, oval swellings, intensely itchy, on fingers and feet, occasionally tips of ears and nose, and especially common in young women. Due to exaggerated and uncoordinated response of the blood vessels in the skin to a lowering of temperature, particularly if combined with damp: even in summer, sometimes!

Treatment: Painting with tincture of iodine, or cooling ointment (menthol). Avoid injury. If chilblains break, an antiseptic cream should be applied, and the part hygienically covered.

Prevention: Warm atmosphere, warm clothes, *not* hugging hot water bottle or fire. Exercise. The main gimmick is not to allow the skin to learn this inconvenient reaction when the autumn weather brings the first taste of cold. Gloves and thick socks then will help prevent chilblains even when the weather is really cold. Not completely cured till the warm spring.

Acrocyanosis [A Ch: N]

Chilblain appearance without much itching, all over hands and feet. A matter of constitution. Treat as chilblains.

Frostbite [A: S]

A severe form of chilblain.

Bluish-red Swelling [Ch: X]

Of outer side, lower third of legs: In girls and younger women.

Treatment: Thicker stockings, longer skirts, or slacks. Very slow to get better—months.

Raynaud's Disease

Spasm of the arteries making the fingers pale and dead when cold. Not a skin trouble.

Granny's Tartan   [Ch: N, 6/12]

Medical term: Ephelis ab igne.

An indirect result of cold weather, a mottling of the legs in a reddish network, due to sitting too close and long by the fire. The mottling turns brown in time.

Treatment: None, but not to sit so near.

Sunburn   [A: N, 2]

Identification: Itching, burning, redness, and sometimes swelling of parts exposed to sun, coming on in about six hours. Blisters may form later. Worse if there is also reflected light from snow, water, or sand.

Duration: Two days to two weeks, progressing through subsidence, peeling, and pigment formation—tanning—a protection for next time.

Treatment: Cooling lotions such as calamine.

Prevention: Applications of calamine lotion, tannic acid jelly, Vaseline. Do not over-expose skin to sun. Particular care if taking tetracycline or chlorpromazine.

Snowblindness   [A: S]

Inflammation of the special skin of the eye due to the ultraviolet rays of the sun, often when reflected off snow, sand, or sea. See doctor.

DRY AND SCALY ERUPTIONS

Psoriasis   [Ch: S, X]

Identification: Irregularly shaped, slightly raised red patches, covered by silvery scales; elbows and knees especially affected; face rarely; scalp often; nails may be pitted or ridged. No itching! Usually starts at 7–15 years, often goes in families.

Treatment: A great many kinds recommended. Occlusive steroid cream dressings in acute stage. No long-term effect.

Duration: Usually remits and recurs for many years. At least it is uncommon after middle age!

Seborrheic Dermatitis   [Ch: S, 2, X]

A misnomer for a disease that is not due to too much oil (sebum) in the skin, but to dandruff having prepared the way for eczema. Constitutional predisposition.

Identification: Scalp trouble extending to face, etc., especially eyebrows; scaly patches, either reddish, or yellow and greasy looking, although this appearance is really because the scales are sodden with sebum. Itching and irritation. There is often acne, also, to complete the miserable picture!

Treatment: A sulphur and salicylic acid ointment or lotion followed by the antidandruff regime. See Head Section.

There is also an acute, weeping form of seborrheic dermatitis [A: S].

Ringworm   [A Ch: S, C, 2]

Medical name: Tinea circinata.

A skin disorder produced by one of several fungi, which attack different areas of the skin. All are infectious, and can be caught from people, cats—especially Blue Persian—and other animals. Common in schools and armed forces establishments. Incubation period 3–7 days.

Identification: Small circular patches spreading at the edges while healing in the center, producing the typical rings. Scaly, spotty, or pustular, depending upon the strain responsible.

Treatment: Whitfield's ointment twice a day, and antifungal powders. Recurrence is common, so treatment must not be stopped too soon. Clothes need to be disinfected.

Special Types

Ringworm of the scalp.

Ringworm of the groin (Dhobie itch). Usually acquired indirectly through the feet, from bath mats, etc. In most boarding schools. Intensely irritating.

Ringworm of the beard: One danger of having a barber shave you with unsterilized equipment. Another type comes from dealing with cattle.

Ringworm of the feet.

Pityriasis Rosea   [A: S, 6]

Usually affects young adults, in winter or spring; perhaps caused by a virus.

Identification: Rash all over, of pink-edged, pea-sized, peeling patches, slightly raised. Usually one "herald patch" has appeared on the body days, or even weeks, before the main attack. Not much itching.

Treatment: Best left alone, except for calamine lotion. Usually better in 6–8 weeks; second attacks are very rare.

Ichthyosis: Xeroderma   [Ch: X]

Dry, scaly condition, from birth, with a tendency to eczema and chapping. No curative treatment, but at least the condition gets no worse after puberty. Emollient creams soften the hard skin, and warm baths with emulsifying ointment help to moisten it.

Diseases Scaly at One Stage

Normal, sensitive skin: Hard water and hard weather.

After measles, scarlet fever, and other fevers: Both scaly and scurfy, especially on the face.

Eczema: There is also weeping, sometimes.

Lupus erythematosus.

Ringworm between the toes sometimes goes through a superficial peeling stage.

WET, WEEPING, OR BLISTERED DISORDERS

Eczema   [A Ch: S, I–X]

A catarrhal inflammation of the skin, not due to any infection, but a reaction to an external irritant, or something in the body, in an especially sensitive subject. There is an hereditary tendency to eczema, linked with allergic conditions such as asthma and hay fever.

Eczema can occur on almost any part of the body and at any age, from the infantile eczema of those under two to that of the dry-skinned over-70's. It can plague those whose work brings them into contact with such substances as nickel, chrome, cement, varnishes . . . or who are exposed to much heat, cold, sunshine, or harsh weather.

Internal contributing factors are less easy to pinpoint. Such general conditions as pregnancy, indigestion, allergy, diabetes, and gout have an effect, as do emotional states such as grief, overwork, and worry.

Identification: The skin goes through these stages:

1. Redness and swelling. It can recover, or go on to

2. Spots and tiny blisters (vesicles).

3. Blisters burst and juice exudes to form crusts: "weeping eczema."

4. Infection, with streptococci or staphylococci may set in, with pustule formation, fissures, and blisters.

5. Chronic stage: no exudation but the surface of the skin flakes off and simultaneously becomes thickened or "lichenified."

Itching, throbbing, and burning accompany these stages, in proportion to the acuteness of the skin process.

SPECIAL VARIETIES OF ECZEMA

Some are named according to their site, i.e., of the palms, of the anal region, etc.

Infantile eczema: Usually on the flush patches of the cheeks, chin, and forehead.

Flexural eczema (*Besnier's prurigo*): In older children who have had a dry eczema at back of knees and front of elbows. Usually disappears at puberty.

Intertrigo (chafing).

Perlèche.

Secondary to an infected discharge from ear, nose, wound, etc.

Occupational: Baker's, grocer's, tar worker's, photographer's. Set up by the materials with which they work, but only if they are themselves sensitive.

Allergic eczema, often in those subject to asthma or hay fever allergy.

Treatment: This differs with stage and variety, but obviously the removal of any cause comes first.

Patch tests: May help to track down an obscure factor. Suspected offending liquids, lipstick, or soap are painted on a circumscribed area of skin, and solid materials can be held on by strapping. Rapidly developing redness reveals a culprit substance.

Water, and especially soap and water, irritate an eczematous skin. Use olive oil instead. Avoid scratching—and worrying! Simple, non-stimulating diet and adequate rest are a background help, but your doctor will supply you with made-to-measure instructions and the medications to suit your particular condition.

Shingles   [A: S, An, 2]
Medical name: Herpes zoster.

Shingles and chicken pox are believed to be caused by the same virus. A child with chicken pox can transmit shingles to an adult, just as an adult with shingles can transmit the virus to a child and give him chicken pox.

Shingles occur most commonly in the age group between 40 and 70. The first sign is usually pain that follows the path of a sensory nerve. It is common on the chest or abdomen, but may occur along the path of the face and eye. Several days after the onset of pain, a rash may follow the same path. The rash consists of small vesicles that look like dew drops. Eventually they become crusted. Usually both the pain and the rash last two weeks, but occasionally the pain may persist. There are no complications except the possibility that the rash may involve the cornea of the eye and cause scarring.

Treatment: none specific. The use of an antibiotic ointment to prevent secondary infection is sometimes recommended. Various analgesics such as aspirin or codeine are used as needed. Very rarely, doctors have used large doses of steroids to abort an attack.

Cold Sore   [A]
Medical name: Herpes simplex.
On the lip.

Chicken Pox   [A]
Spots with blisters on top.

Ringworm on the Body   [A Ch]
Vesicles in a definite ring.

Stings and Insect Bites [A]
May develop small blisters.

Sweat Rash (Heat Rash) [A]
Scattered, pinhead vesicles after overheating from exercise, high temperature in illness, or overclothing (especially in babies). Dust with talc. Rash will disappear in a few days.

PUSTULES

All the troubles among the wet, weeping, and blistered disorders may become pustular.

Impetigo Contagiosa [A: S, C, 2]
Most commonly seen on the faces of children at school, at home affecting the toughest and more delicate alike. It is infectious, but adults are relatively immune.
Identification: Pustules which turn into scabs and come off, leaving no scars; favoring the face, especially around the mouth, the hands, and the scalp. Itching moderate.
Treatment: Through your doctor. Antibiotic cream; cleansing with olive oil. Take care with hand washing, towels, and underclothing.

Barber's Rash: Pustules in the Beard Area [A Ch]
Medical name: Sycosis.
May be due to staphylococcal infection: pull out a hair—it comes easily, with a drop of pus. May be a form of ringworm, or an eczema that has become infected, or due to ingrowing hairs.
    Your own doctor must decide which it is and what to do.

Acne [Ch]
Blackheads, spots, and pustules on face and back.

Drug Eruptions [A Ch]
Medicines containing iodides or bromides, arsenic, mercury can produce pustular spots.

Boil [A: S, 2]

Medical name: Furuncle.

A rapidly formed, localized infection starting deep in a hair follicle, with a concentration of pus at its center. It is almost always due to the skin's chief enemy, the staphylococcus. Common sites are neck, face, and back.

Identification: A little, hard, red lump which increases in size, tension, and pain, until it begins to "come to a head": that is, the middle part softens, shows yellow, and allows pus to escape, followed in a day or two by the sloughing hair follicle itself. The little pit quickly fills but leaves a small scar.

Boils are particularly painful where the skin is tight, for instance, in the ear passage, and particularly troublesome in the armpit, where spread is easy.

Blind boil: Similar start but it either slowly subsides without coming to a head, or takes weeks to reach that stage.

DANGER! Boils on the upper lip or around the nose need prompt professional care, even if they do not seem severe. Infection of the meningeal covering of the brain can—albeit *RARELY*—spread from this situation.

DO NOT SQUEEZE, or even touch.

Predisposing Causes

Scratching.

Friction from clothes, especially grimy ones.

Infection from barbers at the back of men's necks, and chafing of the skin there from the collar.

Diabetes.

Generally rundown, substandard condition, possibly from undiscovered illness.

Infection lurking in the nose, although the boil may be elsewhere.

Treatment: (1) hot, moist applications, (2) antibiotic creams to surround area if discharging, (3) antibiotic medication, (4) occasionally incision if required.

Prevention: antiseptic soaps.

Carbuncle [A: SU, R, 6]

A confluent cluster of boils, usually on the neck, back, or buttock, and commonest in middle age, especially among diabetics, indulgers in alcohol, and the otherwise debilitated.

Identification: Flat, red, painful, hard inflammatory area extending in a week or more to a diameter of several inches, then coming to several heads and pouring pus. Generally ill feeling.

Treatment: Urgent, usually medical, sometimes surgical. The part must be rested. The resistance should be encouraged by plenty of food, rest, and fresh air.

A scar may remain, and occasionally skin grafting is needed, though this is very rare.

Stye [A]
Infected hair follicle of the eyelashes.

ULCERS

An ulcer implies the loss of the whole thickness of the skin, not the superficial place left by, say, a broken blister.

Varicose Ulcer [Ch: S, 6–6/12, X]
Identification: A rounded ulcer, commonly on the inner side of the lower third of the leg, near the ankle, associated with varicose veins, which may not be visible always. The ankle is usually slightly swollen and the skin dusky, and in long-standing cases brown pigmentation appears. May be very painful. Often follows an insect bite, trifling knock, or scratch.

Mechanism: Varicose veins have incompetent valves so the whole weight of the column of blood between the ankle and heart presses against the upward flow. The flow decelerates, stops, and may even reverse, filling the minute vessels of the skin with stale venous blood, instead of the oxygenated blood from the arteries. As in a pond, where there is stagnation, there is trouble: the nourishment of the skin suffers; it becomes purple and scaly, and has a much reduced resistance to infection or injury. The slightest mishap causes the skin to break down, and it remains obstinately unhealed without rigorous and persistent treatment.

Treatment: See doctor.

Exercises: Most important to tap foot with heel on ground a hundred times a day, which pumps blood up leg and maintains the circulation.

Raise foot of bed nine inches in severe cases, to avoid swelling at night.

Walk, but do not stand around.

Course: Should heal in 6–8 weeks.

Be careful not to knock it again!

Long term: A surgeon may advise, and perform, a simple operation on the veins. Some cases are unsuitable, however, and for these, support hose are invaluable, made nowadays in pure, strong nylon, far more effective, as well as more comfortable and sightly, than the former elastic stocking.

Gravitational Ulcer   [Ch: S]

The same mechanism of back pressure in the leg veins may be produced without varicose veins in cases of thrombosis, occupations involving a great deal of standing, obstruction to the return of blood in pregnancy (or other abdominal swelling), sometimes after typhoid or pneumonia. Appearance and treatment as above.

Tuberculous Ulcer   [Ch: S]

Identification: Young people usually affected, either by breaking down of a tuberculous gland, or as part of Lupus Vulgaris, a chronic tuberculous skin disease of small, soft, semi-transparent nodules. Not common, and treatment far more satisfactory nowadays.

Rodent Ulcer   [Ch: SU]

Identification: Men, and less often, women, over 40, who have led an outdoor life, usually. Upper part of face commonly affected, starting with a small, firm nodule, the color of normal skin. Later the surface may be broken and crusts repeatedly form. The skin has a characteristically rolled appearance round the edge of the ulcer.

Treatment: This is the very best type of tumor to have, as it advances very slowly, and is easily and most successfully treated with X-rays, with radium, or by scraping and cauterization.

Outlook: Fine, if treated.

WARTS, TUMORS, AND EXCRESCENCES

Warts [Ch: S, 2]

Medical name: Verrucae.

Overgrowth of the papillae of the skin, caused by a virus. They are mildly contagious, particularly from finger to finger of the same person (autoinoculable).

An injection of ground up wart causes new ones to develop months later!

Identification: Raised, round patches with slightly raspberry appearance; painless unless under pressure; skin-colored unless beginning to go gray.

Commonest in childhood but can be found at any age.

Commonest on fingers, face, or feet, but may be anywhere. Disappear without treatment—but maybe not for years.

No relation to cancer.

Varieties

Plane: juvenile, ½ mm. high; 2–3 mm. across. Many.

Common: ¼ in. high; up to ½ in. across; single or several.

Plantar: on the sole of the foot. The same as above but subjected to pressure. Painful.

Filiform: like small stout threads projecting from the skin, particularly on the necks of middle-aged ladies.

Treatment: Almost anything, from witchcraft to electric cautery, has been known to cure warts. Take your doctor's advice as to which.

"Blood Warts" [Ch: N]

Medical name: Senile ectasia.

Identification: Small ruby-red growths on the skin of the face and neck in persons over 50. Painless. Consist of groups of tiny blood vessels, so they bleed freely if scratched.

Treatment: They are harmless, but can easily be cut out or cauterized if they are in the way.

Moles [Ch: N]

Identification: Dark or light brown, slightly raised spots, like permanent freckles, usually beginning in youth: "beauty spots." Moles may be hairy.

Most of us have several moles all our lives, and they do no harm whatever. *Rarely* a mole, usually a blue-black one, may start growing, and then it requires dealing with promptly.

Blood Vessel Birthmarks [Ch: S]

Port-wine stains, strawberry marks: usually seen at birth, or within a few weeks, but sometimes not until a good deal later. The flat, port-wine type may persist unless treated (results excellent), but the raised strawberry kind usually shrivel up by the fifth birthday.

Wens: Sebaceous Cysts [Ch]

Small, berrylike lumps in the scalp, caused by blockage of glands.

Corns [Ch: N, 2]

Identification: A localized thickening of the horny layer of the skin, as a response to pressure, usually on the feet. A cone of hard material, pointing inward, presses on the sensitive deeper layers, causing pain.

Soft corn: a corn occurring between the toes, which has become sodden.

Treatment: Relieve the pressure. Are new shoes needed? Avoid wobbly types. Use a special medicated corn plaster.

Soft corns: Separate the toes with cotton, powder freely; otherwise as above.

Long term: The foot may require examination in case there is any underlying deformity.

Yellow Nodules on Eyelids [Ch: S]

Medical term: Xanthelasma.

Little yellow lumps just under the skin surface in old people, from deposits of hard fat. Not serious in themselves (though they can be removed easily), but an indication that it is time for a general check.

Skin Cancer [Ch: SU]

See also Rodent ulcer and Blue-black mole.

May begin as a small pearly lump or an ulcer that does not completely heal. Characteristically painless and does not get better of its own accord. Do not neglect any skin abnormality that lasts for several weeks and is no better. Skin cancer is easily and effectively treated—early.

ABNORMALITIES OF PIGMENT

The pigment is the coloring matter of the skin: see also Skin Color for abnormalities due to factors other than the pigment.

Freckles

Tanning in spots, due to pigment-forming cells being arranged in clusters instead of evenly dispersed through the skin. Linked with red hair and sensitivity to sunlight.

Liver Spots

Darker than ordinary freckles, and all shapes and sizes, often occurring in older people.

Both freckles and liver spots can be disguised or removed—if anyone should think it desirable.

Vitiligo

Loss of normal skin color in patches because these parts cannot tan with sunlight, usually beginning between ten and thirty. Completely harmless, mysterious—and embarrassing. Often persists, but sometimes recovers after years.

Treatment: None curative. Cosmetics help. Avoid making the contrast more noticeable by sun-bathing.

Birthmarks

Serum Sickness

Sensitivity reaction appearing within a few hours or days of receiving serum. Intensely irritating rash, hives or other type, around the site of the injection or generally; fever; sometimes a sudden chill, vomiting, or joint pains. Calamine relieves the itching, but the doctor can do better. Occasionally (1 in 70,000) severe symptoms (shock, vomiting, collapse) occur immediately after administration of serum. Treat for shock. Doctor urgently.

THE CHEST

The chest is a box that houses great treasures: the heart, which pumps the life blood unceasingly to every part, and its huge vessels; the lungs, which do the vital job of supplying fresh oxygen to the blood and ridding the body of poisonous carbon dioxide; the tube that joins the stomach to the mouth, without which food and drink would have no value.

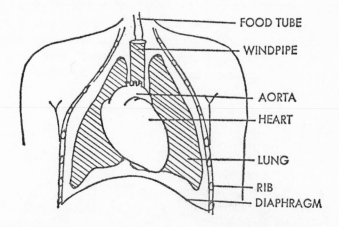

It is not only as a container that the external chest is important; the movement of the cage of ribs with its muscles and ligaments makes possible the mechanics of breathing. The chest wall is at work for us even as we sleep, filling and emptying the lungs.

Symptoms of the chest can be due to the heart, the lungs, or the muscles, bones, and joints surrounding them. Important symptoms we may encounter are:

Heart symptoms: Breathlessness; pain, palpitations.

Lung symptoms: Breathlessness; pain; cough.

Chest wall symptoms: Pain; breathlessness.

The overlapping makes it necessary to consider with especial care any trouble or discomfort in this part of the body.

DEFORMITIES OF THE CHEST

The adult chest if cut across would show the shape of an ellipse, wider from side to side than back to front. In children it is more nearly circular. A man of 5 ft. 6 in. should have a chest measuring 34–35 in. capable of expanding 1½–2 in. In a very fit young man an expansion of 5 in. is not uncommon. Whatever the chest measurement, it should not be exceeded by that of the waist!

There is as wide a variation in shape of chest as of nose. Some are especially narrow with sloping shoulders and long necks; others are thick and square with high shoulders and a nearly nonexistent neck. Each of these extreme types is within the normal range and perfectly compatible with health.

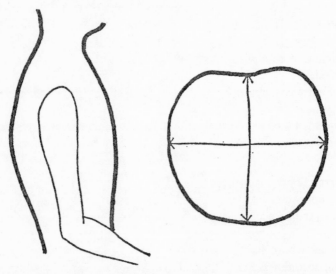

Side View Normal Chest   Cross Section Normal Chest

Pigeon Chest [Ch: N]
Sharply projecting breastbone like a bird's, usually present as long as you can remember; generally a birth defect.

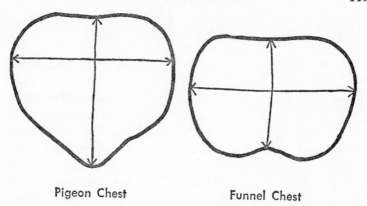

Pigeon Chest   Funnel Chest

Funnel Chest

The opposite of pigeon chest. The breast bone, instead of the ribs each side, is pulled in by the muscles and ligaments. The bone is soft in childhood, and particularly so in rickets, a disease in which there is a shortage of calcium or the Vitamin D necessary for the calcium to be absorbed and used. Usually a funnel chest is a birth defect.

Faulty posture during childhood, for instance at the school desk, may have an adverse effect.

Treatment: None. May predispose to chest troubles in children, but seems to cause no difficulties in later years.

Barrel Chest   [Ch: S]

An appearance as though a big breath had been drawn in and held: the shoulders are unduly high and square also. The chest is, in fact, constantly overexpanded in an attempt to use thinned out ineffective lung tissue whose elasticity has disappeared. This lung condition is known as emphysema and occurs in the older age groups.

An emphysematous, or barrel, chest is capable of very little more expansion, perhaps only ½–1 in., on breathing in. Not all emphysematous people have this deformity, nor may a barrel-shaped chest invariably mean a disordered lung.

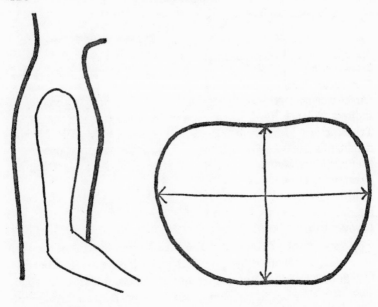

Side View Barrel Chest   Barrel Chest

Asymmetrical Chest   [A Ch: S]
Due to a crooked or curved spine. See Back Section.
Enlargement of an abdominal organ, e.g., liver.
Swelling inside: fluid, tumor or abscess: obviously ill.
In emphysema the ballooned lung may cause bulging above or be-
low the collar bone.
Shrinking on one side may be due to old scarring from pleurisy
or tuberculosis.
A pulsating swelling to the right of the breast bone could be due
to an aneurism, a bulge in an artery. Rare.

BREAST CONDITIONS

See Women's Section.

INJURY TO THE CHEST

Broken Rib [A: S, 6]
Can occur from:
Direct violence: greatest danger is of injury to underlying lung.
Indirect violence, for instance, a crushing injury.
Trivial injury, for instance, coughing or sneezing, after a long, debilitating illness or some general illness affecting the bones.
Identification: Sudden onset, after injury, of pain on breathing in.
Treatment: Depends on severity.
Mild case requires only analgesics. Strapping may not help healing, but it greatly increases comfort.
Course: Ribs, although constantly moving, heal readily and rapidly —in three weeks.

Broken Breastbone
The "steering-wheel fracture." The fractured bone is not important, but damage to the heart and lungs beneath it certainly is—a common cause of death in road accidents, and one for which the safety belt was introduced.

Broken Collar Bone
See Upper Extremities Section.

Pain in Chest Wall
Injury.
Shingles: redness and blistering appear shortly.
Muscle strain: worse on coughing or other muscular effort.
Internal troubles: see Pain in the Chest, below.

PAIN IN THE CHEST

Pain in the chest is always important, but do not jump to the alarmist conclusion that it always, or very often, indicates heart trouble, nor that the severity of the pain is an index of the seriousness of the underlying condition.

Chest pain may originate in *any* of these parts: the breathing apparatus; muscles, bones, and ligaments; the swallowing tube; mind and nerves; the heart and great vessels; the abdomen, indirectly.

Pain over the Heart (Precordial Pain)

Sudden, severe, persistent, accompanied by a feeling of doom, with or without collapse or breathlessness. Central, sometimes radiating across chest, to neck and arms. Consider *coronary attack*. [A: U, B]

Similar pain and feelings but passing off with rest, brought on by effort. Possibly *angina*. [A: B, 1/7]

PAIN DUE TO HEART DISORDER IS CHARACTERISTICALLY PROPORTIONAL TO PHYSICAL EXERTION.

Sudden, severe, left-sided pain, perhaps going down left arm. Skin over heart sensitive. Related to fatigue and emotion more than exercise. [A: S, 1/7]

Dull, persistent ache over the heart. [S]

Dull ache punctuated with sharp stabs of precordial pain, and often fainting. [S]. *NEVER* associated with structural heart disease, though possibly a psychological broken heart. The two preceding types, similarly, are likely to be due to *heart consciousness* or some other anxiety or fear. Has any relative had heart trouble? Go to your doctor for what will most likely turn out to be a thorough examination—and reassurance. Tenderness and pain over upper part of abdomen and chest, associated with cough: *probably muscle and ligament strain.* [S]

Pain produced by pressing on the ribs in the front: *Tietze's syndrome.* Due to soreness of the joints between ribs and breast bone. Heart pain is *never* brought on by pressing on the chest. [S]

Shoulder, arm, neck, and jaw, as well as center of chest, all painful and tender to touch: *aortic trouble* (the aorta is the main artery from the heart). [Ch: S]

Pain over heart area that does not fit any of these descriptions. [S] Consider nervousness; aneurysm; tumor in the middle of the chest. *RARE causes.*

Pain Associated with Breathing

Knifelike, or sometimes resembling a stitch often in the side: *early pleurisy* [A: B, 2], that is, dry inflammation of the lung coverings occurring with many respiratory troubles, from apparently "just a cold" to pneumonia, tumor, or tuberculosis.

Intense pain along lower margin of the ribs, and sometimes radiating to the tip of the shoulder: *inflammation of the diaphragm* [A: B, 2] (the muscular sheet between chest and abdomen). Trouble in the abdomen, especially of liver, spleen, or colon, can irritate the diaphragm from below but give chest symptoms.

Raw soreness behind the upper part of the breastbone; it hurts to cough: *acute tracheitis* (inflammation of the windpipe); *acute bronchitis.* [A: S]

Slight pain between the upper ribs may mean *nothing*—or serious trouble like *early tuberculosis.* [S]

Pain Arising outside the Lungs and Heart

Worse on coughing or effort, and chest hurts when the painful area is pressed on: *strained muscles.* [S]

One-sided, burning and aching, along the slanting line of a rib. Blisters follow: shingles. [S, O, 2]

Bone disorders of spine. [S]

Tietze's syndrome (above). [S]

Note: Lung cancer may cause any of the types of pain described, depending on its position.

ABDOMINAL CAUSES MAY PRODUCE PAIN IN THE CHEST, AND VICE VERSA.

BREATHLESSNESS

Medical name: Dyspnea.

Breathing is a function of the diaphragm, a sheet of muscle separating the chest from the abdomen, and the muscles between the ribs. These muscles alternately expand and compress the cavity that contains the lungs, and they are filled or emptied of air accordingly.

It is natural and normal to feel short of breath, even to pant, after muscular exertion—running a race or for a bus. The amount you are able to do without breathlessness can, in health, be increased by training: that is, practicing the exercise, whatever it is;

and most athletic training programs include cutting out smoking, alcohol, and rich foods, and avoiding late nights, all of which make inroads on the reserves.

SHORTNESS OF BREATH IS AN IMPORTANT SYMPTOM. DO NOT IGNORE IT.

Exercise: Normal unless you find that something you recently managed with ease now leaves you short of breath.

Pregnancy: A mechanical effect of the enlarged womb hampering the diaphragmatic movements. Extra weight to carry increases the effort required for walking uphill, etc., but severe breathlessness in pregnancy requires investigation.

Swelling in the abdomen, even from an over-full stomach, can make breathing difficult.

Obesity: Hampers breathing movements similarly, adds an extra burden to the muscles, and maybe also causes breathlessness indirectly by making the work of the heart harder.

Heart disorders [A: S, B; Ch: S, R]: No special features distinguish the breathlessness from this cause, but the face and extremities may be blue and ankles swollen, and exercise makes the condition markedly worse, often in paroxysms. Breathing is easier if the patient is propped up.

Breathlessness is often present without heart troubles, but rarely vice versa. Sighing is *not* a sign of heart disorder. See discussion of Heart Failure.

Anemia [Ch: S] and other blood disorders. More comfortable lying flat: compare Heart disorders, above. There may also be swelling of feet and ankles.

Debility [S]: Even without anemia, as in convalescents.

Poisons [A: U; Ch: S]: Tobacco, alcohol, gases, snakebite.

A cold or catarrh [A: S, I]: Sniffing and bubbling, and noisy breathing in the night.

Blockage of windpipe or larynx [U, B]: As in laryngitis, inflammation of the windpipe, bronchitis, enlarged thyroid gland, growths or something solid inhaled accidentally. Breathing is then noisy both in and out, and the lower edges of the ribs may be drawn in on inspiration if the blockage is severe.

Bronchitis [A Ch: I]: Often wheezing, too.

Emphysema [Ch: R]: Breathlessness with particular difficulty in breathing *out,* and the chest permanently in the breathing-in position.

Pneumonia [A: S, B]: Rapid breathing (especially in children the nostrils move in and out) coming on suddenly with temperature and ill feeling, or in the course of a bad cold or bronchitis.

Scarred lung, collapsed lung, or pleurisy with outpouring of fluid around the lung [A: S, B]: Continuous breathlessness is the main symptom.

Spontaneous pneumothorax [U, B]: Dramatically sudden, urgent breathlessness, due to air getting into the lung coverings (pleura) from inside or outside, and so preventing the lung from expanding. Can occur in health during strenuous exercise, or less strikingly, in a diseased lung.

BREATHLESSNESS IN BOUTS OR PAROXYSMS

Heart disorders [A Ch].

Asthma [A Ch]: Especially difficult to breathe *out.*

Whooping cough, croup [A: S, I, 6]: Difficulty in breathing *in.* Children mainly, with other signs.

Kidney troubles [Ch: S, B]: Typically the bouts occur in the night and are often thought to be asthma. This breathlessness is due to heart failure following high blood pressure caused by kidney disease—nephritis.

Swellings in the chest [Ch: S]: Anything from enlarged glands to aneurysm (a bulge in the wall of an artery).

Throat abscess [U, B]: Rarely, or swelling caused by wasp sting on tongue or in throat.

Anxiety, or sudden fright.

PALPITATION

Consciousness of the thumping of the heart. There are two main types, the commoner and less serious in which the palpitation comes relatively gradually and goes away perhaps in sleep, but anyway often imperceptibly. This type is not associated with heart disorder.

The other type comes on with complete abruptness and often departs similarly. This is the sort that *may* be due to heart disease.

Type with Relatively Gradual Onset and Cessation
Causes
Unlikely to be associated with heart disease.
Anemia [Ch: S]: Pallor and undue fatigue also probable. The palpitations come on particularly after exertion and are absent in bed at night. They are often accompanied by vomiting.
Dyspepsia [Ch: S]: Frequently comes on in the night, after a heavy meal. There may also be a fear of death, breathlessness, "night starts"; it is particularly common in fat, flatulent, middle-aged females. *Far commoner* as a cause of palpitation than heart disease. Try eating less, especially in the evening; fewer fatty foods; more exercise; check constipation; do not worry.
Hampering of a healthy heart [Ch: S]: By swellings such as tumor of abdomen or chest, dilated stomach, or pregnancy.
Thyroid gland disorder [Ch: S], Graves' disease: nervousness, tremors, sweating and feeling the heat, sometimes bulging eyes or swelling in the neck.
Early tuberculosis [A: S; Ch]: Weakness, fatigue, dyspepsia, cough. (Rare these days.)
Nervous conditions [A: S; Ch]: Acute fright; chronic anxiety; with lassitude, fatigue, pain over the heart, and breathlessness on slight exertion. Particularly in shy, introspective, sensitive personalities. Common in civilian life; prominent in 1914 war as neurocirculatory asthenia, soldier's heart, but not in modern servicemen.
Convalescence after long illness.
Epilepsy [Ch: S]: Thumping heart in bed at night.
Medicines, especially digitalis in heart pills, thyroid pills for gland disorders, insulin in diabetes, morphia, and cocaine.
Tobacco, an effect of the nicotine: any time, but especially noticeable on getting into bed. Alarming thumps.
Tea, coffee, alcohol: Some persons are far more sensitive to their effects than others.
Poisons: Coal gas, car fumes, etc.

Type with Abrupt Onset and Cessation

May be associated with *heart disease,* such as:

High blood pressure.

Coronary disease.

Valve troubles of the heart.

Rapid heart for any reason.

Strain of the right side of the heart which pumps blood through the lungs, from lung disease, e.g., emphysema. [Ch: S, R]

The Heart

How does the heart manage its work as a pressure pump without rest? It does not. The heart snatches its rest between beats, and is actually contracting actively for less than half the time. It has a lion's share of the body's blood supply from the coronary arteries, the fuel pipes to the heart which spring directly from the aorta, the main stream of the blood system.

Nevertheless, the heart's achievement is remarkable. The 11 pints of blood, which are a transport system for oxygen, nutrients and waste, do a complete circuit about once a minute, propelled by the heart. In a lifetime it must beat about 2,500 million times!

The structure of the heart is basically simple. The two halves, right and left, each consisting of a pair of interacting chambers, act separately. The right side sends used blood from the tissues through the lungs for refreshment and re-oxygenation. The left side drives this improved blood to every part of the body, including the heart muscle itself.

An electrically acting pacemaker, connected with the autonomic nervous system, keeps the beat on time.

It is a real engineering triumph. Treat your heart with the respect it deserves and with heartfelt gratitude for its faithful service, and it will last you a lifetime.

Be grateful, too, for the masterly strides made in heart surgery, so that "blue babies" need no longer be blue and delicate; stranglingly tight mitral valves can be operated on; the pacemaker can be replaced by an electric timepiece; even the heart itself can be replaced by a healthy transplant—maneuvers undreamed of a few years ago.

RATE OF HEART

Heart beat: May be felt in the chest, or by the pulse above the collar bone in the neck, or conventionally in the wrist, between bone and tendon on the front of the thumb side.
Normal rhythm: Regular. *Normal Rate:* Adults: 60–80 per minute.
Newborn: 140–120 per minute.
1–3 years: 120–90 per minute.
7–14 years: 90–80 per minute.
14–20 years, or 70+: 80 per minute.

Rapid Heartbeat
Medical name: Tachycardia, i.e., more than 90 beats per minute.
Normal after exercise, big meals, with emotion, monthly periods.
Abnormal Causes
Fever the commonest.
Infections even without fever.
Graves' Disease.
Kidney troubles.
Blood disorder like anemia.
Some common drugs and poisons: tobacco, alcohol, tea, coffee, and belladonna.
Nervous states, merging into the normal raised pulse rate of a thrill!
Heart disorders nearly all cause increased rate (except heart block, when the beat is slow). Usually the heart must beat faster to compensate for any lack of efficiency. See discussion of Heart Failure.

Slow Heart Rate
Medical name: Bradycardia, i.e. less than 50 beats per minute.
Causes
Normal: Personal idiosyncrasy, compatible with perfect health, often running in families, and commonly among such young athletes as boat race crews and marathon runners.

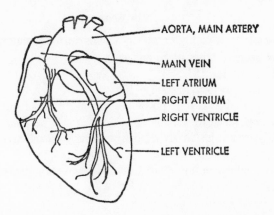

The Heart, from the front, showing the coronary arteries

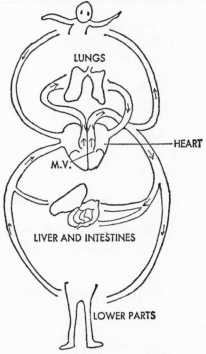

HEAD AND ARMS

LUNGS

HEART

M.V.

LIVER AND INTESTINES

LOWER PARTS

How the Circulation Works

Abnormal

Convalescence, exhaustion, and cold.

Ordinary fainting [S].

Myxedema (hypothyroidism) [S].

Jaundice, diabetes, and poisons coming from outside the body, such as opium [S].

Raised pressure inside the skull from tumor, bleeding, or infection [S].

Typhoid, influenza, most virus diseases, mononucleosis, and some food poisoning. There is fever with a *relatively* slow pulse [S, B, 6].

A few heart disorders.

IRREGULAR HEART RATE

Breathing Irregularity

Medical name: Sinus arrhythmia.

Identification: Speeding up with inspiration, slowing down with expiration, common in young people and convalescents from fevers. Not abnormal, not unhealthy—in fact in a convalescent it indicates that the heart is undamaged. No treatment.

Extra Beats

Medical name: Extrasystoles.

An occasional beat gets in ahead of time, followed by an apparent gap. Really the next beat is at its proper time, but the odd beat before it was too early.

Identification: Flip-flop feeling in the chest. Extra beats can come singly or in runs.

Precipitating factors: Tobacco, alcohol, heavy meals, excitement. Extra beats occur in most people, but to a greater extent, or more noticed, in some.

No significance: Common in health, *and* in heart disorders. Doctor can check, to put your mind at rest, and if the extra beats bother you, take steps to reduce their frequency. Cut out the predisposing factors yourself.

Temporary Speed-up [A: R, S]

Medical name: Paroxysmal tachycardia.

Identification: Palpitation, with heart beating two or three times the normal rate, coming on suddenly, and lasting minutes to hours. Alarming and uncomfortable. May be dizziness and faintness during a bout, and often frequent urination occurs.

Causes: Frequently seen in perfectly healthy hearts, especially in young people, or can occur in heart disorders.

Treatment: An attack can often be cut short by an ice-cold drink, stooping, taking a deep breath, or firmly massaging the side of the neck beneath the angle of the jaw. Also breathing out without letting air out, and at the same time straining as if at the lavatory and pressing the eyes hard enough to cause discomfort. While these attacks are not usually serious, if they are frequent, and to check for underlying trouble, consult doctor.

Fluttering Heart [Ch: S]

Medical name: Atrial fibrillation.

Identification: Rapid, irregular palpitation forms raindrop irregularity in beats, not at all like the usual "marching feet" rhythm. May be in bouts or all the time. Breathlessness and therefore curtailment of activity. Sometimes abdominal pain and fullness.

Causes: Rarely nothing more than a disorder of rhythm; usually a sign of heart trouble, and occasionally thyrotoxicosis. Fibrillation can continue for years without apparent ill effects, but there are dangers in allowing the heart to act so irregularly, so advice and treatment are needed. Rest, sitting up in bed, is a safe first move until the doctor has advised.

Heart Block [A: S, R]

Identification: Missing beats, perhaps one after every two or five. May be shortness of breath, and it is in this condition that sudden blackouts occur without warning (Stokes-Adams attacks).

Heart block is due to a fault in the communication system between the upper chambers of the heart, atria, and the lower chambers, ventricles, so that the latter do not get the message to beat every time.

Causes: Commonest is a heart disorder such as coronary thrombosis; sometimes in rheumatic fever or after diphtheria affecting the conducting nerves of the heart. Occasionally a congenital abnormality.

The doctor's help is of great value for most.

HYPERTENSION: HIGH BLOOD PRESSURE

[Ch: S, W]

Your blood circulates under pressure. If you were to have the misfortune to cut an artery, the blood would spurt out in a fountain. The pressure, obviously, is more when the heart is in the active phase of its pumping than in between. That is why your doctor records your blood pressure by two numbers, systolic and diastolic.

The apparatus he uses to determine your blood pressure, a sphygmomanometer, consists of a cuff which can be tightened to compress the arteries in the arm, and released gradually so that the doctor can read off the pressure at which the heart beats again get through.

There is a normal, individual variation in blood pressure, as in shoe size, and a natural increase over the years. It also goes up temporarily when you are even a little excited: a doctor of the opposite sex often finds a higher reading than one of the same sex as the patient!

So don't jump to the conclusion that a blood pressure higher than the next man's is necessarily a cause for worry. Sometimes, and in 85% of cases we don't know why, the pressure creeps up higher than is good for the heart and arteries, like a water system under too high a pressure.

In this case, there are drugs today which bring the pressure down, so don't be shy about asking advice.

Identification of High Blood Pressure

Maybe—most likely—no symptoms at all.

Headaches, dizziness, ringing in the ears, and tiredness are as likely to be due to *anxiety* as to raised blood pressure. Symptoms of high blood pressure occur only when it affects the heart or arteries, and may then include bouts of breathlessness, particularly in the night; headache, especially on Sunday mornings, after the week's best chance to sleep late; pain in the chest; cough; misty vision in severe cases.

Usually the high blood pressure sufferer is physically fit otherwise.

Causes: A minority of cases are secondary to an anatomical quirk of the great blood vessels, kidney disorder, or glandular trouble. The majority remain a mystery, but there is a familial tendency, and overeating aggravates any tendency that way.

While it can come on in young adults, this is mainly a disorder of the senior years, and one in ten of men over 50 have some degree of hypertension.

Treatment: None may be necessary, except not to worry. For more severe cases the best maneuver is to reduce your activities, and make use of your weekends and evenings for more rest. Modern drugs bring down the pressure, but unfortunately have also some unwanted effects. In no other illness is co-operation with the doctor more important.

Course: The disadvantages of raised blood pressure are the strain imposed on the heart, arteries, and kidneys, all of which may produce symptoms, but many patients have years of reasonable health to look forward to, and in some, especially women at the menopause, the disorder may get better with advancing years.

HEART FAILURE

The heart has considerable reserves of power, and even the possessor of a diseased heart may get by with very little disability unless some other condition crops up to add a burden. Such additional load may be put on by: anemia; infections; pregnancy (the placenta enlarges and alters the circulation); kidney disease, through causing extra fluid to be retained in the body; obesity; excessive physical exercise.

Heart failure itself, however, is no longer the bogey of former decades. Modern drugs can so assist the struggling heart that it can continue to give its possessor reasonable service for many years after failure has first occurred.

Mechanism: When the heart fails, the ventricle (see diagram of heart) does not empty completely with each pump. This in turn prevents the atrium from pushing all its contents through to the ventricle, and so a back pressure is set up in the veins, the vessels which bring blood to the heart. The symptoms of heart failure are due to this back pressure, and often depending on whether the right or the left side of the heart is predominantly affected.

The right side of the heart receives venous blood from all over the body, and the results of its being dammed back may be noticeable even in the fingers and feet. The left side receives blood that has been replenished with oxygen in the lungs, and back pressure here produces chest symptoms.

For clarity we shall consider the two types of failure separately, but naturally a combination of both is very common.

Left-sided Failure   [U, B, 1]
Three times as common as right-sided.
Identification: The dominant symptom is shortness of breath, and there may be an irritating, unproductive cough due to the congested condition of the lungs. Attacks of breathlessness in the night, "cardiac asthma," so that the sufferer wakes up gasping, especially if he has slipped off his pillow. He feels he must open the window to get air, and feels better upright. Bouts last from five to thirty minutes. Palpitation; sweating; faintness.

Muscular fatigue on exertion because the heart is not putting out enough to cope with exercise.

Having to get up at night to pass urine, in some cases.

Bronchitis or pneumonia are likelier in the congested lungs.
Causes: High blood pressure; aortic or mitral valve disease; coronary disease. The first and last are commoner in men, mitral disease in women.

Right-sided Failure   [Ch: O, S]
Identification: Swelling, especially of the feet and ankles, which if pressed upon by a finger remains pitted for several moments. Normal flesh springs back into shape immediately the finger is removed. (*Note:* Similar swelling occurs with varicose veins and in fat people.) Abdomen may be swollen and tender. Veins may be visible in neck. Face and hands and feet may be blue: check

that it is not just due to cold by looking at the warm inner surface of the lip.

Indigestion and loss of appetite if the stomach veins are congested.

Causes: Usually secondary to left-sided failure; mitral valve disease; congenital heart disorders; chronic bronchitis and other lung trouble.

Congestive Heart Failure [Ch: U, B]
Combination of left- and right-sided failure.
Causes: As above; thyroid disorder; rheumatic heart.

Treatment of Heart Failure
Medicines to strengthen heart and reduce the amount of fluid in the tissues: through doctor. Also specific treatment for any associated troubles or anemia, etc.

Rest: Mental as well as physical. In the same way that any other damaged or strained part, for instance a sprained ankle, needs rest in which to recuperate, so does the heart, and it has remarkable powers of recovery given the chance. So that you do not feel frustrated, however, by inactivity, ask your doctor to plan for you how much rest you will need and for how long. In a mild case a rest in the afternoons may suffice for a housewife, or in the evenings and weekends for a worker away from home.

Nor need rest mean, necessarily, complete confinement to bed; in older people, especially, spells out of bed are beneficial. The heart works better when you are sitting up than when you are lying flat, and better still when you are standing.

Sleep: Use a back rest or extra pillows if you find you can breathe more easily propped up.

Diet: Less physical activity requires less food, so make your meals smaller. This will also diminish the strain imposed on your heart during the digestion of a big meal. If you are overweight, of course, you may correct that.

Salt encourages fluid retention which makes the heart's work harder, and leads to swelling. Cut out added salt and salt in cooking, and cut down severely on salty foods such as bacon, cheese, pickles, chocolate, tinned foods, sea fish, ham, eggs, beer, and bottled soft drinks.

Smoking: Nicotine throws an extra strain on the heart, so be moderate. *Alcohol,* on the other hand, may help by its sleep-inducing and relaxing effects.

Outlook: Cheerful! An indefinite period of activity lies ahead, with modern treatment. No need for depression. See notes on how to live after a heart attack (below).

Acute Heart Failure [U]

Symptoms as above, coming on rapidly. Treatment is in the doctor's hands—and bag.

Rheumatic Heart Disease

Rheumatic fever and the related disease chorea are less common nowadays with better living conditions, and less severe with modern therapy. However, many hearts are still damaged by rheumatic fever. The heart trouble is not usually noticeable until ten years after the fever, and only in two-thirds of cases can any attack be remembered.

The valves which prevent the blood from going back the wrong way when the heart contracts are the parts most usually affected, and of these the mitral valve (see diagram of heart) is the most vulnerable, and the usual effect is that it becomes narrow and stiff, or stenosed.

Mitral Stenosis: valvular disorder of the heart [Ch: S, W]

Identification: Commoner by 3½ to 1 in women; ages 18–55, especially the late 20's. Breathlessness on less and less effort, dry cough, tendency to bad colds on the chest, cold hands and feet, blueness, fatigue. Occasionally, blood may be coughed up.

Treatment: If the symptoms are enough to be bothersome, operation is excellent: rapid, dramatic recovery, increased longevity —and no age limit for the operation.

Outlook: Indefinitely good.

Other Heart Disorders

The signs of incipient heart failure (above) will bring to your notice any significant heart trouble, and it is for your physician with his armory of diagnostic aids to take over the problem from there.

Remember, however, that there are more people who think they have heart trouble than actually have, so do not be surprised if your symptoms turn out to be based on anxiety and misconception.

"HEART ATTACK": CORONARY DISEASE: CARDIAC INFARCT

Coronary disease, one of the more alarming manifestations of our Western civilization, accounts for the deaths of a large and increasing number of men, many of them in their early forties, and a large proportion professional. It seems to be taking the place, more seriously, of the "businessman's ulcer." Among women, although less often affected, the rate is rising steeply.

Mechanism and Causation

The coronary arteries are the most important in the body, for they supply the heart itself with the oxygen, glucose, and other substances which it needs. If they fail, the heart stops beating, which means death. "Death from a coronary" is such a failure.

Coronary occlusion
Coronary thrombosis } means blockage of a coronary artery.

If the blockage is large, death occurs; if it is moderate in size, the victim collapses in severe pain but survives; if only a small branch is affected, there are attacks of pain which pass off.

The pain is caused by the heart muscle having to work without adequate supplies. Any muscle hurts in such circumstances.

How does the blockage occur? As age advances, and beginning in the twenties, changes occur in the arteries.

Atheroma is a laying down of fatty material from the blood in patches inside the arteries, narrowing the channel. The main constituent of the deposits is called cholesterol.

Hardening: The atheromatous plaques gradually become impregnated with calcium, which makes them stiff and brittle (it is calcium that makes teeth and bone hard). This is hardening of the arteries, or arteriosclerosis. The hardened narrow arteries readily become blocked by *clot formation,* but exactly what makes this occur is still obscure.

What we do know: Research is still actively proceeding in the United States, Sweden and other European countries, and under the auspices of the Medical Research Council in Britain. It has been observed that the amount of cholesterol in the blood, and the number of coronary deaths, is lower among the Italians, who use olive oil; the Eskimos, who use fish oil; and the Chinese, who use sunflower seed oil and corn oil, than in the Westerners, who prefer animal fats, butter, and egg yolk. In Norway, during the German occupation when food was scanty, particularly the fats, the mortality from heart disease fell dramatically.

Big eaters, who are obese, have been found usually to have *atheroma,* the possible forerunner of coronary disease, and it also seems likely that a large fatty meal may start off a clot. Also, if there are beta-lipoproteins in the blood from such a meal, the process known as fibrinolysis, which "dredges" the arteries of blockage, may be inhibited.

The importance of exercise: an ordinary, healthy man's heart is capable of immense adjustment to the demands of its possessor, and in exercise the coronary arteries may enlarge to three or four times their usual size. Small vessels are also capable of opening up to assist or replace others, and this is the basis not only of athletic training, but of the heart's wonderful recuperative powers after it has been damaged, as by coronary blockage.

It has been found that heavy workers such as miners, bricklayers, and farm laborers are relatively immune from coronary disease, whereas doctors, lawyers, and clergymen head the list of its victims.

On the strength of the above we know and can deduce:

How to Avoid a Coronary

Keep or become slim.

Step up your physical exercise, not more violently but more regularly, especially if you are over 35. Consider the tonic effect of a walking or golfing vacation compared with a food-centered, beach-lounging one.

Stop cigarette smoking.

Do not eat excessive amounts of fatty meats or dairy products.

Use instead vegetable oils (chemically unsaturated fats). Eyelid nodules (xanthelasma) of yellowish hard fatty material often occur in middle-aged people with high blood cholesterol levels; they are an indication that your doctor should examine you and check. *If you suspect* you may have high blood pressure or anemia, have a check, and treatment if necessary. These disorders aggravate coronary difficulties.

Or view it in reverse. In a recent issue of the journal *Heart*, there were these "Rules for Admission to the Coronary Club."

1. Make sure you have a positive grievance, a real chip on your shoulder. A promising candidate has to make resentment part of his life.

2. Never smoke less than fifty cigarettes (preferably more) per day. A mild cigar in the evenings is no substitute.

3. A man who can afford a bottle of whisky per day is a ground floor candidate.

4. Make sure you add a few pounds to your body weight each quarter. An ambitious candidate must put up with shortness of breath. The bull-neck and hippo-belly are excellent qualifications.

5. Keep your nose near the grindstone. Take work home in the evenings—seven nights a week. Make yourself so tired that you need a sedative. Cut down that vacation! An idler won't be admitted here.

6. Eliminate walking—it's a waste. Go everywhere on wheels. Put effort into your leisure. Don't let yourself relax. You owe it to your employers. Make your games a science. Never play golf without business talks at the same time. Run for that train!

7. Cut out the optimism. Let your mind dwell on tax problems. Remember the boss is out to get *you*. Keep the nuclear bomb well in mind. Work up a nice obsession about the state of the world.

If you fulfill these main qualifications for getting into the Coronary Club, we can't say you will be admitted, but the application will be kept on file.

"Heart Attack" [A: U, B, 6/12, X]
Identification of Coronary Attack
Sudden severe pain in the center of the chest, sometimes radiating across the chest, into the neck, or the arms. Tight or crushing

sensation and feeling of impending death. Breathlessness often, because of the pain.

Treatment

Immediate: Sit or lie at an angle of about 45° in bed or on armchair. Send for doctor urgently.

Later: If the pain lasts for up to six days and then gradually recedes, you will need absolute bed rest for three weeks at least, and three months' convalescence, since it takes around two months for a firm scar to form in the damaged section of the heart, and longer still for small vessels to open up and take over.

Convalescence: Aim at gradually increasing your activity, without incurring pain or breathlessness. In this way you will stimulate the development of a compensating, collateral circulation. Heavy work is not for you, however, and for a year at least, make sure of generous night and weekend rest.

After a Heart Attack: How to Live Wisely and Well

Medicine provides the drugs to help your heart; you provide its tasks, its stimuli, and its rewards with your way of life. A heart attack does not mean a short and invalid life; many people I know, leading an active social life in their eighties, have had heart disorders for twenty years and more, but their habits suit both themselves and their hearts.

You must start at the zero, that is, after having completed—to the letter—the period of treatment and convalescence recommended by your doctor.

After that, get on to a permanent re-ordering of your life.

Keep your weight at what is normal or desirable for your age, height, build, and sex. Make adjustments gradually by modifying your diet and taking moderate exercise. Never overload your stomach at one meal.

Slow down: don't run for a bus, dart upstairs, hurry anywhere.

Save your energy all for digestion after meals.

Do nothing that makes you short of breath or brings on pain.

If you are short of breath or feel a chest pain, lie down.

Cut down brain strain. Do your thinking jobs only when you are fresh. You will do them better.

Cultivate a calm outlook. Don't be proud if you are "quick on the trigger"—change your ways.

Avoid moods, unless they are all colored cheerful.
Don't smoke.

These are reasonable tenets by which to live; at any rate your heart will think so, and serve you better and longer.

Angina [A Ch: U, B, 1/7]

A condition in which the coronary arteries are constantly on the borderline of insufficiency, so that there are often attacks of the same type of pain as in a coronary heart attack, but with rest, the pain passes off.

Identification: Gripping pain in upper chest, often radiating up neck and down left arm. The word angina means suffocation, for that is how it sometimes feels. The pain is brought on typically by:
Effort after a meal: One man walked easily from his office to his luncheon restaurant, but had anginal pain when he attempted the return walk.
Effort and anxiety: e.g., hurrying when late for an appointment.
Effort alone; emotional upset alone.

Treatment: Immediate: Stop. Place tablet from your doctor under your tongue; it is inactive if swallowed whole. These tablets act like magic.

Later: Regulate life within the limits of your heart's comfort along the same lines as After a Heart Attack (above). Use the tablets as your doctor advises—try to anticipate the pain by taking them before exertion or physical strain of any kind. He may need to treat associated conditions, too, such as anemia or hypertension.

Note: The tablets themselves occasionally cause headaches and a feeling of heat, which show that they are working in your case.

Outlook: You can look forward to a fairly active, comparatively painfree existence—going on into really old age, if you live wisely. Anginal patients in their 80's are not rare.

The Breathing Apparatus

This comprises the lungs, the bronchial tree, and the expansion mechanism.

The absorption of oxygen, vital to every bodily function from reading to running, and the disposal of poisonous carbon dioxide, produced as the oxygen is used, occurs in the lungs. They are composed of myriad tiny air-filled balloons in whose gossamer walls the capillaries run, so small that the red blood cells must pass along them in single file.

For the used blood to be re-oxygenated, air must reach these distant chambers. Warmed and moistened in the nose (it should not be by-passed through the mouth), it travels through the larynx into the main air passage. This divides, behind the breast bone, into right and left tubes, and these redivide into smaller bronchi and finally bronchioles, like branches and twigs. To deal with the dust inhaled at each breath, there is a comprehensive sweeping system of flailing microscopic hairs, wafting the debris upwards twelve times a second, night and day. A cough is an emergency clearing measure.

To work the lungs, a partial vacuum is produced around them by enlarging the chest. The ribs swing outward on their hinges to the spine, the diaphragm descends: air sucked in. Normal breathing out is the recoil.

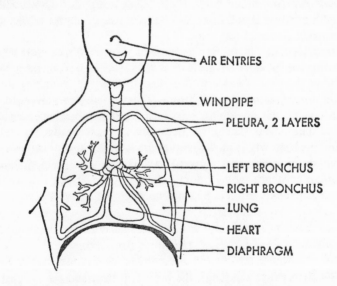

This, in brief, is the apparatus that, acting twenty times a minute, year on year, provides for you the breath of life.

Sputum (phlegm): Material that is coughed up

Types and Causes

Mucoid: Clear, jellylike, with frothlike detergent water on top. This occurs in acute or chronic bronchitis (irritation or inflammation of the air pipes to the lungs) when there is *no infection.*

Mucopurulent: A mixture of mucus, as above, with pus so that it is opaque: the commonest type of sputum, and usually associated with bronchitis that has become *infected,* and needs treatment *now.*

Purulent: Nearly all pus, yellow or green, depending upon the organism responsible. *Infected.* (Acute or chronic bronchitis, bronchiectasis, tuberculosis, pneumonia.)

Extremely sticky, sometimes containing small pellets which are casts of the smaller air passages. Feels "heavy on the chest."

Typical of *asthma.*

A viscid sputum is also produced in *pneumonia,* often tinged with blood to a rusty color, and it is sticky and frothy in the early stages of acute bronchitis.

Blood flecked: Bronchitis or whooping cough or any violent coughing; tuberculosis, now much less common and far more easily cured; cancer of the lung.

Note: Blood in the sputum may not come from the lung. Nose bleeding or blood from the stomach may be mixed with the sputum.

Thin, frothy, dark red, or "prune juice" appearance; associated with cough, loss of weight, and fatigability, may occur in cancer of the lung.

Thin, pinkish, frothy, with breathing difficulty and other symptoms: water-logged condition of the lungs as in asthma; in heart troubles.

Large quantities, say a cupful, on waking, and especially on leaning down. This is suggestive of a cavity, due to *bronchiectasis* or *tuberculosis,* probably, which fills with mucopurulent material in the night.

Black or gray: A sign of the city dweller, or the coal miner. Fog makes it worse.

Apparent sputum: Mucus, pus, and blood from the nose, sinuses, or the back of the throat, or possibly the stomach, may mistakenly be considered to be sputum. Sputum is coughed up from the bronchi and lungs.

Importance of Sputum

Twofold: the presence of pus is an indication of infection and the first sign of it is the signal for energetic treatment.

The presence of blood is important in revealing the presence of a serious disorder in some cases.

How to Bring the Sputum up

It is inefficient and a strain on the lungs, and often causes bleeding, to try to cough the sputum up all at once by a tremendous effort, and a savage paroxysm defeats its own purpose by pumping up the pressure inside the chest. The best method, when there is material to be coughed up, is to ease it up little by little through the complex tree of tubes, by small gentle coughs, using particularly the lower part of the chest and the diaphragm. In bronchiectasis or other cases in which there is a cavity full of pus, drainage can be helped by position, leaning over first to one side and then the other.

Coughing up of Blood   [U]

Medical name: Hemoptysis.

See Blood-flecked sputum, above.

Tuberculosis, especially in a young adult. Can be the first sign. Not nowadays nearly such a misfortune to contract.

Heart trouble, mitral stenosis. Not usually the first sign.

Cancer of the lung: middle age, repeated small bleedings more likely than one copious hemoptysis.

Other lung disorders, as asthma, bronchitis, pneumonia, but not as common as foregoing causes.

Note: Blood from the nose, gums, or other parts of the mouth, throat, or stomach may be confused with blood truly coughed up from the chest.

Treatment: Rest in a propped-up position. Send for doctor urgently.

Give no alcohol or other stimulant.

COUGH: COMMON CAUSES IN BRONCHIAL TREE AND LUNGS

(See Cough in Throat Section.)

Bronchitis

An inflammation of the lining of the bronchial tubes, the commonest disease of the breathing system.

Acute Bronchitis   [A: S, B, 2]

Often follows "catching cold," or as a herald or complication of measles, influenza, whooping cough, or typhoid. People with chronic bronchitis (below) are very likely to have an acute attack in smoggy or cold weather, and when there are colds or influenza about.

Identification: Cough, at first barking and painful, with a very little sticky sputum, becoming looser and easier in a few days with more sputum, mucus and pus mixed. Tightness in the chest. Mild fever. Huskiness. Coated tongue. Feelings of languor and oppression.

Treatment: A vaporizer is helpful, and hot fruit drinks, as much as you like.

Doctor's treatment will include medicines to deal with the infection, loosen the sputum, and calm the cough at night. A productive cough in the day is a good thing and should not be suppressed. The tubes need to be cleared.

Outlook: Dangerous in infants, invalids (from other causes), and the aged. Usually acute bronchitis subsides in a week, and you are back to normal in a fortnight. It is important not to jump the gun and go back to work before this is completely cleared, however, for acute bronchitis readily leads to chronic bronchitis.

Prevention: Babies, chronic bronchitics, and the very elderly should stay indoors in smog.

Chronic Bronchitis   [Ch: S, W or I, X]

What happens: The lubricating glands of the bronchi are enlarged, and the sweeping system of the bronchial lining is disorganized: in places the tiny hairs are completely absent. The airways become

clogged with mucus and have to be cleared by a routine of coughing, which may strain the delicate air chambers and cause emphysema. The debris blocking the bronchi and bronchioles in turn
causes further irritation, and bacteria settle and multiply, bringing
on an infective element. The initial damage usually occurs in an
attack of acute bronchitis, which is never completely cured, or a
run of acute attacks.

Identification

Shortness of breath: Hills that used to be nothing now seem troublesome to climb; you would rather not walk *and* talk.

Cough that is present for at least three months of the year and
probably never clears completely; moist, productive; disturbs the
sleep; characteristically there are bouts of coughing, not on waking, but the moment you put your feet to the ground.

Sputum is coughed up, stringy, jellylike, or frothy, often gray from
city grime, and in bad spells streaked with pus and occasionally
blood. Wheezing, loss of weight, and anxiety are also fairly frequent, and true asthma with paroxysms of breathlessness may
supervene.

Treatment

Medicines: Inhalers and tablets to expand the tubes help some patients particularly; sedatives and expectorants to loosen the
phlegm help others.

Some doctors are trying long courses of antibiotics, all winter;
others prefer to give each bronchitic a supply of tablets to use at
the very first sign of a cold.

Breathing exercises: Including reading aloud, and humming, for a
slightly longer time each day. Try to breathe with the lower part
of your chest and by using your diaphragm, as this aerates the
lungs completely.

General measures: Of course, *NO SMOKING.* Smoking does not
start chronic bronchitis, but it keeps it going and makes it worse;
it is as though you cut your hand while gardening, and then took
a handful of earth and rubbed it into the wound. Consider your
bronchitic chest as wounded. If you have a dusty job, swap it.
Wintering in a warm, dry, equable climate is a pleasant ploy for
the wealthy bronchitic. Otherwise, there is a divergence of opinion
on fresh air.

One school advises cool bedrooms, open windows; the other and larger group recommends a warm bedroom, heated all night, door open instead of window.

Outlook: Modern drugs greatly help, particularly in avoiding or dealing with acute phases, but do not completely cure chronic bronchitis. Some chronic bronchitics are active in their mid-eighties, so it is worth taking care.

Factors that Favor the Development of Chronic Bronchitis

Sex: Men affected four times as often as women.

Age: Over 40's mainly, but not exclusively.

Occupation: Professional, clerical, and skilled workers less liable than the unskilled. Of manual workers those who fare worst are either in dusty jobs such as mining or textile manufacture, or must work outdoors in all weathers, like mailmen.

Air pollution: Smoky industrial cities.

Housing: Damp and overcrowded.

Personal: Smoking; obesity; other lung disorders; curvature of the spine, hampering the breathing; chronic infection in nose or sinuses; hereditary tendency.

Emphysema [Ch: S, X]

A wearing out of the elastic tissue of the lung, rare before fifty, and comparable with the similar loss of elasticity of the skin with advancing age. In the lungs, however, it means a loss of their normal tendency to spring back into shape after being stretched by breathing in, so that they remain partly inflated, and the chest stays in a partly expanded position. This reduces its range of movement, and the rib joints themselves become stiff.

The cause is uncertain, though the blowing of wind instruments, traditionally blamed, has now been exculpated. There may be a family weakness of the lung elastic; the changes of age itself come on sooner in some than others; and the condition is at least aggravated by bronchitis and asthma, with which it is often associated.

Identification: Increasing shortness of breath, with special difficulty in breathing out; dry hack of a cough, unless there is accompanying bronchitis and sputum, in which case there will be the symptoms of chronic bronchitis; barrel chest; blue lips and face.

Treatment: As after chronic bronchitis. Stop smoking.

Outlook: The worn tissues cannot be rejuvenated, but care can prevent bronchitic complications.

Bronchiectasis [Ch: S, X]

A ballooning enlargement of the bronchial tubes.

Causes: An after effect of bronchopneumonia, measles, influenza, or whooping cough, or from chronic bronchitis. Some babies are born with cysts in their lung tissue: congenital bronchiectasis.

Identification: "Just not feeling well"; continual slight fever; mild bronchitis every winter; moist cough; sputum, coming up in a large quantity all at once, especially in the mornings and on leaning in one particular position, sometimes very offensive, and causing unpleasant breath; clubbing, that is a thickening of the last part of the fingers, in some cases.

Treatment: As for chronic bronchitis, with plenty of antibiotics to control infection.

Postural drainage: The positions of the cavities which fill with sputum overnight are determined by X-ray. It is then possible to work out the best position to put oneself in each morning to empty them. Deodorant inhalations are necessary for some, and in some cases, especially children, the affected part of the lung may be removed surgically.

Outlook: Complete cure only by operation, but even without, a ripe old age can be obtained.

Asthma [A: U; Ch: S, W. X]

See also Allergy.

Characterized by bouts of panting breathlessness, due to temporary closure of the smaller airways deep in the lung tissues where effective breathing takes place.

Identification: Children often, young adults most commonly, and sometimes those over 40 affected for the first time. Attacks of *tightness* in throat or chest, with a feeling of suffocation, labored, *wheezing* breathing with special difficulty in breathing out, and paroxysms of *coughing*. *Sputum* at first sticky, then comes freely and spasm relaxes: relief but exhaustion. Attacks come commonly in the night or early morning, and last from minutes to hours, occasionally days. They can recur several times in the twenty-four hours, or not for months.

Wheezing may persist, and there may be the signs of accompanying chronic bronchitis.

What happens: The lining of the small tubes suddenly swells up, and the automatic muscles in their walls contract; there is also increased production of mucus in the bronchi. Breathing out is usually a gentle process, mainly the passive recoil of lung and chest wall, but in these circumstances it is long and difficult. The wheezing is the whistlelike effect of air being forced through the narrowed tubes.

Causes: Basically an inborn bodily trick: some people react with headaches or tummy aches, some with asthma. Factors are:

Heredity: relatives with asthma, hay fever, or hives.

Other lung trouble. The first attack often comes on during an attack of bronchitis.

An allergy to, for instance, house dust and other dusts, animal or human dandruff, shellfish, pork, eggs or milk, aspirin, molds, and pollens.

Emotion: children typically get an attack on Christmas Eve or the night before the family vacation; adults may bring on an attack by fear of it!

People who have asthma often had eczema, hay fever, or hives (all allergic troubles) when younger.

Treatment and Prevention

Immeasurably improved in the last five years.

Skin tests may establish that you are sensitive to certain substances, in which case a course of injections may make you able to tolerate them. Tablets to chew and rapidly acting inhalers will help you to avoid and to deal with attacks; in a severe or persistent spasm, your doctor can give dramatic relief by an injection.

Measures You Can Take

Breathing exercises. Do not smoke. Do not get fat. Do not let yourself get upset.

Find out, and avoid, what affects your bronchi. It is a highly individual affair: some do well, some do worse, by the sea; others thrive in sooty, city air.

Special precautions if you are sensitive to house dust, animals, etc. See Allergy.

Outlook: Better now than it has ever been. Children usually grow out of it, and many of those who start in adult life are very much benefited by steroids and other new drugs, though not cured.

Pregnancy and feverish illnesses both keep asthmatic attacks at bay.

Chronic bronchitis and *emphysema* associated with asthma are the likeliest causes of trouble.

Pneumonia

Inflammation of the lung itself, with fluid from the irritated tissues exuding into the tiny air sacs, so that the usable lung area is diminished, and breathing must be more rapid to make up.

NOWADAYS RARE because our antibiotics and chemical medicines deal so efficiently with the responsible organisms before pneumonia has a chance to develop. Bronchitis is as far as most infections go.

BACTERIAL OR LOBAR PNEUMONIA   [A: S, B, 2]

Due usually to the pneumococcus or staphylococcus, both of which are knocked out by antibiotic drugs. What was once a deadly disease is now no longer to be feared, and is increasingly uncommon.

Identification: Suddenly "taken ill" with headache, shivering, perhaps vomiting, and backache. Temperature rockets to 103° F. the first day. Short cough with sticky, blood-flecked sputum, sometimes rust-colored later. Severe pain on one side of chest. Shortness of breath, shallow breathing, almost panting. Color high, but tinged with blue. Lips dry and cold sore may be present. Tongue furred. There may be delirium at night.

VIRUS PNEUMONIA   [A: S, B, 2–6]

Identification: "Out of the blue" or following a cold (also caused by a virus). Similar to but much less severe than lobar. Temperature around 100°–101° F. Dry hacking cough, without much to bring up. Usually both sides affected. Great fatigue and limb pains as in influenza.

BRONCHOPNEUMONIA   [A: S, B, 2–6]

A patchy inflammation of the lungs and tubes, which may be due to a variety of organisms. It can occur at any age, but is especially frequent in infancy. Usually it comes as a complication of acute fever, like measles and whooping cough, influenza; spread of acute bronchitis; chronic illness, and long lying in bed; inhaling infected material after a throat operation.

Identification: Merges into *acute bronchitis,* gradual turn for the worse taking two or three days. Temperature goes up and down, about 100° F. in the morning, up to 103° F. in the evenings. Cough, with mucus, pus, and sometimes streaks of blood in the sputum. Breathlessness. Face pale and bluish. Languor.

Treatment of Pneumonia

Medicines—from doctor. Antibiotic drugs for bacterial pneumonia produce a dramatic improvement in 24 hours; tetracycline prevents the virus of some virus pneumonias from multiplying, which allows the natural defenses to work more easily; there is no hard and fast rule about what works in bronchopneumonia, and different medicines may have to be tried.

General: Prop up; minimum talk and disturbance. Hot water bottle for pain in side. Inhalations to ease the tubes and loosen the sputum. Tepid sponging if temperature 103° F.

Breathing exercises started as soon as possible, and continued into convalescence. Warmth and fresh air.

Outlook

Bacterial pneumonia: No longer the deadly "old man's friend" that snatched so many to a speedy departure. Much better in a week nowadays, and back at work in 6 weeks.

Virus pneumonia: If the virus responds to the antibiotic, cure and convalescence may take 3–4 weeks, otherwise 6–12 weeks.

Bronchopneumonia: Also depends on response to drugs. May remain ill for weeks with correspondingly long convalescent period. Keeping up the nourishment is therefore important. Bronchiectasis can follow bronchopneumonia unless it is vigorously and seriously treated, and work is not resumed until the lung is absolutely clear, as shown by X-ray, preferably.

Pleurisy

The lungs are enclosed in a double bag called the pleura. Pleurisy is inflammation of this bag; it can be either *dry,* painful because of the sore surfaces rubbing on each other, or *wet,* because fluid has formed inside the bag, keeping the surfaces apart.

Either type can arise apparently without cause after a cold or a chill, or over an inflamed area of lung as in pneumonia, lung cancer, bronchitis, or when there is a general illness such as kidney disease, ear trouble, blood poisoning.

DRY PLEURISY   [A: S, B, I]

Identification: Sudden, severe, stabbing pain in side or shoulder, aggravated by breathing, coughing, moving, pressing; short, dry, distressing cough—or none; fever 100°–102° F., or none.

Treatment: Appropriate antibiotic. Local heat—hot water bottle. Breathing exercises later.

WET, WITH EFFUSION   [A: S, B, 6; Ch]

All the causes already mentioned apply, and also tuberculosis.

Identification: As in dry pleurisy, but pain disappears as fluid separates the inflamed surfaces, while lassitude and feeling of illness increase. Temperature continues moderate. Slight to marked breathlessness. Sometimes no cough.

Treatment: Medicines appropriate to cause, as prescribed. Prolonged rest and convalescence.

Outlook: Small collections of fluid absorb in a matter of weeks, larger ones, unless drained surgically—months. An aching corner may persist for some months, and the two layers of pleura tend to stick together, which give breathing exercises an importance.

Thirty percent of wet pleurisies are tuberculous in origin, so the original treatment needs be thorough, and X-ray checks are advisable for the next three years.

Pus in the Pleura   [A: S, B, 6; Ch]

Medical name: Empyema.

Usually comes on at the verge of convalescence from pneumonia, but can arise with tuberculosis or other lung illnesses.

Identification: Temperature climbs up again, higher at night than in the morning; pain in the side which soon passes off; ill.

Treatment: Medicines, especially penicillin; surgery, brilliant results. Walking and breathing exercises as soon as possible.

Tuberculosis of the Lung [Ch: X]
Medical term: Phthisis.

This is the "consumption" of literature: infection of the lung substance with tubercle bacilli.

Now becoming rare, but important because it can be treated satisfactorily if recognized early; untreated there is a danger of infecting others.

Identification: Onset varies, and may be dramatic or insidious. Take note of, and seek advice for:

Sudden coughing up of blood: the mouth is unexpectedly full of something warm and salty, in someone in apparently perfect health (10% of cases).

Wet pleurisy.

Feeling unwell, fatigue where formerly easily able to manage, loss of weight, and loss of appetite at breakfast, sweating in the night, periods irregular or stopping in women. Slight fever, cough, and then the coughing of blood-stained sputum may follow the general symptoms.

Unexpected detection from routine mass X-ray, or other X-ray. The mass X-ray system is one of the factors responsible for the stamping out of this once dread disease.

Age range: Unexpected divergence between the sexes:

Women   19–25 years ⎫
Men   60+   ⎬ commonest ages of onset.

Treatment: Streptomycin, PAS, and isoniazid, powerful drugs used in combination so successfully that many patients who would have required sanatorium treatment can now be managed at home.

Sanatorium treatment is still advisable for a large proportion; where it is does not matter, provided that skilled care is available. There is no danger of catching further infection from other cases at a sanatorium.

For a selected few, surgery has a wonderful contribution to make.

Rest, rest, rest, whatever else. Then graduated re-education to outdoor exercise.

Outlook: Never so good as now, but a sensible life must follow, with regular rest and meals, cutting out hurry and stress. X-ray checks. A woman should get a doctor's advice before having a baby.

Prevention

Nearly all of us have had tuberculosis (40% at 21, 95% by 50) but have never even noticed it—only the scars remain to be seen by X-ray, and the immunity acquired protects from further infection.

BCG vaccination, with very weak bacilli, produces an immunity in those who have not been infected, such as children and young adults.

Factors which predispose to tuberculosis are contact with an infected person, often an elderly granny or grandfather who may be thought to have simple bronchitis; poor diet; diabetes; smoking; silicosis; unpasteurized milk; overcrowding.

Lung Cancer [Ch: SU]

We hear a lot about this disease, but it is not nearly as common as, say, coronary disease or high blood pressure. It is important, however, because it is a killer; it is on the increase, but it is much more effectively treated if detected early. *It is to a large extent preventable.*

Identification: Cough, productive sometimes of blood-stained sputum, a "prune juice" mixture of old blood and mucus, or blood; cough may be brassy in character, maybe wheezing. Vague ill-health. Chest pain. Lassitude and loss of weight come later.

Age: Usually over 40, commonly 50–60 years.

Sex: Six men to one woman.

Treatment: Operation, X-ray, etc. Lung surgery is nowadays far easier, largely because the problem of anesthetics has been solved by tubes slipped down the windpipe.

   IF YOU SUSPECT LUNG CANCER, SEE YOUR DOCTOR AT ONCE.

Causes

The trouble starts in the lining of a bronchial tube, the part of the lung that can be irritated by what is breathed in. It seems beyond doubt that cigarettes are the chief culprit in this way, although air pollution and personality have been suggested as possible factors.

Relation between Smoking and Lung Cancer

The Royal College of Physicians, hardly a sensationalist outfit, published a report in Britain in 1962, based on surveys and studies from nine countries. It shook the doctors and became a best seller —but has not convinced the public, which continues to spend increasing amounts on cigarettes.

In 1964 the U.S. Government published their report, confirming the findings.

Quotes

- Death rates from lung cancer increase steeply with increasing consumption of cigarettes.
- Cigarette smokers are much more affected than pipe or cigar smokers (who do not inhale).
- The risk is greater for the heavier smokers.
- Heavy cigarette smokers may have thirty times the death rate of nonsmokers.
- No other explanation fits all the facts as well as the obvious one that smoking is a cause of lung cancer.
- The lungs of smokers without cancer show signs of chronic irritation, of the sort which might precede cancer, more often than the lungs of nonsmokers.

The Magnitude of the Lung Cancer Problem

From 1916 to 1959 lung cancer death rates increased forty-four times; the trend continues.

Sex: Five-and-a-half times as many men as women die (*but* five-and-a-half times as many men as women smoke more than twenty cigarettes a day).

Age: Most deaths occur in age range 60–70, very few before forty-five years. Dr. Alton Ochsner, recent president of the American Cancer Society: "It is probable that lung cancer will now become more frequent than any other cancer of the body unless something is done to prevent its increase."

But Professor Harold Burn, Emeritus Professor of Pharmacology at Oxford: "If men were as reasonable as women, the lung cancer problem might disappear."

And Doctors Hammond and Horn, 1962, who had been following the fortunes of 188,000 American men for nearly four years: "The [lung cancer] rate for cigarette smokers who had given up the habit for a year or more was considerably lower than the rate for men who were smoking cigarettes regularly at the start of the study."

So it is not too late—it is worth while changing your ways even now!

Note: It has been suggested that

(1) *Air pollution* is the snag, not smoking. How come then that Finland, a 90% rural country, has the second highest lung cancer rate in the world, and that on the Isle of Jersey, where the air is clean but cigarettes are cheap, the rate is higher than anywhere else in the British Isles?

(2) *Personality* is the underlying factor. The type that smokes is a type that has a predisposition to lung cancer always—a book by psychologist Dr. Hans J. Eysenck, 1965. Dangerous stuff. Can human personality have changed so markedly (and continue to do so) since the turn of this century, when cigarette smoking got its hold?

And if you give up smoking—and reduce your chance of lung cancer—are you a different person?

Other Results of Smoking

Lung cancer is frightening; there are other diseases as important in which the villain of the piece is again the cigarette.

The main constituents of tobacco smoke are benzpyrene and allied tar products, nicotine, and a variety of irritants. There is a little carbon monoxide, not normally enough to do harm. The benzpyrene is the substance most closely associated with lung cancer, and it also causes the brown staining; nicotine, colorless, gives tobacco its particular character and has effects on the circulation; the irritants affect the lining of the breathing system.

Cough with Phlegm—Smoker's Cough

The irritants in smoke make the mucus glands in the tubes pour out more of their secretion, and at the same time the sweeping system is slowed down so that phlegm accumulates and must be cleared by explosion—cough. Productive cough is directly related to the amount of cigarette smoking. Pipes and cigars have less effect.

Bronchiectasis

Smoker's cough may be irritating; it is dangerous as the forerunner of chronic bronchitis. Heavy smokers stand five times the chance of disabling bronchitis as other people, and run an increased risk of chest infections after operations.

Tuberculosis of the Lungs

Tuberculosis is on the way out—except in elderly men. It seems that heavy smoking is a factor, but alcohol also is associated.

Coronary Heart Disease

The shocker of the century dealing sudden death particularly in the age group 45–54, when a man has much to give to the community and very much for which to live.

One-quarter of all male deaths at ages 40 plus are due to coronary thrombosis, and the rate is increasing for both sexes. Smoking is concerned. The American Heart Association and Dr. Beric Wright of The Institute of Directors' Medical Centre in England agree that "heavy cigarette smoking contributes to or accelerates the development of coronary disease," and this most markedly in men under 55.

Other factors may be concerned, but there is no doubt that those who give up smoking reduce their coronary risk.

Angina: Not a disease in itself, but heart pain due to inadequate blood supply. It can be brought on directly by smoking.

Palpitations can be brought on by smoking, but these are not a disease.

High blood pressure: Nicotine raises the blood pressure, but only temporarily. There is no permanent effect.

Buerger's disease (*thromboangitis obliterarus*), an illness in which the arteries to the legs close up, occurs almost exclusively in smokers.

Other artery diseases are slightly likelier in smokers.

Minor disorders of digestion: Heartburn, nausea, flatulence, loss of appetite are all improved when smoking is given up.

Gastric and duodenal ulcers heal more slowly in smokers.

Cancer of throat, mouth and gullet: All increasing, all commoner in smokers than nonsmokers.

Babies: Tend to be born underweight if mothers smoke during pregnancy—or their fathers before! These are confirmed facts.

With all this against it:

Why Do We Smoke?

Children: Curiosity; parental example.

The rest: Sociability; fashion; for a possible sense of relaxation: psychologists say that a cigarette in the mouth of an adult is equivalent to thumb-sucking in a baby; because it helps concentration; nicotine addiction; help in avoiding obesity, because smoking certainly assuages hunger by suppressing stomach movements. Psychological type: the extrovert, sociable and outgoing, tends to smoke cigarettes; the pipe smoker turns his thoughts inwards—in general.

The benefits of smoking are 99% social and psychological; the price is physical: three times the danger of death before 45 if you smoke heavily; twice the chance of death before 65.

Only a minority of smokers shorten their lives by their habit, but we have no way of telling which they will be.

For the present: Do not smoke:

If you are adolescent; the habit is hard to break once you have started.

If you have smoker's cough, emphysema, or bronchitis.

If you have a peptic ulcer, or even simple indigestion.

If you have any heart or artery trouble.

If you are over 50, and entering the cancer-prone age.

If you *must* smoke, then moderate your appetite to less than fifteen a day; do not smoke fast, for the smoke is then hotter, more irritating, and contains more nicotine; do not inhale; do not smoke the last inch, concentrated with benzpyrenes and nicotine.

Better still, take up a pipe or cigars.

The Esophagus, or Swallowing Tube

The esophagus is a 10-in. tube that carries the nourishment from mouth to stomach, past such vital structures as heart and lungs. It is narrowed in three places: at its upper end in the neck, part way down the chest where the left bronchial tube crosses it, and where it goes through the diaphragm just before entering the stomach. These are the places where trouble, if any, arises.

The swallowing tube is one of the simplest organs, but even so, swallowing is an active process: the food is massaged along, so that it is possible to swallow something solid even standing on your head!

Two troubles can arise with swallowing: pain; difficulty.

Painful Swallowing
Causes in the neck (see Neck Section).
Causes in the esophagus: acute inflammation; heartburn; ulcer, e.g. in hiatus hernia; cancer.

Acute Inflammation of the Swallowing Tube   [A: 48, D, I]
Medical name: Acute esophagitis.
After swallowing hot or corrosive liquids, or a solid that becomes stuck; as an extension of inflammation of the throat in some fevers.
Treatment: A tablespoon of olive oil, ice to suck. See doctor if pain is severe.
Outlook: Not usually more than a passing inconvenience, but with some types of injury, scarring may occur and make a narrow place in the tube, causing difficulty in swallowing much later.

Heartburn   [A: N, 1/7]
Nothing to do with the heart, except that the pain is in the chest.
Identification: Sharp, burning feeling in chest, coming on about an hour after a meal and lasting a few minutes or much longer, relieved by drink of milk or an antacid such as sodium bicarbonate.
Mechanism: Painful contractions of the circular muscle of the esophagus often brought on by the irritation of the usually acid stomach contents backing up into the tube.
Causes: Any weakness of the muscle closing the stomach off from the esophagus, a faulty passage through the diaphragm, pregnancy or obesity pushing the stomach contents upwards, and in association with esophageal peptic ulcer (below). Overwork, overanxiety, or overtiredness cause heartburn directly through the nervous pathways to the swallowing muscles.

Treatment: Milk or antacid, soda water or even plain water gives immediate relief. Change of diet to simpler, less seasoned foods, and a vacation—or at least a more leisured outlook—are long-term measures.

Underlying trouble, if any, to be dealt with by doctor.

Waterbrash: Acid Regurgitation

Rising up into the mouth of sour or burning fluid, is sometimes confused with heartburn. See Dyspepsia.

Ulcer of the Esophagus   [Ch: S, 6]

Similar to peptic ulcer in the stomach, and caused by stomach juices acting on the swallowing tube, usually due to a quirk of development in which the tube is unduly short, and its entrance into the stomach inefficient in closing; or after long illness, lying down, so that stomach contents are not helped on by gravity. Rare before 40. See Hiatus hernia.

Identification: Heartburn behind lower one-third of breastbone, and burning sensation as food is actually swallowed. Worse lying down or leaning forward.

Treatment: As peptic ulcer in stomach. No smoking. Stay upright as much as possible. Sleep with many pillows.

Difficulty in Swallowing Due to Trouble in the Esophagus

See Difficulty in Swallowing in Neck Section.

Cancer of the Esophagus   [Ch: SU]

The commonest cause of a swallowing difficulty *after middle age,* especially in men.

Identification: Occasional tendency for solid food to "stick." Often the trouble goes away for days or weeks, but then becomes more frequent, and happens even with soft foods. Pain—usually none, but this is not invariably so.

Important to get help *QUICKLY.*

Treatment: Operation or X-ray, with medicines to increase comfort.

Simple Stricture of the Esophagus   [Ch: SU]
A narrowing due to the contraction of scar tissue in the esophagus following the accidental swallowing of a corrosive—or even very hot liquid.
Identification: Progressive difficulty in swallowing.
Treatment: Gradual stretching or replacement with plastic tube of the narrow place, by surgeon. Important to have this trouble investigated because of the possibility of cancer.

Pouch of the Esophagus   [Ch: S]
Medical name: Diverticulum of the esophagus.
A weak spot in the wall of the tube which has ballooned out. Food may stick in it.
Identification: Long continued swallowing difficulty, but not complete blockage. Food sometimes comes up. Only X-ray can identify for certain.
Treatment: None usually necessary except care with foods, once it is certain that this is the only cause of the trouble.

Hiatus Hernia   [Ch: S, X]
See also Hiatus hernia in Abdominal Section.
Part of the stomach protrudes upwards through the gap (hiatus) in the diaphragm intended for the esophagus to pass through. May occur as a developmental abnormality in children or, more usually, in those over fifty, especially women, following pregnancy, or, lifting heavy weights, or with obesity.
   A cause of inflammation of the esophagus and possibly ulcer: see above.

Achalasia of the Cardia
The entrance to the stomach does not fully open, causing difficulty in swallowing.

Anemia and Swallowing Difficulty
Rare combination which occurs in middle-aged women.

THE ABDOMEN

This is the factory area, where a wide variety of materials from ice cream to steak are processed and converted into—you.

> It's a very odd thing
> As odd as can be
> That whatever Miss T. eats
> Turns into Miss T. . . .

Not just a childish jingle but sober scientific fact. So individual is the rearrangement of amino acids to form your particular protein that your body reacts at once if a strange type is introduced into the blood.

The stomach is the collecting bag and partial digester of the raw materials; in the 22 ft. of coils and loops of small intestine, digestion continues, and the resultant milky fluid is absorbed by many fingerlike processes which dip into it from the lining. The large intestine, a mere 2 ft. festooned around the internal borders of the abdominal cavity, receives the waste products, reabsorbs some of the water, to conserve it and to make the movement

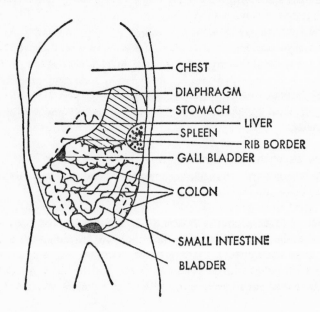

firmer, and in turn passes it on into the sensitive rectum. It is from there when it is loaded, that the message to evacuate is sent.

The whole complex process from stomach, by the conveyor system of squeezing muscles, to rectum takes an average of eighteen hours, but we know far less about the way it works than we do about the working of the heart, lungs, or nervous system.

The Stomach

It is situated higher than you think, behind the lower ribs, just left of center; that is how heart and stomach pain come to be confused. When empty, it hangs in a limp "J" from the esophagus; full, it assumes the generous curves of a summer squash.

The food arriving in the stomach is not much altered: roughly mashed up by the teeth and mixed with saliva, which partly digests the starch foods (if you keep a piece of bread in your mouth long enough you will taste the sweetness of the sugar being formed). From solid chunks of meat, pellets of bread—whatever—the stomach makes a souplike fluid which can be acted on by other parts of the digestive system.

The stomach juices contain three important substances:

(1) Hydrochloric acid, a disinfectant and dissolver of the solids.

(2) Pepsin, to break down (digest) meat and other protein foods.

(3) Mucus, a thick material which protects the stomach from being digested by its own juices, by acting as a barrier cream and neutralizer.

The stomach juice also contains substances which turn cane sugar into glucose, begin the digestion of fats, and one which is essential for the making of blood.

A great deal of knowledge of the stomach is due to two men, neither of them scientists! Alexis St. Martin was shot in the stomach when he was 17, in 1822, and lived into his 80's with a hole in it large enough to put his finger in. Tom ——, in our century, burned his gullet with hot clam chowder; and by the time he was 57, there was such severe scarring that an opening into his stom-

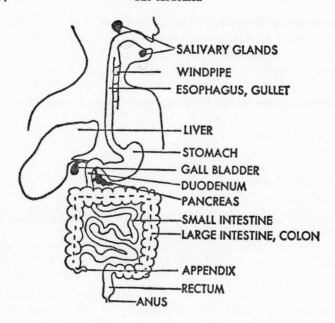

SALIVARY GLANDS
WINDPIPE
ESOPHAGUS, GULLET
LIVER
STOMACH
GALL BLADDER
DUODENUM
PANCREAS
SMALL INTESTINE
LARGE INTESTINE, COLON
APPENDIX
RECTUM
ANUS

Diagram of Digestive System

ach had to be made through his abdomen, to get his food in. It was also a medical peepshow.

Among a mass of fascinating information, it was discovered that emotion had a marked effect on the stomach lining. It became red and produced juice with plenty of acid, not only when a savory meal was in preparation, but also with anxiety and resentment—even when no food was in prospect.

When Tom and Alexis were sad or despondent, their stomachs went pale inside, less acid was produced—and they had no appetite. These facts are of particular interest when we consider that important disorder *peptic ulcer*.

> "Better is a dry morsel and quietness therewith,
> than a house full of feasting and strife."
>
> —*Proverbs* XVII

Symptoms of Disorder in the Stomach

Discomfort ⎫ In the upper abdomen, sometimes in the back,
Pain ⎭ or between shoulders.
Nausea.
Vomiting.
Tenderness over the stomach.
Dry mouth, furred tongue.
Unpleasant taste.
Unpleasant breath.
Thirst.
Wind and distension.
Heartburn.
Hiccup.
Waterbrash.
Acid regurgitation.
Altered appetite.
Loss of weight.

The first four are most commonly encountered, and any may occur in several disorders, not necessarily in the stomach.

Pain in the Stomach (or Upper Abdomen)

May go through to back or between the shoulders.

Discomfort Rather Than Pain

Gastritis, acute: relieved by vomiting. Gastritis, chronic: relieved by belching, alkalis, food.

Colitis, inflammation of the large intestine: comes on after meals, accompanied by wind below. Pain usually low in abdomen, however, in this case.

Functional (anxiety) dyspepsia, nervous causes, many other symptoms.

Normal eating after being on a diet.

Constant Pain

Cancer of stomach: no appetite, wind, distension, loss of weight.

Chronically inflamed gall bladder: made worse by food, especially greasy; wind, not relieved by belching.

Several uncommon causes.

Intermittent Pain

Peptic ulcer: related to food.

Gallstones: severe, unrelated to food.

Angina: brought on by effort.

Esophageal disorders: pain immediately after swallowing, e.g. hiatus hernia.

Acute gastritis, comes on suddenly, with tenderness, nausea, vomiting.

Nausea (Feeling Sick) and Vomiting

Causes in the Stomach

Wrong foods: too much, too fatty, spicy, or hot, with too much alcohol.

Special sensitivity to certain foods such as shellfish, pork. Hives, diarrhea also, maybe. See Allergy.

Medicines, particularly in certain people, especially aspirin, antibiotics, sulpha drugs. Expectorants and emetics.

Poisons, e.g. turpentine, household disinfectants.

Fermentation due to blocked exit to stomach. *RARE.*

Stomach diseases: See Table, page 175.

Gastritis, acute or chronic.

Ulcer, gastric and duodenal.

Cancer.

Bleeding into the stomach from any cause.

Hiatus hernia: green fluid brought up.

Stimulated via the Nerves

Anxiety or other emotional disturbance. Vomiting is as likely after a digestible food like milk as an indigestible one such as a pickle. Sometimes little more than a regurgitation: not an urgent affair.

Migraine. Headache. No relation to food.

Trouble inside the skull affecting the vomiting center in the brain: injury, abscess, tumor, meningitis, bleeding. Maybe no nausea. No relation to food; urgent vomiting.

Travel sickness.

Mountain sickness, also occurring at high altitudes in unpressurized aircraft. Due to lack of oxygen to the brain. Other symptoms: lassitude, insomnia, irritability, lack of concentration, headache.

Early pregnancy.

Reflex vomiting, that is, the stimulus to the vomiting center comes from some part other than the stomach, commonly in ear infections and tonsillitis in children; in all people often in infections of the intestines, disorders of the liver, pancreas, kidney, gall bladder, appendix, and sex organs; or hernia. Reflex causes outside the abdomen include Ménière's disease (associated with dizziness), glaucoma, and irritation of the pharynx in alcoholics and smokers. There may be much hawking, bringing on the vomiting. The vomiting that often accompanies bouts of coughing in whooping cough is also brought on mainly mechanically.

Toxic Causes

Beginning of some feverish illnesses, such as measles, typhoid.

Toxemia of pregnancy. Later months.

After anesthetics.

Jaundice.

Some general illnesses: pernicious anemia; Addison's disease; thyroid disorder.

Cyclical or recurrent vomiting in children. "Acidosis."

Treatment: Of cause. Meanwhile rest horizontally and take nothing by mouth. Sips of iced water, or milk diluted with barley water may be tried after an hour or two. Plain water induces further vomiting; it should be salted, one teaspoonful per pint, to match the body fluids, until the tendency to vomit is over.

Note: Vomiting is not the spitting out of fluid that has come up into the mouth, but the expelling of the stomach contents by retching, in which the diaphragm goes down and the abdominal wall is drawn in, automatically, to press on the stomach. The muscles involved ache afterwards from the exertion.

Vomiting of Blood [A: U, B]

Medical name: Hematemesis.

To be taken seriously. Gravity depends on cause.

Any appreciable quantity of blood in the stomach causes nausea and vomiting; if the bleeding is coming from the stomach itself, there is a feeling of faintness before the vomiting, there may be food mixed with the vomit, or the blood may be partly digested to produce a "coffee grounds" appearance.

Causes in the Stomach

Peptic ulcer, occasionally the first sign.

Cancer, seldom a large quantity. Over 50's.

Chronic gastritis, especially in alcoholics. Morning vomit of mucus streaked with blood. Occasionally in acute gastritis.

Irritants: aspirin and its derivatives in some sensitive people; chemicals; mechanical injuries from swallowed objects.

Causes Not in the Stomach

Nose bleed, blood swallowed.

Bleeding from gums or throat, mixed with saliva. Look and see.

Lungs: See Coughing up of Blood in Chest Section.

Swallowing tube disorder.

Blood disorders.

Liver disorder.

Tropical diseases: malaria, yellow fever.

Heart disorders.

Treatment: Absolute rest, horizontal. Warmth. *Doctor—urgently.*

Hiccup [A: N, 1/7]

A disturbance in the normal synchronization between the movements of the lid that shuts off the airways during swallowing, and the diaphragm, the muscular sheet between chest and abdomen that is used in breathing. It is the diaphragm that gets out of step.

Causes

Simple indigestion: over-distention; hot, peppery foods; exercise after eating.

Wind, in either stomach or colon.

Faulty swallowing: food "trying to go the wrong way."

Nervousness.

Hiatus hernia.

Rarer causes of more persistent hiccup:

Pleurisy, near the diaphragm.

Inflammation in the abdomen, e.g. appendicitis.

Serious disorders of liver, kidney, brain.

Epidemic hiccup, probably an infection.

Treatment: Most hiccups go away within an hour. Traditional maneuvers to stop the spasm and make the diaphragm work normally are sipping water, sucking sugar, holding the breath, or deep breathing. Breathing into a paper bag to produce air with a high concentration of carbon dioxide, which stimulates the breathing center, may be tried. Any of these measures may help, and hiccup due to indigestion is quickly cured by sodium bicarbonate, one teaspoonful to a glass of water. Do not worry if a baby hiccups, and do not try to cure him.

Hiccup is not serious in itself, but see the doctor if it goes on for more than three hours.

Waterbrash, Acid Regurgitation, Heartburn
May be confused.
Waterbrash: Gush of clear fluid from mouth, with or without staining, usually in the morning. Due to excessive production of saliva overnight, which is swallowed.

May be nervous, due to any form of dyspepsia, or peptic ulcer, as may acid regurgitation and heartburn.
Acid regurgitation: Rising of sour, burning fluid into the mouth, usually met in conjunction with heartburn.
Heartburn: Burning sensation behind the breast bone.

Flatulence: Wind
Distension by gas, which escapes either upwards or downwards.
In the stomach (may cause hiccups or palpitation).
NOT due to decomposition of food.
Air swallowing: Commonest cause and leading to the severest belching.
Anxiety dyspepsia. Emotional stress. An attempt (unavailing) to relieve discomfort from gas in the intestine by regurgitating and swallowing air.
Indiscretion after being on a diet.
Chronic gastritis.
Gall bladder trouble, worse after fatty foods.
Hiatus hernia.
Ulcer of stomach or duodenum.
Cancer of stomach.
Faulty emptying of stomach; the alkaline juice from the intestine may enter the stomach backwards, mix with the acid stomach juice, and liberate carbon dioxide; or the stomach may fail to empty

and a wave of muscular contraction drive up the normal gas bubble in the stomach, together with some of the food.

In the Intestine

Air swallowing, the gas passing all the way down.

Constipation—damming back of normal intestinal gas.

Diarrhea ⎤ decomposition in the colon of
Laxatives ⎦ undigested food.

Fermentation in intestine of milk, starches, and sugars.

Treatment: Of cause. Break the air-swallowing habit. Let the wind come up, but do not try to help it up. Break the laxative habit, also; it brings more discomfort than it relieves.

Babies' Wind. See Children's Section.

Acute Dyspepsia, Acute Gastritis, "Bilious Attack" [A: 48, B, 1]

A sudden disturbance of digestion, so common that we have all had it; it is gastritis if the stomach lining is actually inflamed.

Identification: Stomach discomfort rather than pain; nausea, usually vomiting; tenderness of upper abdomen; headache; no appetite. May be slight fever.

Causes: Too much food; too rich food; too much alcohol, especially when tired; contaminated food—but see Food poisoning; poisons; as part of some fevers.

Treatment: Usually self-curing—a few hours without food is sufficient. Fruit drinks and dry crackers, and care with meat, skins, and spicy foods, or those too hot or too cold. See Vomiting. Back to normal, in an average case, in three days. Be careful about excesses next time!

Chronic Gastritis [Ch: S, R, X]

Not a forerunner of peptic ulcer but sufficiently unpleasant in itself.

Identification: Lack of appetite, nausea, and sometimes small vomits of mucus and fluid *in the morning,* getting better during the day. Feeling of fullness, drowsiness, and discomfort after meals, not helped by stomach medicines. Furred tongue, headache, undue fatigue. See Table, below.

Predisposing Causes

Regular, liberal use of alcohol.

Smoking.

Hurried meals, bolted unchewed.

Excessive tea or coffee drinking.

Too much carbohydrate: bread, cakes, buns, jams, pastries.

Chronic infections, especially in throat, mouth, and nose.

Aspirin, too much or too often.

Treatment: Cut out predisposing causes. Rest, particularly before and after meals. Bland diet.

Outlook: Good, if stomach given a chance. It will recover completely even from prolonged and severe ill-usage.

Functional Dyspepsia, Anxiety Dyspepsia, Nervous Dyspepsia, "Chronic Indigestion"   [Ch: S, 2]

Important, because it is so common, incommoding, and depressing; all ages, both sexes.

Identification: Variable appetite; heavy sensation in abdomen; fullness, discomfort, and wind above and below, sometimes after meals, or any time; nausea; gurgling abdomen; heartburn and acid or bitter risings.

Commonly associated symptoms: headache, depression, lassitude, lack of concentration, insomnia, palpitation.

Mechanism: Anxiety, worry, disappointment or overwork, and/or unintentional misuse or mismanagement can upset the delicately balanced nervous mechanism controlling and synchronizing the continuous movements of stomach and intestine. The digestive system is basically a muscular tube, and if parts of it go tight (spasm), there is discomfort. Flatulence arises as described.

This is the long-term version of the situation: "sick with fear."

Digestion itself, the rendering soluble of the foods for their absorption proceeds normally, except that rarely, and usually in children, there may be some difficulty with starches.

The other symptoms are not due to the dyspepsia, but are other, common, manifestations of anxiety.

Causes

Factors which may interfere with well co-ordinated working of digestive tract.

Constitution: your abdomen may be the part that, for you, reflects your feelings most.

Bad habits: fads of diet; smoking too much; too much tea, coffee, alcohol; too much drink with meals.

Misuse of laxatives.

Self-treatment, especially cutting out meat and going over to milk, carbohydrates, and medicines.

Introspection: brooding over your own bodily workings.

Emotional stresses, including an undercurrent of fear of cancer, ulcer, or appendicitis.

Treatment

Visit doctor for check, reassurance, and chance to air difficulties.

Normal diet, including meat. Cut down milk and sweet foods.

Drink less at mealtimes, and *moderate* amounts of tea and coffee.

Don't worry!

Hiatus Hernia [Ch: S, X]

See also Hiatus hernia in Chest Section

A bulging upwards into the chest of part of the stomach, due to weakness of the muscular sheet, the diaphragm, between chest and abdomen. Extra pressure in the abdomen, as in pregnancy and obesity, may be the final straw.

Age: Usually 50 plus; occasionally infants born with a defect.

Sex: Women more than men.

Identification: Heartburn and sometimes severe pain, worse on stooping and lying down, behind lower end of breast bone. Dyspepsia, wind, difficulty in swallowing on occasion. Bringing up of small amounts of bitter greenish material, maybe bloodstained. Hiccups. Cough.

Treatment: Sleep propped up with pillows. Small frequent meals. Avoid heavy work with much stooping. Reduce weight, if fat. Suck antacid tablets.

Operation may be advised but is not always necessary.

Outlook: Not dangerous.

Peptic Ulcers [Ch: S, B, X, 6]

These are a minor cause of death, although the accident of perforation in which the ulcer eats right through the stomach wall is not excessively rare. However, a more than average number of cases of coronary disorder occurs in peptic ulcer patients, and the ulcers themselves are painful and incapacitating.

There are two types: one in the stomach, mainly a wear and

tear process, and the other, four times as common, in the duodenum, the part of the intestine into which the stomach first sends
its contents. This type is associated with a high degree of acidity
in the stomach juice.

Identification: See Table, page 175. Pain may be felt in the back
if the ulcer is on the posterior wall of the stomach, or (rarely) it
can resemble angina. One-third of those with duodenal ulcer are
waked up in the night by the pain, but pain noticed on waking
early in the morning is likely to be due to anxiety dyspepsia. Occasionally, particularly in alcoholic subjects, there is no pain, and
sometimes instead of pain there is nausea and a sinking feeling,
especially in women. A feeling of fullness in the upper part of the
abdomen, "hunger pain" relieved by food, coming on regularly,
with periods of remission which become shorter as the disease
progresses, aggravated by fried and highly spiced foods, and accompanied by acid regurgitation (something like vinegar or lemon
juice rises in the throat), characterizes a duodenal ulcer.

Occasionally vomiting of blood "out of the blue" is the first
indication.

Although constipation occurs with peptic ulcers, excess of stomach medicine may cause diarrhea instead.

Weakness and tiredness are not usual symptoms: they more
commonly arise in anxiety dyspepsia.

X-ray and other tests will clinch the diagnosis for your doctor.
Treatment: Immediate: To heal the ulcer: rest in bed, perhaps
reinforced by sedatives; no smoking. To relieve the pain: two-
hourly insoluble antacid, for instance magnesium trisilicate; light
milky diet of many small meals, with plenty of eggs, buttered toast,
poached fish, custards, gelatins.

Long term: Do *not* become a food faddist. Do not stick to a
melancholy regime of steamed fish, puréed vegetables, tapioca.
Eat all you like except those foods which you know by experience
upset you. These will usually include fried foods, pickles, curries,
and spices. Have, *in addition,* a milky drink mid-morning, mid-
afternoon, and at bedtime.

HOW YOU EAT MATTERS AS MUCH AS *WHAT.*

Meals should be regular, unrushed, and well masticated. No

medicines, tablets or alkalis unless you have a relapse: in that case suck magnesium trisilicate malted milk tablets, or take other alkaline powders or medicines between meals, and step up the milk.

Do not feel you must change your job to one with less responsibility: it might carry less pay and produce more anxiety; but plan your day reasonably, *cultivate calmness,* and try not to bicker with your family at meals.

Surgery: Operation may be necessary in emergencies such as perforation, or advisable in ulcers that are slow to heal.

Outlook: Symptoms tend to come in bouts, and without treatment these may become so frequent as to be almost continuous, or in an equal number may gradually go away. Treated, the outlook is good: pain relief occurs in a matter of days, even hours, cure usually in six weeks. Insurance companies nowadays accept on normal terms peptic ulcer patients whose last attack was 3–5 years ago.

Cancer never develops from duodenal ulcers, although in the U.S. the less common gastric ulcers are considered suspect.

Causes of Peptic Ulcer: Prevention

Age and Sex: Nine out of ten occur in men, especially in their 40's and 50's; the tenth is likely to be a woman of 50+. Rare in children —perhaps because they can eat all day if they want. Heredity. Blood type O. Nonsecretors of antigens in the mouth. All these factors have a moderate effect only.

Personality: All types, but conscientious, hardworking, anxious men preponderate.

Job: Involving responsibility, as doctors, foremen, business executives.

(Note: shift work and irregular meals do not cause ulcers.)

Diet: No evidence incriminates even hot, spicy dishes.

Smoking: May not cause, but certainly, through the action of nicotine, delays healing.

Corticosteroid treatment: Ulcer may begin or worsen during treatment with these modern drugs.

Chronic bronchitis: Doubtful association. Drugs such as ephedrine may cause gastritis.

Cheering tailpiece: Peptic ulcer seems to have been diminishing in frequency in the last fifteen years.

Comparison of Symptoms of Some Important Digestive Disorders

	Duodenal Ulcer	Gastric Ulcer	Chronic Gastritis	Inflamed Gall Bladder	Cancer of Stomach
SITE of pain	Varies with ulcer site	Varies with ulcer site	Always central	Upper right abdomen	Varies with growth site
WHEN	Before meals (or 2–2½ hrs. after)	½–2 hours after meals	Immediately after food	Most noticeable after fatty foods. Irregular	Not much relationship to meals
MADE BETTER by food	Yes	Sometimes	No	Not usually	No, never
MADE BETTER by alkalis (indigestion medicine)	Yes	Yes	No	Not usually	No
VOMITING	Rarely	Common	In the morning	Not usually	Yes, common
APPETITE	Good	Fair	Bad in the morning	Variable	Very bad
BRINGING UP BLOOD	Occasionally	Occasionally	Very rarely	No	"Coffee grounds" (altered blood)
LOSS OF WEIGHT	Slight	Slight	No	No	Yes
TEST FOR BLOOD IN STOOLS	Yes	Yes	Sometimes	No	Yes, always

Stomach Cancer [Ch: SU]

Far less common than ordinary stomach ulcer, but nevertheless a common form of cancer.

Sex: Twice as many men as women.

Age: Over forty-five.

Heavy drinkers, those with chronic gastritis and family history of the disease stand a greater risk. The wealthy are least often affected.

Identification: Vague sick feeling in abdomen, spoiling appetite and causing loss of weight. Pain, fullness or discomfort may be associated with meals, or not. Nausea and "coffee grounds" vomiting, or ordinary vomiting may occur. The pallor and easy fatigue of anemia may be an early sign. See Table, above. Early diagnosis is vital; your doctor can do it by special tests and X-ray, so *GET ADVICE ABOUT DYSPEPSIA IF YOU ARE OVER FORTY.* The chances are your symptoms are due to something else, but if it is cancer, it needs catching—quickly.

Treatment: Surgical.

The Liver

Giant gland and master laboratory: its functions even today are imperfectly understood. Indications of its importance are its size, 5–8 lb.; its site, tucked safely yet centrally under the dome of the diaphragm; its capability of containing a quarter of the body's blood.

All the blood from the stomach and intestines passes through the liver, to emerge much altered. The liver prepares proteins, carbohydrates, and fats for storage or immediate consumption, working with the pancreas to keep a constant amount of sugar in the blood. It produces the substances that make the blood clot, so that a cut finger does not involve bleeding to death. It detoxicates bodily poisons and those from outside, including viral and bacterial, entering through the intestine. It makes bile, which is necessary for the digestion of fats, stores the anti-anemic factor that guards against pernicious anemia, and disposes of the unwanted blood pigment from worn-out cells.

To crown all, the liver, alone among the organs, can regenerate its own tissue.

Jaundice, "Yellow Jaundice"

An abnormal state in which bile accumulates in the blood stream and colors all the tissues yellow, including the whites of the eyes. A foremost warning of *liver trouble* or some blood disorder.

Causes

Blocked bile duct, preventing the bile from passing out in the normal way through the intestine.

Eyes look yellow before skin does. Dark urine. Bowel movements pale. Skin itches. Gallstones: in middle-aged women, healthy till now; color fluctuates with passage of stones. Pain. Common.

Inflammation, spreading from duodenum.

Tumor of neighboring organ, e.g. pancreas, stomach. Color steadily deepens.

Cirrhosis.

Inefficiency of liver cells: Comes on gently, skin yellows before eyes. Itching and pale movements, maybe.

Infective hepatitis. Fever for several days before going yellow. Common.

A complication of pneumonia, yellow fever, etc.

Chemical poisons, especially in munitions.

Too much blood pigment for the liver to deal with: Pale yellow only, movements and urine normal, no itching.

Less common than other types; due to pernicious anemia, faulty blood transfusion, Rh factor in new babies, snake venom, some bacteria, easily broken red blood corpuscles.

Treatment: As cause.

Fallacies: Conditions that may be mistaken for jaundice:

Yellow fat under the white of the eye—irregularly placed.

Sallowness of anemia—the whites of the eyes are not affected.

Certain medicines, especially atabrine.

Infectious Hepatitis [A: S, B, C, 6]

Inflammation of the liver by a virus.

Identification: Comes on gradually. Fever, distaste for food, diarrhea and vomiting for several days; then jaundice, and an improvement in other symptoms. Any age.

Treatment: Rest in bed until movements and urine are normal color.

Later: No alcohol for six months, but plenty to eat, because much weight will have been lost.

Infectious hepatitis is slightly catching, and particular care is needed over washing after toilet.

Cirrhosis of the Liver   [Ch: S, R, X]

Failure of the liver cells to renew themselves as they wear out, so that gradually they are replaced by useless scar tissue which impedes the circulation.

Identification: Dyspepsia, because of associated chronic gastritis, spider blood vessels on face, deep fatigue, muscular weakness, loss of sex urge, jaundice, piles, yellow nodules round the eyes. Not all of these symptoms, probably.

Causes: Not all unravelled. Chronic alcoholism especially in *men in their 50's and 60's.* Aftermath of liver infection, or its damage from gallstones.

Treatment: No alcohol. Highly nourishing diet with extra glucose and vitamins. Rest.

The Gall Bladder

A little muscular bag, offshoot of the main bile duct, in which bile is collected, concentrated and delivered in measured doses into the intestine to assist the digestion of fats at a signal from the intestines that food has arrived there.

Gallstones   [Ch: S]

Medical name: Cholelithiasis.

The function of concentration can be overdone. Gallstones, consisting basically of fatty cholesterol, are common, present in around 30% of those who reach 70 and commonest of all, according to the old age in "fair, fat, and forty" females.

Most of us are not aware of it if we have gallstones, but unto-

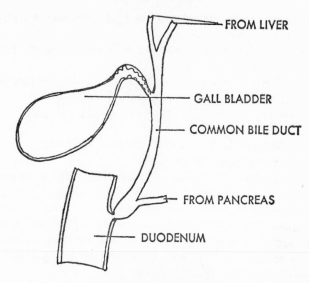

FROM LIVER

GALL BLADDER

COMMON BILE DUCT

FROM PANCREAS

DUODENUM

Diagram of Gall Bladder

ward effects can sometimes ensue and draw attention to their existence. A stone pushed into the main bile duct may pass down quite painlessly, but on the other hand it may cause severe *colic,* or by blocking the escape of bile, produce *jaundice* or irritation and *inflammation* of the gall bladder.

Treatment of "silent" gallstones, i.e. causing no symptoms:

It seems logical, when it is known that the gall bladder is working under difficulties, to restrict fatty foods and correct obesity if present.

If an operation is advisable, how do you guard against possible ill effects in the future? Your doctor must decide. *NO MEDICINE OR MANEUVER OTHER THAN SURGICAL REMOVAL OF THE GALL BLADDER CAN DISSOLVE, DISPERSE, OR OTHERWISE DISPOSE OF ANY GALLSTONE.*

Biliary Colic, "Attack of Gallstones"   [A: U, 1/7]

Due to a stone passing down the narrow pipe from the gall bladder.

Identification: Agonizing, colicky pain, with sweating, nausea, vomiting, and inability to keep still. The pain, starting high in the abdomen, may shoot up towards the right shoulder or shoulder blade.

Jaundice, with pale stools, may follow in a day or so, fluctuating with the movement of the stone.

Treatment: Pain relief by doctor. Recovery rapid—but the whole episode is likely to be repeated, so consult doctor about possible operation later.

Chronic Inflammation of the Gall Bladder [Ch: S]
Medical name: Chronic cholecystitis.

Stones predispose to infection, infection to stones . . . the gall bladder may become scarred and unable to function.

Identification: Oppressive fullness, flatulence, and distension (clothing needs to be loosened) coming soon after meals, especially fatty ones and most especially fried. Heartburn. Evanescent attacks of definite pain or jaundice, or undoubted *biliary colic*.

Usually in a plump, middle-aged woman.

Treatment: Turns on the presence of stones: X-ray needed.

Stones present: treat as *silent gallstones*.

No stones: treat as functional dyspepsia.

Antibiotics may help.

Outlook: The main difficulties, which make chronic cholecystitis worth taking seriously, are the chances of its flaring into:

Acute cholecystitis; gallstones leading to *biliary colic;* or possible cancer of the gall bladder.

Acute Inflammation of the Gall Bladder [A: U, B, 7]
Medical name: Acute cholecystitis.

Usually because of a gallstone obstructing the gall bladder.

Identification: Sudden onset of fever, pain in the upper abdomen on the right, continuous with spasms of being worse; usually vomiting, tenderness, sometimes jaundice.

Treatment: Operation to remove gall bladder, at once or after acute infection has been calmed by antibiotics.

Outlook: Good, after operation; constant trouble without.

Cancer of the Gall Bladder [Ch: SU]
Uncommon.

Identification: As chronic inflammation of gall bladder with constant discomfort, loss of appetite and weight, maybe jaundice.
Treatment: Surgical.

Abdominal Pain

[A: U]
See Pain in the stomach.
Nature's danger signal. Do not ignore it. It is foolhardy to be brave about abdominal pain which, although it is often due to trivia like dietary indiscretion, constipation, or mild food poisoning, can be a pointer to serious disease.
Particular Attention If
Pain severe and recent.
Distension accompanies it.
Nausea and vomiting also.
Abdomen hard.
Great tenderness to pressure.
Blood or tarry color in movements.
Severe abdominal pain lasting several hours, after previously reasonable good health, requires immediate investigation by a doctor: *THE SOONER, THE SAFER.*

It is particularly dangerous to take a purgative when suffering from unexplained abdominal pain, even if the bowels have not been opened.
Types of Pain
Colicky.
Peritonitis-type.
Inflammatory.
Others.

Colicky Pain

Sharp, agonizing bouts that cause writhing or doubling up, and are sometimes associated with cold and vomiting. The abdomen is not hard except during the spasms of pain, nor is it particularly distended. Pressing the abdomen, which the sufferer does automatically, slightly relieves the pain of colic, but of no other abdominal pain.

Intestinal colic: That which is usually understood by the term *colic*. Pain griping, in upper abdomen and around navel, sometimes gurgling sounds and patches of gas; sometimes vomiting.

Infection: enteritis. Diarrhea follows pain.

Irritation from indigestible or tainted foods, or the toxins of some fever, e.g. typhoid.

Lead poisoning, in painters or in children eating wall plaster.

Constipation.

Obstruction by enlarged glands, adhesions, tuberculosis, cancer, *strangulated hernia.*

Distension. No diarrhea.

Colic of colon: Commoner and less acute than small intestine colic described above. Pain mainly below navel. Colitis. Dysentery. Very severe constipation. Cancer, with recurrent attacks of distension, colic, and constipation, should be considered.

Appendicitis colic: In early appendicitis the pain is like intestinal colic, around the navel. Pain. Much restlessness. Due to overstretching of one of the muscular tubes of the abdomen, either because of a stone or in an effort to get the normal fluids past an obstruction.

Kidney stone colic: Sudden pain in loin shooting down into groin, testicle, or urethra in some. Frequent and painful passing of water, which may be bloodstained in some cases. Vomiting common.

Gastric colic: Pain in upper abdomen, due to blockage of stomach exit by ulcer or cancer. Stomach hemorrhage is similar but blood is vomited.

Womb colic: Pain felt in lower abdomen, lower back and sometimes down thighs. Due to passage of a clot, miscarriage, a polyp or—childbirth. Period pain may be severe. Bleeding likely.

Gallstone colic: Pain on right side either just below ribs or by shoulder blade, or sometimes right around: "girdle pain." Very severe. Maybe also jaundice. Abdomen may be rigid if there is inflammation of the gall bladder.

Tubal pregnancy, causing colic: A developing egg may lodge in the narrow Fallopian tube instead of the womb. As the egg grows, it may cause the tube to be painfully overstretched, or actually burst.

The pain can occur on either side and come on with such sudden severity as to make the sufferer faint. Missed or irregular periods provide a clue.

Peritonitis Pain [U]

Great, extensive, and persistent abdominal pain, usually coming with catastrophic suddenness, severe enough to cause fainting. May wake the victim from sleep. Cold sweat and vomiting, and a hard tender abdomen are associated. Breathing rapid and shallow. Abdomen becomes distended. Caused by:

Perforation, i.e. bursting of an abscesslike area, or gradual erosion by an ulcer, of the appendix, gall bladder, any part of the intestine, or peptic ulcer. In the latter case the pain is of a burning character, and there may also be pain in the shoulders.

Spread of infection from, for instance, womb, tubes, appendix, colon, gall bladder, pancreas.

Doctor immediately.

Inflammatory Pain

Constant, not spasmodic: sharp or dull aching, followed by slight vomiting and slight fever. Localized.

Right upper quadrant of abdomen: due to inflamed gall bladder, pancreas, or liver, or to duodenal ulcer.

Right lower quadrant: inflamed *appendix,* enlarged glands in children.

Lower part of abdomen (including right lower quadrant): diverticulitis, often on the left side; other colitis; inflammation of female organs, or bladder.

Loin, coming around and down to groin: kidney infection.

Other Pains

Shingles: burning pain in the side, skin very sensitive.
Distended bladder, becomes very painful if it cannot be emptied.
Aneurysm, pain felt first in chest, then descends to abdomen.

Conditions that May Be Mistaken for Acute Trouble

Influenza and other fevers, especially in children, may start with abdominal pain and vomiting.

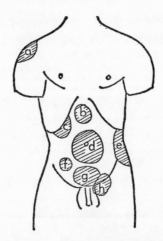

Front: Sites of Pain in Acute Trouble in the Abdomen

(a) Gall Bladder
(b) Stomach; Duodenum; Pancreas
(c) Gall Bladder
(d) Small Intestine; Appendix
(e) Kidney
(f) Appendix; Pregnancy in a tube; Inflammation in a tube
(g) Colon; Bladder
(h) Hernia; Kidney trouble

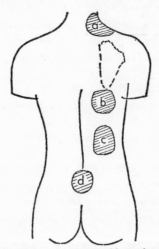

Back: Sites of Pain in Acute Trouble in the Abdomen

(a) Perforated Ulcer
(b) Biliary Colic; Gall Bladder
(c) Kidney; Pancreas
(d) Rectum; Womb

Diabetics have abdominal pain and vomiting often before a coma.
Food poisoning: Several people probably affected at same time.
Pneumonia.
Pleurisy.
Heart attack.
Kidney failure: Vomiting and distension.

ABDOMINAL DISORDERS

Swelling of Abdomen
Many causes.
General Enlargement
Gas in the intestines, associated with constipation, dyspepsia, air-swallowing; also, *accompanied by pain and obvious illness,* obstruction; inflammation of intestines; peritonitis.
Obesity.
Pregnancy.
Cyst of the ovary.
Fluid in the abdomen, usually accompanied by swelling of feet and legs.
Disorder of important organ: liver (may be jaundice also), heart, lung, kidney.
Investigation urgently needed.
Swelling in One Area
Pregnancy.
Full bladder, particularly if emptying is obstructed by enlarged prostate gland (middle-aged men) or displaced womb (women).
Gas: lower abdomen only may be affected.
Constipation: the swelling, often on the left side, can be indented by the fingers, unless it is in hard balls.
Cysts or tumors of female reproductive organs: ovaries or womb.
Tumors of any abdominal organ, due to either inflammation or new growth.
Lump in groin, bigger on coughing or straining: rupture (not strictly in the abdomen, but closely associated, since the swelling is composed of abdominal contents).

Acute Appendicitis   [A: U, 2]

The appendix is a fingerlike, finger-sized offshoot from the intestine, where the small intestine and colon join, in the lower right hand corner of the abdomen. It is thought to be the obsolete remains of an organ for digesting grasses, and in horses and rabbits the appendix is large. It is a mystery why the appendix should relatively commonly become inflamed, especially in Europeans and North Americans, and particularly amongst the better-off of these. (See diagram of digestive system, page 164.)

Identification: Pain, which may wake the sufferer in the night, starting in the middle of the abdomen but shifting in a few hours to the right lower quadrant. Vomiting, usually only once, may occur, or merely nausea and a distaste for food. Tenderness to pressure in one spot may be found. Slightly raised temperature: 99–100°F.; constipation usual.

For a few days before the attack, there has often been indigestion or flatulence, typically in one not subject to such troubles.

Age: Rare before two years, increasingly common through childhood; peak age: 15 years and 18–30, then a gradual decline. *NO AGE IS EXEMPT.*

Treatment: Operation to remove the appendix (appendectomy) as soon as possible. A safe, trouble-free procedure if performed without delay.

Outlook: Complete recovery; the appendix will not be missed.

RECURRENT APPENDICITIS

There is no such thing as chronic appendicitis, but repeated, mild attacks are common, usually culminating in a particularly sharp one that leads to the removal of the offending organ, which is the only cure.

Rupture, Hernia   [Ch: SU]

A bulge of the abdominal contents, usually a loop of intestine, through a weak place in the muscular wall.

Sex: Males much more than females.

Age: From birth to old age, less in the middle years.

Causes: Primarily, a weak part in the wall, particularly where the testis descends in the male.

Secondarily, conditions raising the abdominal pressure and

putting a strain on the weak place: chronic cough, straining at stool, heavy manual labor, pregnancy, abdominal tumors; and conditions weakening to the abdominal wall: old age, prolonged rest in bed, debilitating illness, lack of regular exercise.

Identification: Lump under the pubic hair by the groin on one or both sides. Coughing and straining make it larger, but it may disappear on lying down.

Pain in groin on exertion, sometimes in testicle. Dragging or heavy feeling if hernia large.

Treatment: Operation, for comfort, convenience, and SAFETY. An untreated hernia may become strangulated (see below).

A truss may be used while waiting for operation, or on those for whom operation is unwise because of heart or lung conditions. It is particularly important for those with a cough, who are fit enough, to have the operation, since it is they who most often get strangulated hernia.

Outlook: After operative repair, very good.

STRANGULATED HERNIA   [A: U, 6]

A loop of gut in the hernia may become twisted or constricted so that the blood supply is cut off. A DANGEROUS condition, since gangrene can set in in as little as six hours.

Identification: Sudden coming down of the rupture, abdominal pain, vomiting, tense tenderness of the rupture itself.

Treatment: Urgent operation.

Outlook: After operation, good, back to work in 21 days. Without operation: fatal.

Diarrhea

Frequent stools of loose or watery consistency that is more frequent than the individual's normal bowel habit.

A frequent desire to pass a movement may occur without its consistency being abnormal. This is not diarrhea.

Types of Diarrhea

Yellow, pea-soup appearance: small intestine affected, and food hurried by undigested.

Bulky and greasy stool, but not much pain: failure of fat digestion.

Pain when the motion is passed: usually colon affected. This is certain if blood and mucus are passed.

Alternating diarrhea and constipation: *IMPORTANT* as possibly due to a cancer beginning.

ACUTE

Virus gastroenteritis: commonly affecting whole household at few days intervals. *NOT* due to food.

Food poisoning, contaminated food. Several affected simultaneously.

Bacillary dysentery often in schools; slime in stools; doubling up with pain.

Traveller's diarrhea: infectious types, or from unaccustomed fatty foods, e.g. fried in olive oil, during a vacation trip.

Too much fruit.

Typhoid fever, rare in the U.S.

Part of other acute illnesses, e.g. infectious hepatitis.

CHRONIC

Colitis, inflammation of the colon: mucous colitis (mucus, white and gelatinous, in movement), ulcerative colitis (blood and mucus in movement), diverticulitis, rarely, not very common. Hyperthyroidism: nervousness, tremor. Malabsorption syndrome: offensive, porridgy stools, wind below.

Cancer of rectum or colon: typical alternation with constipation.

Functional, or nervous, diarrhea set off by unusual food or emotional upset.

Treatment: Of cause.

Bismuth and kaolin mixtures reduce the sensitivity of the intestine; agar stiffens the movement by absorbing water.

   Replacement of the fluid and minerals lost can be achieved with broth and soft drinks. Nourishing diet later to make up for food loss.

Constipation   [Ch: N, A, X]

Millions of dollars are spent on laxatives every year. A nation of neurotics, or unduly sluggish guts? No, there has been concern over the bowels since Biblical days; the ancient Egyptians had enemas, the Greeks had a word for it—dyschezia—and 70% of the concoctions from the medieval herbals were purges.

Identification: Prolonged gaps between evacuations, or difficulty in passing of the movements. (Remember, however, that each has his individual pattern, and movements every 48, 24, or 12 hours can be equally compatible with perfect health. *THERE IS NO LAW ABOUT THE BOWELS OPENING ONCE A DAY.*) Abdominal discomfort.

Headache, furred tongue, and wind are more likely to be the results of using laxatives, or of anxiety because the bowels "won't move," than of the constipation itself.

Most women have a tendency to constipation.

Causes

Faulty habits, maybe from childhood, usually later. Ignoring or resisting the call to evacuate, because of inconvenience, lack of time, or laziness, leads to the feeling's passing off, and the sensitivity of the rectum to being full diminishes.

Laxatives—strange though this may seem! Chemical laxatives act by irritating the intestine. Undigested food arrives in the colon, where it decomposes, giving off gas with an offensive smell. The colon's reaction is an attempt to delay the too-rapid passage of the undigested material, which makes matters worse. A further larger dose or series of doses has the same effect, more so.

It is then that the well-known symptoms of malaise, headache, furred tongue, wind, and distension develop. Bad dreams are not uncommon.

Weak muscles, as in old age, after pregnancy, sedentary life.

Locally painful troubles, like fissure or piles disturbing the habit.

Inadequate diet: In amount, in fluid, or in roughage, so that the stimulus is insufficient for a call to evacuate. (Commonly on a slimming diet.)

Spasm of the colon, spastic constipation. Some people react to anxiety or stress by a tightening of a section of their colon—other people react by headache. While the spasm lasts, maybe on and off for weeks, the material cannot pass. Dark people, rather than fair, in cool, rather than mild, climates tend to have this trouble the most.

Strange surroundings: An unfamiliar routine and an unfamiliar lavatory seat, such as obtain in the first few days of a vacation, put off the natural reflexes.

Nothing to do with the water!

Thinking about your bowels: "There is nothing like worrying

about the bowels opening to stop them opening": Dr. Clark-Kennedy, consulting physician at the London Hospital.
Depression.

CONSTIPATION ALTERNATING WITH DIARRHEA   [SU]
Or any sudden change in bowel habit in middle age: see doctor, to check for cancer or colitis. *IMPORTANT.*

STRANGULATED HERNIA   [A: U]
Great pain, lump in groin. Acute condition.

DIVERTICULITIS   [Ch: S]
Irregular bowels.

HIRSCHSPRUNG'S DISEASE   [Ch: S]
Rare, present since birth.

Treatment and Prevention
Stop laxatives.

Use bulk producers like agar, or mineral oil (it is said to interfere with the absorption of Vitamin D) or the so-called wetting agents like dioctyl, indefinitely.

Set aside a regular adequate period of time for the job. Never fail to respond to the urge to evacuate.

Diet: Plenty of fruit and fluid, but do not make a fetish of, say, prunes for breakfast. The less you think about your bowels, the likelier they are to act naturally.

Exercise: Take more, particularly if you are elderly. A brisker circulation and brisker muscular activity encourage a brisker set of intestines, and general toning up, even mental.

Defeatist's regime: Senna preparations two or three times weekly; but do try the other measures first, for a month.

Outlook: No one was ever much harmed by constipation, though *piles* are possible result.

Cancer of the Rectum or Colon   [Ch: SU]
An ulcer in the large intestine that does not heal by itself, usually in those over 60, and more often in men.

Identification: Diarrhea, especially "morning diarrhea," in which unsatisfying small mucoid or bloodstained movements are passed after several efforts, but there is really constipation, and laxatives are needed to pass a proper movement. Wind. Loss of weight.

Loss of energy. Maybe anemia and backache. Have any change of bowel habit, past 50, checked.
Treatment: Surgical.

Ulcerative Colitis [Ch: S, X; A: S]

An inflammation, with ulcers, of the large intestine, which appears to be the weak spot in some unusual personalities. They are more often women than men, commonly young adults of extreme conscientiousness. Emotional upset, particularly a blow to the self-esteem, often sets off an acute phase of what is a fickle and irregular disorder, coming and going in an unexpected fashion.
Identification: Gradual or sudden onset of diarrhea with blood, slime, and mucus in the movement. Fever. Abdominal pain.
Treatment: Through doctor: sulpha drug tablets; corticosteroids; possibly operation in severe cases. During active phases: *rest,* and full, appetizing and varied *diet,* but puréed. Not much milk. Plenty of vitamins.
Outlook: Medicine usually has effect in 3–4 days; some recover naturally, while others need prolonged care.

Mucous Colitis [Ch: S, X]

Commoner in women, but becoming rare. Important only because its symptoms may cause confusion with more serious disorders.
Identification: Alternating diarrhea and constipation, with white gelatinous material in the movements, but not blood. Flatulence. May be abdominal pain or discomfort.
Treatment: Vacation or change, non-irritating diet. A new outlook, new interests, and less concern with the bowels are needed.
Outlook: Fine.

Diverticulitis: "Left-handed appendicitis"
[A: S, B, 2; Ch: S, An, X]

With advancing years weak areas in the wall of the colon may bulge into flabby little pouches. These may become inflamed, perhaps sometimes due to a fruit pit becoming lodged in one. The symptoms are similar to those of inflammation of the appendix, but on the left-hand side.

Identification: Pain in the abdomen; tenderness on the left; fever.

Chronic diverticulitis: constipation, irregular bowels, some pain.

Treatment: Drugs via doctor. Avoid constipation.

Virus Gastroenteritis; Intestinal Flu   [A: 48, B, I]

A very common infection, particularly among children and in groups of young people like recruits. Due to several strains of virus, probably entering the body with food that has been contaminated by unhygienic handling, or coughing or breathing over by someone harboring the virus. The effects may be mainly abdominal or mainly in the nose and throat.

Identification: Sore throat, sore eyes, "cold," fever, headache, muscle pains; abdominal pain, diarrhea, vomiting. Only some of these may be present.

Treatment: None special, nor any means of prevention as yet. Bed, sweet fruity drinks only for 24 hours, then gradual addition of plain crackers, custard, and gelatin, small pieces of fruit, toast, egg, fish. . . .

Much better in 48 hours: completely recovered in a week usually.

See Children's Section.

FOOD POISONING

Many organisms enter by the mouth, but only a handful produce what we understand by food poisoning.

Staphylococcal Food Poisoning   [A: 48, B, 1/7]

Usually due to contamination of food by someone suffering from an infection of skin, nose, or throat with staphylococci. The staphylococci multiply in the food and produce a toxin (or poison) which does not alter its taste, and is *not destroyed by further cooking.*

Chief sources: Ham, cold meats, milk.

Identification: Abdominal pain, nausea, vomiting, diarrhea: coming on rapidly one-half to four hours after the meal, for instance, before the end of afternoon school, or after the wedding reception.

Treatment: None specific. Bed for 24 hours. Hot water bottle.

Sweet, fruity drinks, sips of warm, boiled milk; nothing solid while symptoms last. Kaolin mixture may help if diarrhea is troublesome.

Outlook: Nasty, but short. Ill for six to eight hours, recovered in twenty-four.

Prevention: Care about health and hygiene of whoever prepares the food. Eat food fresh, so that organisms have no time to multiply. *NOT* infectious from case to case, as it is the poison, not the germs that cause the symptoms.

Salmonella Food Poisoning [A: S, B, C, I]

Due to contamination of food by rats, mice, flies, birds, and humans. Often present in animal feeding stuffs, bone meal, fish meal, and duck eggs. Likeliest if food is kept too long, and warm. Foods may look, smell, and taste normal.

Chief sources: Cold cuts, sausages, pies; cream, ice cream; bread, cakes.

Identification: Sudden onset, but about 12 hours after meal. Nausea, vomiting, colicky pain, abdominal tenderness, and diarrhea. Headache and slightly raised temperature. Sometimes: cold sweats, shivering, cramps.

Significant if several members of the household or institution are affected simultaneously.

Doctor may wish to have stool examined at laboratory.

Treatment: Rest in bed, hot water bottle, sweet fruity drinks, warm boiled milk in sips, and no food until symptoms cease. Kaolin mixture. Drug, from doctor.

Outlook: Often continuous diarrhea for several hours, rarely continuing for more than two to four days. Recovery within a week.

Prevention: Movements of infected patient are infectious, therefore careful hand washing after toilet and before meals. The infection cannot be considered to have gone without laboratory check.

Care should be taken about buying cooked meats, especially from shops of doubtful hygiene, but thoroughly (freshly) cooked food is safe from this type of trouble, as salmonella is destroyed by heat.

Note: There is a wide individual variation in susceptibility, and some people eating the same contaminated food as those affected may have no symptoms at all.

Fungus/Mushroom Poisoning [A: U]
Identification: Abdominal pain, vomiting, much watery diarrhea, watering of the mouth, disturbance of vision—after eating dish with mushrooms.
Treatment: Antidote or stomach wash-out by doctor.

Can be due to an inedible fungus having been mistakenly used, or to a personal bad reaction to edible mushrooms.

Shellfish Poisoning
May occur similarly to mushroom poisoning, and also in some cases is due to allergy.

Allergic Food Poisoning
See Allergy.

OTHER INFECTIONS AND INFESTATIONS

Dysentery
A looseness of the bowels, usually with blood and mucus in the movements, and abdominal discomfort, due to certain organisms.

Common in tropical countries; formerly a scourge of armies in the field.

Only one form is nowadays prevalent in temperate climates:
BACILLARY DYSENTERY [A: S, B, C, I]
Acute infection of the intestines with Sonne's bacillus, via milk, food, or possibly water contaminated directly by an infected person, or indirectly through dust or flies. A common cause of epidemics in schools and other institutions.
Incubation period: One to seven days.
Identification: Abdominal pain, diarrhea, nausea, vomiting, headache. Very like food poisoning (above), but there is more pain, doubling the patient up, a definite feeling of illness; the diarrhea lasts longer, and there is slime usually, and blood sometimes, in the movements. Laboratory tests are needed to make certain.
Treatment: Antibiotic drug through doctor: the laboratory tests

can ascertain which is best in your particular case. Absolute rest in bed. Fluids only, at frequent intervals until symptoms subside. Then gradual reintroduction of foods.

Outlook: Much better in thirty-six hours; complete recovery in five days, a week if severe.

Infectious until laboratory tests are clear.

Prevention: Protection of food from flies, particularly.

Typhoid Fever [A: S, B, C, 2–6]

Occasional outbreaks in U.S., and isolated cases among those who travel abroad. Usually from contamination of water supply or foods such as watercress, milk, ice cream, and oysters. Flies spread it, and materials handled by carriers of the bacillus, who may have no symptoms.

Incubation: Seven to twenty-one days (time to have returned from overseas trip).

Identification: Insidious onset of headache, constipation, maybe nosebleed. Temperature rises gradually, over several days; diarrhea and abdominal pain and rash may occur.

Treatment: This, though rare, is a serious disease, both for the sufferer and his contacts.

Antibiotics, through doctor, are very effective. First class nursing essential.

Prevention: By inoculation. Immunity lasts about a year.

Internal Parasites

Except for the pinworms in children, worms, etc., are *RARE* in this country. If you see something unusual in your movements, take a specimen in a sealed jar to your doctor for identification. Cure is usually easy with our modern battery of medicines.

ANO-RECTAL SECTION

In 1686 Louis XIV had an operation on his rectum; court mourning was scarcely appropriate, but bottom bandages were ordered to be worn. Pain in this area requires the utmost sympathy.

The rectum, which is the last section of the digestive tube, and the ring of muscle, the anus, which forms its outlet, are to the lower end of food tract what the mouth and lips are to the upper. They are highly sensitive. The lower rectum is the area from which the call to evacuate arises, and the anus, or outlet, is dual-controlled, part automatically, part voluntarily.

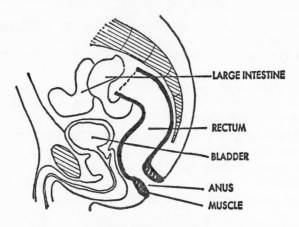

Section through Pelvis

Abnormal Stools [A Ch]
Too fluid: Acute: as in diarrhea; from food poisoning; gastro-enteritis, influenza, etc.

Chronic: colitis, small intestine infections, causes of chronic diarrhea.
Too hard: Constipation; lack of fluid, as in hot weather or fever.

Typically *woody hard* in the constipation associated with inactivity in the debilitated or bedridden.
Pencil-shaped [S]: Muscular spasm of the outlet, due to irritation by fissure; abscess, etc.; growth, making the passage narrower; after diarrhea when there is not much material to form a stool.

Pale, gray or clay-colored [S]: In and after diarrhea, due to the bile which normally colors the stool having been washed out more quickly than it is produced; liver disorder, usually the skin becomes yellow; milk diet; incomplete absorption of fats as in disorder of the pancreas or in sprue.

Black: Iron, bismuth, or charcoal medicines. Most tonics contain iron.

Bleeding from stomach or intestine: blood turns black after contact with stomach acid, and 3 oz. is enough to make the whole stool tarry. Blood (but not medicines) causing a black stool reddens the water into which it is passed.

Red blood [S]: The water is reddened, as above.

Streaks on the outside of the stool: piles, fissure. Mixed with the stool: ulcerative colitis; growth of the colon or rectum; acute dysentery.

Floating stool: Hard, dry balls (medical name: scybalae) mean lack of fluid, see above. Occasionally stools float because they contain a lot of undigested fat due to an unusually fatty meal, or a disorder of the pancreas.

Pus and mucus [S]: Ulceration of the rectum or colon as from ulcerative colitis; growth; infection; abscess; fissure; mucous colitis.

Undigested food: Overfeeding, in children; in adults, disorder of digestion or pancreatic trouble.

Worms [S].

Unusual odor: We barely notice the smell of our own bowel movements in health, but when, as in illness, odors come from other than the usual bowel element, they are immediately obvious.

Bleeding from the Rectum   [A Ch: SU]
Causes
  Piles
  Fissure
  Fistula
  Polyp ⎫
         ⎬ in the rectum
  Growth ⎭

For other causes, in which the blood is mixed with the stool, see Abnormal stools (above).

Pain in the Rectum

Each trouble has its characteristic pain.

Hemorrhoidal: Sudden, intense, constant, not made worse by bowel movement, painful to touch. Lasts ten days, then disappears.

Probably due to a clot forming in an external pile.

Abscess: Severe pain at one side of the anus, with throbbing, hard swelling under the skin. Takes 1–2 days to come on, and does not get better until the abscess bursts or is drained surgically.

Fistula: Soreness rather than pain, unassociated with bowel movement; always discharging.

Fissure: Pain coming on only with bowel movement, though there may be aching for some time after. Slight to knifelike.

Internal hemorrhoids: Itching pain in sore moist skin, and very sore anus, from excessive mucoid material.

Cancer: An uncomfortable ache, and the rectum may feel full all the time. Discharge may occur.

"Fleeting pain." Medical name: Proctalgia fugax.

Severe, even alarming pain inside the rectum, coming on sporadically, sometimes in the night, but not associated with bowel movement. It is due to muscle spasm, and may be more likely during a period of anxiety. Not serious. A glass of water may help the spasm to pass off.

Protrusion from the Anus

Causes

  Piles

  Prolapse of rectum

  Sentinel pile

  Warts round the anus occasionally cause confusion

  Polyps of the rectum

Piles, Hemorrhoids   [Ch: S]

Varicose, that is, swollen and tortuous, veins of the rectum, similar to varicose veins in the leg. They are not important in themselves, but are troublesome because the constant loss of blood may cause anemia, and they are liable to repeated attacks of inflammation, which is very painful. They may also be the first indication of a more serious disease. *You should consult your doctor if you suspect piles.*

There are two types: those arising inside the rectum and those arising outside the anus, and covered by skin.

Both types may be present together.

INTERNAL PILES

Identification: Bright red blood on toilet paper may be the only indication. Later the piles may come down when a stool is passed, and later still remain prolapsed and cause a feeling of heaviness. Discharge of mucoid material. Itching. Constipation usual.

"Attack of piles": a pile may be nipped by the anal muscle and strangulated; then it clots, and causes considerable pain.

EXTERNAL PILES

Identification: Merely a feeling of fullness around the anus; or if a clot forms: sudden, painful swelling, tense and tender, in one side of the anus.

A sentinel pile is a particular type of external pile.

General enlargement of the veins round the anus on straining means too sedentary a life is being led.

Causes of Piles

There are many superstitions about this, sitting on wet grass and eating various foods being falsely blamed.

Family tendency, as with other varicose veins.

The erect posture: animals do not have piles except for a few elderly, obese dogs.

Straining because of constipation or purgatives.

Diarrhea (less often a cause).

Pregnancy, due to pressure on veins by the womb and also because of hormonal effects.

Some other disorder, less common, but important:

    Tumor or inflammation low in the abdomen.

    Heart disorder.

    Liver disorder.

    High blood pressure: in this case the bleeding may be a useful safety valve.

Treatment

Internal Piles

No pain: laxatives and, if necessary, a small dose of senna preparation at night. Lubricant suppositories inserted into the rectum at night.

Permanently prolapsed: injection or operation. Age and infirmity no bar.

External Piles

No pain: no treatment but to take more exercise and treat constipation, if present.

Painful lump: can be cured at once and permanently by small operation if seen within 36 hours. Otherwise, ice packs or hot baths and suppositories, prescribed by doctor.

Outlook: Good so long as the underlying cause, if any, is dealt with. The piles that frequently arise during pregnancy disappear naturally after the birth of the baby, and a change in habits of eating and taking exercise is all that is needed for many others with the common types of piles. Surgical treatment is excellent for the remainder.

Prolapse of the Rectum   [Ch: S]

Commonest in those under three and over seventy. The lining of the rectum sticks out at the anus; in adults usually there are already bad piles, or straining; in the female an unstitched tear after childbirth, and in old age a weak slack anal muscle. In children it may come on after diarrhea, much loss of weight, or whooping cough.

Identification: Pink mass protruding from back passage (piles are plum-colored). Pain.

Treatment: In children the prolapsed rectum may be pushed in again. If not better in a month, and in an adult anyway: operation.

Rectal Polyp   [Ch: S]

Usually in children of one to six years.

Identification: Blood, or blood and mucus from the rectum, and sometimes a round lump comes down during the passing of a movement.

Treatment: Diathermy. Simple. This is a harmless tumor.

Rectal Warts, or Papillomata   [Ch: SU]

Usually in the middle-aged or elderly.

Identification: Passage of large amounts of clear mucus, with bleeding only from time to time. Doctor can feel or see it.

Treatment: Diathermy or operation. Medical checks in the future are important, as this type of warty growth can become cancerous if not removed completely.

Pilonidal Cyst, "Jeep Disease" [Ch: S]

Age: 18–25 years.

Sex: men, four times as often as women.

Due to a deep vestige of skin forming a cyst which gets infected.

Identification: Inspection reveals one or two dimples at the end of the spine. The surrounding area may be tender or painful. Pain on sitting or riding in an automobile. (During World War II, the condition was commonly aggravated by riding on hard Jeep seats.)

Treatment: Hot "sitz baths"; occasionally antibiotics; sometimes surgical excision.

Anal Fissure   [A Ch: S, 6]

A crack or narrow ulcer in the skin of the anus, something like a crack at the corner of the mouth, but it drains pus from deeper infected tissue.

Commoner in middle age, and women.

Identification: Very sharp *pain* on passing a movement, but lasting an hour or more; slight discharge, and stools may be blood-streaked. A sentinel pile at the anus: a tag of skin in line with the fissure.

Treatment: Xylocaine lubricant, and gentle stretching of the anus; laxative to keep movements soft.

Operation sometimes necessary.

Abscess near the Anus   [Ch: S, 2]

A boil-like condition near the outlet.

Identification: Intense, throbbing pain unrelated to bowel movement, but more agonizing on sitting down. Red, hard swelling at one side of the anus. Temporary relief from a hot bath.

Treatment: Drainage by operation. Antibiotics.

Fistula [Ch: S]

An established drainage tract from an abscess, leading to the skin surface near the anus.

Identification: Small, red, discharging pimple near the anus, which will not heal untreated. Irritation and soreness of surrounding skin.

Treatment: Antibiotics, operation.

Worms which May Be Seen in the Stools [Ch: S]

Roundworm: General resemblance to an earthworm, tapered at both ends, yellowish—6–16 inches. May cause cough, irritability, vague indigestion.

Pinworm: May be numerous in the stools, like short pieces of thread, moving slowly, 4–10 mm. Much itching around anus at night. Children mainly.

Whipworm: Whip shaped, much thinner at one end, 2 inches. May cause anemia.

Tapeworm: Flat tapelike segments. Whole worm 5–45 mm. long, but usually only segments are passed. May cause capricious appetite and loss of weight. All ages.

Hookworm: Eggs more likely than worms in stools: 1 mm. or less in diameter, but occasionally embryo worms are seen. Itching, small blisters on the skin, *anemia,* blood in the stools, and sometimes diarrhea.

Very common in tropical and subtropical countries.

Treatment: Varies with the parasite. There are effective methods for dealing with most of them. Doctor's help needed.

Pain on Passing a Stool

Causes

Fissure of anus.

Constipation: hard or impacted stools.

Piles: if inflamed or clotted.

Prolapse of rectum.

Growth in rectum: harmless or cancerous.

Fistula, or boils near rectum.

Diarrhea: pain all over abdomen, not at the outlet.

Purgatives and some other medicines: as with diarrhea.

Inflammation or disorder of the womb or prostate gland: uncommon.

Pain on Sitting Down
Inside Causes
Dislocation, fracture, or tenderness without obvious cause, of the end part of the spinal column, the coccyx.
Strain, or after childbirth.
Arthritis of the joints at the lower end of the back.
Inflammation in the lower abdomen: other signs of ill-health.
Constipation.
Outside Causes
Piles.
Fissure of anus.
Fistula.
Boils.
Carbuncle.
Prolapse, rectum or womb.

THE URINARY SYSTEM

This is the plumbing system of the body with a chemical works, the kidneys, at its head. Blood pours through the kidneys at the rate of 2½ pints per minute, to be processed, and the waste is passed down twin pipes, the ureters, to the expandable collecting chamber, the bladder. From here a single drainage tube, the urethra, conveys the urine to the surface for disposal.

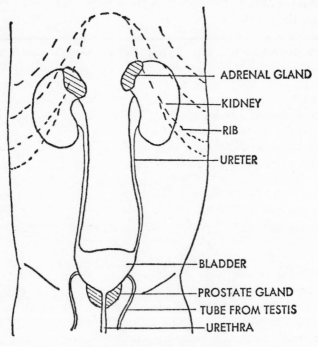

The Urinary System (Male)

The working unit of the kidney is the nephron, a two-part structure the size of a grain of sand, consisting of a coiled and convoluted mass of blood vessels and tubing, called the glomerulus, and a simpler, delicate pipe called the tubule. There are over a million such units in each kidney, which provide for a large reserve of power.

The function of the kidney is to rid the blood of harmful waste products, while allowing it to retain such essentials as amino acids, proteins, and glucose; to maintain a constant blood volume, a steady mineral and water balance; and to keep it from becoming unduly acid or alkaline.

The glomeruli extract, by a process of ultra-filtration, the fluid part of the blood, or plasma. The tubules then pass 99% of this filtrate back into the blood stream. In cold weather, however, or under the influence of certain drugs called diuretics, so useful in dropsy, the tubules reabsorb less, and large quantities of urine are passed, but of paler color.

The kidneys in health work with silent efficiency; their cry of distress in disorder is pain, pallor, swelling up, sometimes a raised blood pressure, and abnormalities, for instance blood in the urine. But antibiotics have revolutionized the outlook for the kidneys by greatly reducing the likelihood of their becoming involved in such diseases as scarlet fever and tonsillitis.

The other dramatic advance of the century is kidney transplantation: replacing two diseased kidneys by one from a healthy living person. The donor's single remaining kidney will have reserve enough. The difficulty, except in the very first patient, whose donor was his identical twin, is to get the recipient's body to accept the strange kidney, but this problem has been to a large extent solved.

Examination of the Urine

The Greeks, the Egyptians, the doctors of the medieval Dark Ages —all looked upon examination of the urine as a divining rod in diagnosis. Chemical analysis brought scientific exactitude and was a tremendous advance on naked eye inspection, although that can still tell us much with the variations of color, sediment, cloudiness, odor.

Our present decade is that of the dipstick: chemical testing refined to a mere matter of moistening a treated sliver with urine and reading off the significance of the color change.

Urinalysis is now an integral part of any physical examination. Interpreted expertly, it will give your doctor information that will enable him to safeguard your health better. He may, for instance, find clues to perhaps unsuspected kidney disorder, toxemia of pregnancy, nervous illness, diabetes, dietary traits and drugs, bone disease, cancer, pregnancy, glandular abnormality, liver disorders, and, of course, trouble in the bladder itself.

Frequent Passing of Water
Medical term: Frequency of micturition.
An adult in full health passes, on the average, 50 ounces of urine in 24 hours, divided among 4–6 occasions, none of these in the night. Variations in quantity and frequency vary normally, depending on how much is drunk, on the one hand, and how much fluid is lost, on the other, from sweating, vomiting, or diarrhea.
Commonest Causes
Young persons: diabetes mellitus.
Elderly people: kidney disease; enlarged prostate gland (rising at night often first sign).
Cold weather.
Wives: early pregnancy.
However, there are many other causes to consider.
Frequency and increased amount (polyuria) of urine:
Old age: kidney has diminished concentrating power.
Diabetes mellitus: fatigue, loss of weight, thirst, large appetite (sugar present in urine).
Chronic nephritis: kidney disorder. Urine tests confirm.
Convalescence after feverish illness.
Temporary effect of excitement, or following an attack of asthma.
After taking *diuretics,* i.e. medicines intended to produce polyuria.
Some heart disorders, and rare glandular troubles.
Frequency without increased amount:
Causes may be: local irritation; general conditions; fault at the outlet.
Local irritation:
Inflammation of the bladder.
Stone, ulcer, or tumor in the bladder.
Stone or inflammation of the kidneys.
Enlarged prostate.

Reflex irritation, i.e. trouble elsewhere is referred to the bladder, worms, fissure, piles, prolapse, caruncle.

Pressure on the bladder in pregnancy (first and last three months), or tumor, cyst, or inflammation in the lower abdomen.

Urine too acid.

General conditions:

Nervous disorders, hysteria.

Fault at the outlet:

Too tight a foreskin, too small an orifice, downward displacement of bladder after childbirth.

Rising at Night to Urinate

Medical term: Nocturia.

Causes

Extra drink.

Advancing years.

Enlarged prostate, for any reason.

Inflammation of bladder.

Growth of bladder.

Heart disorder, glandular disorder.

Inability to Pass Urine with Bladder Full

Medical term: Acute retention.

ACUTE   [A: U, 1/7]

Identification: Inability to pass water, even after several hours; spasms of pain in lower abdomen, where the swollen bladder may be felt and is tender to the touch.

Causes

Children: stone, congenital abnormality, tight foreskin, ulcer of the outlet with scabbing.

Women: fibroid, misplaced womb, nervousness, temporarily after childbirth, disorder of the nervous system.

Young or middle-aged adults: inflammation of urethra, gonorrhea, spasm due to exposure to cold or much alcohol.

Elderly men: *prostatic enlargement* (commonest).

Stone or tumor or paralysis of the bladder from nerve disorder can occur at any age.

Treatment: Try passing water while in a warm bath, and hot water bottle on abdomen, while waiting for doctor. He can give immediate relief, and treatment of the cause.

CHRONIC

[Ch: S] Long-standing obstruction, e.g. prostatic, or narrowing of the urethra may cause gradual distension of the bladder and dribbling overflow, but acute retention may supervene.

Bladder Empty [A: S]

No urine is being formed. A very serious condition.

Medical term: Anuria.

Identification: No urine passed, maybe for days; drowsiness, muscle twitching, headache, vomiting.

Causes: Obstruction to outflow from kidney: stone far the commonest, especially in men of about 40; cancer of bladder or womb; kidney disease.

Collapse after injury or operation.

"Crush injuries" as in street accidents, or under debris.

Treatment: Surgical, and/or expert medical.

Diminished Quantity of Urine

Medical term: Oliguria.

Causes

Kidney disorder.

Fever.

Much vomiting, diarrhea, or sweating.

Drinking too little liquid.

Pain on Passing Urine [S]

Scalding, during the act: Inflammation of the urethra, the tube from bladder to exterior, including gonorrhea. Discharge of pus may be also present; narrowing of some part of the urethra; ulcer or cancer of urethra; urethral caruncle.

Tingling or pricking in the penis, or in the female at the urinary orifice, immediately after passing water: stone in the bladder; inflammation of the bladder (cystitis) with blood and pus, possibly, in urine, and abdominal pain; inflammation of the prostate gland in men; growth of the bladder.

Pain in part between anus and urethra, or anus only, during the act and after: disorder of the prostate, especially if there is straining; growth in the bladder.

Very severe pain at the outlet of the urethra at the end of the act: stone impacted in tube from kidney to bladder.

Associated with lower abdominal pain: cystitis; inflammation of ovary, appendix, or other lower abdominal organ. Early stages.

Brief, but knifelike, at the end of the act: cystitis, as the two inflamed sides of the bladder press together at the final moment of emptying.

Burning pain outside when urine comes in contact with vulva: skin disorder, cancer of vulva.

See also Men's Section.

Changes in the Stream

Weak and slow, even dropping straight down; maybe inability to expel the last few drops, but they dribble out.

> *Enlarged prostate gland* (gradual onset in elderly men, with increased frequency).
> Inflamed prostate.
> Narrowing of urethra, by inflammation or stone. In the latter two conditions a discharge may be present.

Sudden stoppage of flow: Stone becoming stuck; tuft of growth blocking outlet of bladder; blood clot doing same; nervous spasm of bladder exit, especially if other people present.

Thin, forceful stream: Narrowing of urethra (stone or inflammation) near tip of penis.

Difficulty in starting or strain in continuing: prostatic enlargement; narrowing of urethra; way blocked by stone or blood clot; disorder of the nervous system; old, weak bladder muscle; overstretched bladder, often from prostatic enlargement of longstanding.

Alteration in pressure in or on bladder: increased, in pregnancy, uterine tumor, reduced, after childbirth, temporary effect.

Dribbling away of urine, involuntarily: usually overflow from a bladder that is not being emptied properly because of obstruction (prostatic enlargement or narrowing of urethra), or nervous disorder; rarely, due to injury or paralysis of the exit from the bladder.

Stress Incontinence [Ch: S]

Commoner in women, especially those who have had children, from weakening of the muscles of the urethra and anus.

Identification: Escape of urine during any strain such as coughing, sneezing, crying, laughing, or even emotion on its own.

Treatment: Exercises to strengthen muscles; operation.

Outlook: Persistence in exercising is very effective unless there is a clear cause. Operation also gives good results.

Color of Urine

Straw-colored: Normal.

Yellow and orange: Concentrated, because of fever, hot weather, lack of fluid; in liver disorder, jaundice, the foam is also yellow; drugs like rhubarb, senna, picric acid, nitrofurantoin tablets.

Pink and red: Dyes in sweets, tonics, and vitamin preparations, may have a green fluorescence; blood.

Brown and black: Already dark when passed: some medicines including aspirin derivatives; long-standing jaundice.

Darkening on standing: a few rare conditions, but important to see doctor.

Milky: see Cloudy Urine, below.

Green and blue: Most striking, but least important. Nearly always due to methylene blue in sweets or medicines.

Pale urine: Not concentrated, due either to too much to drink or other causes of increased amount of urine.

Foaming Urine

As though full of detergent on shaking. May be due to protein or bile in the urine, in kidney disorder.

Abnormal Odor of Urine

Normally aromatic.

Foul: Infection in the urinary tract.

Sweet and fruity: Diabetes.

Blood in the Urine [A: S, Ch: SU]

Medical name: Hematuria.

The blood of the monthly period in the female must not be confused with blood coming from the urinary orifice. Other causes of red urine are eating beets or rhubarb in certain individuals, and dyes in foodstuffs, especially sweets.

Characteristics and Causes

Bright crimson, mainly at the beginning of passing water: Infection of the urethra, the pipe from bladder to exterior; infection or congestion of the prostate gland in the male, may be pain and tenderness, and signs of irritation in the rectum; urethral caruncle, a visible red lump at the urinary orifice in the female.

Mainly at the end of passing water, clots: Indicates trouble in the bladder.

Acute inflammation (acute cystitis). Bleeding slight.

Stone in the bladder. Pain, often felt at the tip of the penis, or vulva, worse after exercise or jarring. Moderate bleeding.

Growth, either simple and warty, or cancerous, in bladder or surrounding organs. Considerable blood loss. Weakness.

Enlarged prostate with bulging veins, in men.

Uncommon: tuberculosis of the bladder; parasites, after residence in Egypt or South Africa; scurvy; varicose veins of the bladder.

Blood intimately mixed with the urine giving it a smoky tint or red if the quantity is large: indicates bleeding from the kidney.

Inflammation, acute or chronic, of the kidney (nephritis).

Congestion, commonly from heart trouble, or suddenly, from clotting in the kidney vein during an infection, or on getting up after months in bed from any cause.

Stones or crystals in the kidney. Kidney pain.

Growths of the kidney. Often painless.

Injury or accident: a blow on the loin.

Blood conditions: Scurvy, malaria, leukemia, purpura.

Drugs: Especially aspirin and its derivatives; phenol; cantharides; sulpha drugs, turpentine.

Foods in some persons, by causing the formation of oxalate crystals: rhubarb, tomatoes, spinach, strawberries.

Ache in the loin. Dyspepsia maybe. Bleeding slight.

Anyone who has had blood in the urine should have a laboratory examination: this means *you must see your doctor.*

Early or precancerous conditions may this way be detected and dealt with.

Cloudy Urine

Some of the normal constituents of the urine may produce turbidity or sediment after the urine has cooled.

Clear when first passed, becomes cloudy, and when cool forms a pink sediment: due to urates, the commonest deposit. Shows that the urine is concentrated, either normally as in hot weather, or after exercise, or in disorders such as fever and heart disease.

Sandy deposit like cayenne pepper: likely to be uric acid. Occurs normally in some healthy young people, especially boys, after heavy meat meal; or in gout or stone formation.

White cloud or milkiness, immediately on passing urine, especially the last part. May also form an iridescent deposit on the surface of the water. Most noticeable on waking, and after a meal. Due to phosphates: significant of eating a heavy meal (e.g. children); large quantities of fruit and vegetables; loss of weight for any reason; depression, anxiety.

Specks of white on a mucus deposit: "powdered wig" appearance. Due to oxalates: occurs in some after eating rhubarb, spinach, tea, coffee, cocoa—in abundance. Not usually significant.

Fine cloud of mucus, made visible by entangled debris. Indicates kidney disorder. Microscopic examination needed.

Long thin white threads indicate disorder of the prostate gland in men.

Blood: Gives a smoky appearance unless copious.

Pus: Appearance similar to phosphates (above) to the naked eye, but easily distinguished microscopically.

Accompanied by feeling ill, listless, and perhaps feverish.

Bacteria or fat in the urine may also cause a cloudy appearance.

Pus in the Urine   [S, U]

Mainly in the first bit, scalding on passing urine: inflammation of the urethra or abscess of prostate.

Mainly at the end of passing water; pain in lower abdomen, frequent passing of water: inflammation of the bladder, acute or chronic.

Pus mixed through the urine, but forming a sediment later, pain in the back. Fever: inflammation of the kidney, pyelitis.

"Gravel" [Ch: S]

Identification

A gritty sensation on passing urine, may be slight smokiness, due to blood, in urine.

Due to aggregations of uric acid crystals, or small stones in the urine. See Stone and Gout.

Inflammation of the Bladder

Medical name: Cystitis.

Age: Any.

Sex: Women, especially.

ACUTE [A: S, B, 2]

Identification: Pain in lower abdomen and between the legs; frequent desire to pass water, even just after the bladder has been emptied. May be agonizing pain in bladder and tip of penis at end of micturition. Urine may feel scalding as it is passed. May be blood in urine, and it may become thick and ropy. Fever and feeling ill may not always occur.

Treatment: Bed. Plenty to drink (five pints of water daily).

Drugs via doctor. Hot water bottle to abdomen to relieve pain.

Outlook: Much better in seven days, back to normal in two weeks usually. If not, there may be a predisposing cause which must be dealt with, for instance, something obstructing the outflow of urine such as prostate enlargement, pregnancy or just after childbirth, a stone or tumor of the bladder, or a generally run-down condition from other illness.

CHRONIC [Ch: S, 2, X]

Identification: Similar but less severe symptoms than in acute cystitis.

May follow acute cystitis or come on by itself.

Treatment: Medicines as prescribed by doctor. Copious fluids. Rest.

Outlook: No danger to life, but a troublesome painful complaint that tends to recur, so any underlying cause needs to be rooted out.

Inflammation of the Urethra   [A: S, 2]

Medical name: Urethritis.

The urethra is the pipe from the bladder to the exterior.

Often venereal in origin: see Venereal disease.

Identification: Itching, redness, and stickiness of urinary outlet; discharge; scalding pain on passing water. Slight fever often.

Treatment: Varies with the organism causing the urethritis, which will have been identified by laboratory tests.

Growths of the Bladder

These are becoming more common, particularly among those who have worked in the rubber industry for many years, using benzidine and naphthylamine. The growths may not be dangerous at first, but tend to lead on to cancer, and the loss of blood is undermining to the health.

Identification: Blood in the urine, now and again. *This symptom always calls for investigation,* although it may have a simple cause.

Treatment: Surgical: the sooner the better.

Kidney Pain

Either: *Fixed dull ache* in loin and/or under ribs in front.

Or: *Agonizing paroxysms* of ureteric colic (renal colic) going on and off for as long as 24 hours, with sweating, vomiting, doubling-up, and writhing.

Causes

Obstruction to the flow of urine from the kidney, due to blockage in or above the bladder: *kidney stone;* tumor or tuberculosis of the kidney (uncommon); stone in the ureter or pressure on the ureter from elsewhere in the abdomen; clots of blood blocking the ureter; stone or tumor blocking outlet of ureter into the bladder.

Deformed kidney: Hydronephrosis, the kidney is swollen out of shape.

Infection: Pyelitis or abscess of kidney.

Swelling in the Loin

Causes

Enlarged kidney, blocked by stone.

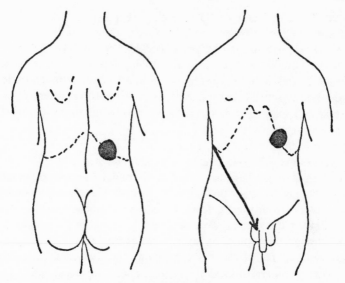

Sites of Kidney Pain

Kidney abscess.
Inflammation of kidney.
Deformed kidney.

Acute Infection of the Kidney [A: S, 2]
Medical name: Acute pyelitis, acute pyelonephritis.
Commoner in females than males, particularly in early childhood, adolescence, shortly after marriage (*"honeymoon pyelitis"*), in midpregnancy, and at the menopause.
More often on the right than the left.
Identification: Usually comes suddenly: shivering attack, acute pain in flank and under ribs at front, occasionally shooting down to groin. Fever 102°–103° F. Soon there follows frequent need to urinate, with scalding pain.
Urine may become cloudy in 24 hours, and scanty.
In men: Pyelonephritis occurs most frequently in the elderly whose enlarged prostate glands are holding back the urine. Stagnancy leads to infection, as in a pond. Both sides are affected.

Treatment: Hot water bottle to loin. Five pints of such fluids as lemonade and very weak tea daily. Sulpha drug or antibiotic, and alkalinizing mixture may be prescribed by doctor.

Outlook: Usually back to normal within a fortnight, but it is important to follow up the recovery by checks by doctor later; for recurrence is not uncommon, nor chronic infection, which is important and ultimately dangerous.

Chronic Kidney Infection   [Ch: S, 6]

Medical name: Chronic pyelitis, chronic pyelonephritis.

May follow acute infection, may be secondary to obstruction to the outflow of urine, or may arise on its own with bacteria arriving in the blood from tonsils, teeth, boils, or carbuncle.

Age: Under 40, women; over 60, men.

Sex: Women three times as susceptible as men.

Identification: Dull back pain; pain on, and increased frequency of, passing water; lassitude; lack of appetite; nausea; headache. Attacks of fever of about 100° F.

Treatment: Dealing with predisposing causes such as stone, and sources of infection elsewhere in body. Medicines depend on doctor's opinion: operation occasionally useful.

Plenty of bland fluids to drink.

Outlook: Patience is required, and medicines may have to be taken over a long period to effect a complete cure. Raised blood pressure may occur in long-standing disorder.

Kidney Stone   [Ch: S, X; A: U]

One of the commonest disorders. Stones vary from sandlike "gravel" (above) to chunks of stone as big as a golf ball. Tiny ones slip out harmlessly, or merely cause transient pain; bigger ones may be agonizing as they travel down the fine tubes from the kidneys to the bladder. They may get stuck on the way or lodge in the bladder, causing characteristic symptoms.

Age: Any, but especially 30–50.

Sex: Males more than females, four to three.

Identification: Pain in loin and under the ribs in front, often worse on walking, especially going upstairs. Colic: agonizing bouts of pain from loin to groin, sudden, and severe enough to cause doubling up and rolling about, with sweating, vomiting, and the passage of a few drops of urine after painful straining.

Smoky urine due to slight bleeding; occasionally profuse. Turbid urine due to pus, if, as commonly occurs, there is infection associated with the stone.

X-ray diagnosis is essential.

Treatment: Must be assessed by doctor. Antibiotics if there is infection. Operation may be needed.

Outlook: Operation very successful. Since there is a known tendency to form stones, it is wise, henceforth, to drink plenty of liquids, including a nightcap before retiring, to produce a flow of dilute urine with no likelihood of crystal formation, and have any infection of the urinary tract treated promptly and vigorously.

Kidney Abscess [A: S, B]
Two types: inside the kidney: pyonephrosis; surrounding the kidney: perinephric abscess.

Identification: Constant pain and tenderness in the loin; swelling; fever; pus in the urine.

Treatment: Antibiotic and surgical.

Kidney Tumor [Ch: SU]
Not very common.

Identification: Blood in the urine; persistent pain in the loin; swelling in the loin; loss of weight. None of these symptoms is necessarily associated with a kidney tumor, but they require investigation, including examination, microscopically, of the urine.

Treatment: Operation. Risks much reduced recently.

Nephritis, Bright's Disease
A disordered working of the kidneys characterized by the escape of protein into the urine (albuminuria). Normally, while waste products are present in the urine, valuable constituents of the blood like sugar and protein are not.

ACUTE NEPHRITIS [A: S, B, 6]

Identification: Sudden onset around ten days after a sore throat, which has apparently completely recovered, usually in a child or young adult. Swelling of face and legs, blood in the urine, headache, pain in the loin. Usually no fever.

Treatment: Absolute bed rest, diet that puts least possible strain on kidneys, that is, with little sodium and reduced protein. Drink as much water as was passed in urine the day before, and one pint extra.

Antibiotics sometimes helpful.

Outlook: In most cases (80%) complete recovery after 4–5 weeks in bed. Go to doctor for check three months later, as chronic nephritis can follow.

SUBACUTE NEPHRITIS (nephrotic syndrome) [Ch: S, B, X]
Identification: Gradual onset; pale, puffy face; lassitude; headaches; often in children.

Diagnosis by urine test.

Treatment: Hospital. Steroid treatment for weeks or months, and low sodium, high protein diet.

Outlook: Recovery slow, especially in adults, but steroids often work dramatically, though a further course may be required later.

CHRONIC NEPHRITIS [Ch: S]
Identification: Increased quantity of urine, probably causing rising at night; headache, especially on waking; blurred vision; easily tired; vomiting may occur. Diagnosis by urine test.

Treatment: Varies absolutely with the individual. None may be required, or such dramatic affairs as kidney grafting may be employed.

Tuberculosis of the Urinary System [Ch: S]
Always secondary to tuberculosis elsewhere, and since that is becoming less common and much more efficiently treated, tuberculosis of kidney or bladder is now unusual.

Symptoms that might suggest these troubles:

Frequent passing of urine, blood or pus in the urine, loin pain.

Treatment and Outlook: Good, revolutionized by new drugs.

Stone in the Bladder [Ch: S]
Especially children, the elderly, and the male.

Identification: Pain and a few drops of blood at the end of

micturition. Water is passed extra frequently by day, but not at night. Child may appear to masturbate.
Treatment: Surgical removal.

Urethral Caruncle   [Ch: S]
A result of chronic inflammation, not cancerous, in women.
Identification: Brilliant scarlet, visible swelling the size of a cherry stone at the urinary outlet. Exquisitely tender, causing pain on passing water and with intercourse; bleeds easily, staining the urine.
Treatment: Surgical removal.

THE UPPER EXTREMITIES

Raise a cup to your lips, or take your handkerchief from your pocket. Fifty muscles acting on thirty joints from shoulder to fingertips must cooperate to achieve your will. The hand, so mechanically complex and so exquisitely sensitive, is the slave of the mind, and the whole upper limb is an apparatus to enhance its usefulness.

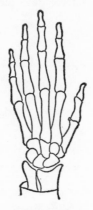

The Hand

The shoulder joint is a ball and socket type, with universal movement. The elbow is a hinge which straightens to convert the arm into a rigid rod, extending your reach. The final refinement is the carrying angle: when you bring home the shopping, for instance, the elbow locks so that the forearm is held out a little from the body, and your basket does not bump against your legs.

The curious sliding and twisting movement of the forearm bones permits the hand's complete rotation, palm up, palm down. There is no part of the body which one hand or the other cannot touch, though the hardest is the spot between the shoulder blades.

Each member of the hand is an individual. The powerful, squat thumb is the most valuable, for it alone can cross over to work with any finger. Of the fingers, the middle is the strongest, and the index finger quickest and most sensitive. The little finger is the slowest, but the proud ring finger is the most difficult to teach to typewrite or to press a piano key.

Hands are as characteristic as facial features, and just as you can eat, or smile, with any normal mouth, so hands of any shape or size, stubby or slender, may serve a musician or a carpenter, a conjuror or a coal-miner.

The hand is the main organ of sensation, the "eyes" of the blind, and to all of us the informant about texture, size, shape, and temperature, even for what we cannot see: the keys in our pocket, the thread on our needles. It is an instrument of expression: clenched to show aggression, twisting in anxiety, as vociferous as a cheer in applause.

Your hand and the limb that serves it are fit partners for your miraculous brain.

PAIN AND STIFFNESS IN SHOULDER, ARM, AND HAND

Often arises in parts other than the upper limb itself, because of the shared nerve supply.

Causes

Direct: Injury, sprain, overuse; arthritis; inflammation; muscle and fibrous tissue pains, especially after exposure to drafts or to cold and damp; and awkward posture, e.g. reading in bed, driving. See Frozen shoulder and Slipping shoulder, below.

Indirect: Disorders of the heart, e.g. angina, coronary disorder; disorder of lungs, pancreas, liver, gall bladder, stomach, diaphragm. Disorders affecting the nerves, e.g. poliomyelitis, shingles (acute), or nervousness.

Disorders of the spine: see Neck, shoulder, arm syndrome.

Note: Since they bear no weight, the joints of the upper limb, at shoulder, elbow, and wrist, are less subject than others to arthritis, especially osteoarthritis or arthrosis, or to severe sprains.

Stiff, Painful Shoulder

The shoulder joint itself, a shallow ball and socket in a roomy, tough, protective bag of tissue, is seldom sprained in youth or severely affected by arthritis in age. However, there are subsidiary moving parts round the joint which may give trouble.

Stiff, painful shoulder is a common complaint from middle age onwards, and usually falls into one of two groups:

Tearing of the Cuff of muscles and tendons round the joint [A: S, 2–6/12].

Identification: Middle or old age after minor injury or none. Pain growing worse in a few hours, starting in shoulder but radiating through neck and arm. Arm held to side; it cannot be raised sideways. Tenderness over joint, felt in thin people.

Treatment: Sling for a few days, then try swinging the arm loosely. Active movements when pain has subsided.

Injections sometimes help; operation occasionally needed.

Outlook: Recovery takes a variable time: two weeks or several months.

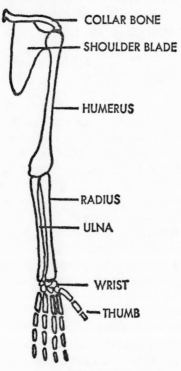

COLLAR BONE

SHOULDER BLADE

HUMERUS

RADIUS

ULNA

WRIST

THUMB

The Upper Extremity

Frozen Shoulder [Ch: S, 6/12]

Gradually increasing stiffness, with pain, until arm cannot be moved. Often follows injuries or fractures near the joint, but may occur without apparent reason.

Age: 45–55 is the peak.

Sex: Women more than men. Nearly always physically inactive people.

Identification: Pain felt deep in shoulder, later involving back, chest, and arm. Noticed during such movements as brushing the hair, later more constant, even interfering with sleep. The joint may be tender to press.

Treatment: There may be an underlying cause of pain remote from the shoulder itself (above). This must be treated, but in such cases it is important (and does not make the pain worse) to keep the joint moving, because any joint left immobile becomes stiff.

Manipulation under anesthetic may be required.

Injections and heat treatment help others.

Outlook: "Frozen shoulder" without apparent cause usually clears up by itself in a year or two.

Bursitis [S]

If pain in the shoulder is not due to injury, it is probably bursitis: a disorder of tendons and tendon sheaths near the bursa. In most cases, calcium deposits form in the tendons and can be seen on an X-ray. Pain may be acute. Acute symptoms can last several days.

Treatment: Rest, aspirin, phenylbutazone or derivatives, X-ray or the injection of cortisone.

Slipping shoulder [A: U; Ch: S]

Due to its shallowness, the shoulder joint readily dislocates; it is also easily replaced. Some people find that after one dislocation, the shoulder constantly slips out.

Identification: Injury causing the original dislocation: the round knob at the upper end of the arm bone usually bulges forwards, and the arm cannot be moved. Later, recurrent dislocations occur during normal activities such as swimming or washing the neck.

Treatment: Operation is the only cure; a sedentary worker might not think it worth while, though a tennis player would.

Broken Collar Bone [A: U, 6]

Extremely common, at any age, from a fall on the hand or shoulder, for instance, at football or horseback riding.

Identification: Pain eased by holding head to injured side to relax the neck muscles attached to the bone, and by supporting the arm on that side with the other hand to relieve the drag. Tender place on the bone.

Treatment: Doctor. Sling or brace for about three weeks.

Outlook: Heals very well.

Pain in the Elbow

Pain in the outer side of the elbow apparently connected with *any* energetic use of it.

"TENNIS ELBOW"   [A: SU, 2]

Identification: Aching pain in elbow and forearm coming a few hours after exercise. Better with rest, worse with use, and especially with gripping tightly. Tender place at side of elbow.

Treatment: Go to doctor promptly. Splint, to rest the elbow, for ten days. Strapping is less efficient, though easier for dressing, etc. Do not undertake energetic exercise until all pain and tenderness are gone. Injections and massage help some.

LESS COMMON TYPE OF TENNIS ELBOW   [A: U, 2]

Identification: Sudden onset of pain during game or exercise: arm cannot be used. Straightening the arm is painful.

Tenderness exactly over the dimple of the elbow joint.

Treatment: Manipulation: relief dramatic.

Stiff elbow from untreated tennis elbow of this type is also much improved by manipulation.

Osteoarthritis [Ch: S]

Unusual in the elbow except in those who have injured the joint at some time, and those who have used pneumatic drills. Pain and stiffness are the main symptoms.

Bone Formation Around Elbow   [Ch]

Occurs after injury; new bone is produced where there has been bleeding next to the bones. Stiffness is the main result and can be very severe, so it is important to avoid the situation by having any elbow injury treated promptly. Rest is the best treatment if the condition has started.

Cystic Swelling at Wrist or Elbow   [Ch: S]

Medical name: Ganglion.

These swellings, full of a jellylike material, occur in association with joints and tendons. They are common on the back of hand and wrist, or foot, sometimes occurring by the elbow or other joints. Harmless.

Identification: Slowly growing swelling, painless in itself, but occasionally causing aching and weakness of the hand.

Treatment: The fluid can usually be dispersed by pressure but often recollects. However, in the end ganglia usually disappear.

Note: There are several other, far less common, fluid or soft swellings which may occur at wrist or hand, but all are harmless, and your doctor can distinguish them.

Pain, Numbness, Pins-and-Needles in Hand and Arm

"NECK, SHOULDER, ARM SYNDROME"   [Ch: S, 6/12]

Due to various degenerative changes in the neck bones and the discs between them. The nerves that supply the upper limb are pressed upon or restricted so that they are painfully stretched with arm or neck movements. Early middle age onwards.

Identification: Gradual onset of attacks of painful, stiff neck or shoulder, sometimes dating from a jar or stumble. Made worse by cough, sneeze, or arm movements. Arm also becomes painful, later. May be tender around shoulder. Numbness, tingling, weakness of hand and forearm, especially on waking.

Treatment: Manipulation in some cases; rest in others: doctor's assessment. One pillow only at night.

PRESSURE ON NERVE IN WRIST   [Ch: S or N, 6/12]

Medical name: Carpal tunnel syndrome.

Often no apparent cause, but it may be associated with arthritis of the wrist, inflamed tendon sheath (see below), old dislocation of a small wrist bone, injury or ganglion (see above). Not uncommon in pregnancy.

Sex: Mainly women.

Age: Mainly middle-aged; can be young or old.

Identification: Burning, tingling, numbness, pins-and-needles, feeling of swelling and impaired sense of touch (e.g. picking up a needle) in thumb and *three* fingers. The little finger is not as often affected as the others, a characteristic identifying pointer. Occasionally, pain in the forearm, but this is not severe: the hand is the nuisance. Worse at night, disturbing the sleep, and hand is clumsy and weak first thing. Hanging it down, rubbing and moving the fingers sometimes helps. Worse if hands are used energetically; one significant pain-causing movement is to bend the hand back with the elbow straight.

Treatment: If mild, recovery probable in a few months without any treatment, although analgesics are useful to ease the discomfort at night.

Splinting the back of the wrist may help.

Severe cases: Operation is uniformly successful. Any special cause in the wrist, e.g. ganglion, must also be dealt with.

Outlook: Recovery always occurs, but doctor's advice needed in severe cases, which may not get better without help.

PRESSURE ON NERVE AT ELBOW   [Ch: S]

Medical name: Ulnar palsy.

Usually occurs after an injury of the elbow—much later, say ten years—or from pressure by a cyst or ganglion (above); or occasionally the ulnar nerve slips out of place, over a knob of bone. The ulnar nerve runs in a groove of bone just under the skin near the point of the elbow and is responsible for the odd "funny bone" sensation when the elbow receives a knock.

Identification: Numbness and tingling over the little finger side of the hand, and pain on that side of the elbow, coming on slowly. Loss of sensation in little finger, and weakness: it tends to bend like a claw.

Treatment: Operation, the sooner the better, for the condition is progressive.

FAR LESS COMMON.

Extra Rib in the Neck

It is not unusual for there to be an extra rib, or the rudiments of one, above the normal uppermost rib. This may give no symptoms, but occasionally, especially in women of middle age or more, when the shoulders tend to sag instead of being held firmly back and up as in youth, the nerves to the arm may be dragged.

Identification: Burning, tingling, and numbness of fingers and forearm, especially the little finger side. Pain comes in spasms. Weakness of arm and hand.

Treatment: Better postural habits, and exercises to strengthen the muscles supporting the shoulders. Operation if pain severe.

RAYNAUD'S DISEASE   [Ch: N or S, X]

First described by a Frenchman, 100 years ago, it consists of a tightening of the arteries to the hands, and less often to the feet, when they are cooled. This is an exaggeration of the normal state, because when it is cold there is less blood sent to the skin, where it would be cooled even more, and so the outlying arteries contract accordingly.

Sex: Women more than men.

Age: Adolescents and young adults mainly, but the trouble may continue past middle age.

Identification: When cold, fingers become white and clumsy in handling for instance, change, or a doorkey. Then they turn a dusky red and swell, so that they feel like a bunch of bananas. When the attack passes off, usually with warmth, the skin goes bright red, patchily at first, and there is a burning and tingling sensation.

Treatment: Keep warm, and take particular care of infections around the nails, pricks, etc., as they get worse quickly while the blood supply is cut off, in an attack. Drugs to keep the arteries dilated may be prescribed, and occasionally operation on the nerves that make the arteries contract is useful.

WRIST AND HAND

Injured Wrist; Broken Wrist   [A: U, 3/12]

Common, especially among elderly ladies who fall on an outstretched hand. The most usual type is called a Colles's fracture.

Identification: Pain and tenderness about 1 in. above wrist. It is out of shape, with the hand displaced upwards, the so-called "dinner fork deformity." Hand cannot be moved.

Treatment: Replacement of deformity under anesthetic. Plaster of Paris splint for four to six weeks: it is important to keep the fingers in use throughout or they will become stiff.

Outlook: Perfect recovery probable in two to three months.

Sprain or Cracked Wrist Bone   [A: S, 6–3/12]

After a fall on the hand.

Commonly in men of 20 to 40.

Identification: Pain, swelling, and tenderness after injury. May be one especially tender spot on the wrist, and fullness on the back of the hand near the thumb. (Put both hands down flat to compare). X-ray may be useful but is not infallible.

Treatment: Sprain of the wrist is uncommon, break of a small wrist bone far likelier; and if a fracture is inadequately treated, crippling arthritis and weakness may be the final, permanent result. Cock-up plaster cast, allowing finger movements is safe, good treatment. Three to ten weeks.

Inflamed Tendon Sheath in the Wrist   [Ch: S, 6]

Medical name: Tenosynovitis.

Identification: Gradual swelling and stiffness of the fingers, which tend to remain in a half-curled position. Numbness and tingling in the thumb and adjoining three fingers, and occasionally pain in the forearm or palm. Grating sometimes felt in the wrist when the fingers are moved.

Treatment: Rest in a splint; if unsuccessful after a few weeks, operation. Occasionally this condition is tuberculosis, in which case a long course of medicine is necessary.

De Quervain's Disease   [Ch: S, I]

Sex: Women more than men.

Much use of the thumb seems sometimes to bring on this trouble. A common complaint.

Identification: Pain in thumb, forearm, and wrist, made worse by using hand. Swelling on thumb side of wrist, and tenderness.

Treatment: Only lasting benefit is from operation: dramatic relief, and back to work in a few days.

Rheumatoid Arthritis   [Ch: S; A: S, X]

A general disease which shows itself in the joints. The fingers are the most commonly affected part.

Age: First half of adulthood: average 42 years.

Sex: Women three times as often as men.

Identification in the hand: Gradually increasing pain, tenderness, swelling and stiffness, the latter showing its progress by the time taken for it to wear off after waking up. The swellings are symmetrical and spindle-shaped, usually involving several joints on each hand; the skin is smooth and shiny and the nails brittle, sometimes discolored. The onset can be more acute, when the joints are hot as well as swollen, and there is a low irregular fever, loss of weight, and general ill feeling.

Late stages: Deformity of the hand: fingers slide towards the little finger side of the hand and the tendons give, producing a dip in the back of the hand and drooping fingers and thumb.

Treatment: Rest in bed, *large and varied diet,* extra iron, in early stages. Physiotherapy to keep a good range of movement. Butazolidine is the drug usually used now, and aspirin type medicines are very helpful indeed, but in severe, resistant cases, cortisone is used.

Outlook: Do not be disheartened. This illness always burns itself out so that the joints, though stiff maybe, are ultimately painless.

Trigger Finger   [Ch: S, I]

Any age, but in children the thumb is usually the one, in adults the ring finger.

Identification: Finger straightens with snap, audible and visible. Due to a lump in the tendon on front of the finger slipping through a tight place in its sheath.

Treatment: A nick in the tendon sheath produces immediate, permanent relief.

Hammer Finger   [A: SU, 6]

Due to snapping or tearing of the tendon that straightens the last joint of the finger. A trivial injury can cause those to occur, and then the end of the finger cannot be straightened voluntarily, though it can be pushed into position. The bent joint is inconvenient and awkward, for instance, when tying a knot or putting on gloves.

Treatment: Wearing a special finger splint of plastic or metal. Get it as soon as possible.

Operation not usually helpful.

Hammer Thumb [A: S]

A similar breaking of the tendon that straightens the thumb; sometimes occurs especially if, in the past, there has been a sprain or fracture near the wrist. The thumb cannot be held straight: awkward for any work.

Treatment: Operation.

Clubbed Fingers [Ch: S]

The end joints of the fingers are bulbous and the nails unduly curved over them.

Causes

A family tendency, of no significance.

Chronic disorder of heart, lung, or liver.

Not important in themselves.

Swelling of the End Finger Joints [Ch: N]

Medical name: Heberden's nodes.

Runs in families. Usually in the elderly; the swellings are at first soft, then become hard and bony.

Painful at first; this subsides, but the appearance is somewhat ugly. No treatment. No harm.

Osteoarthritis, which more usually attacks the large joints, can produce a similar appearance to these nodes in the fingers.

Tremor of Fingers and Hand [A Ch]

Common Causes

Nervousness.

Thyroid overactivity.

Parkinson's disease.

Weakness, especially in convalescence or advancing years.

Infection Around a Nail

Medical name: Paronychia.

ACUTE [A: S, 1]

All ages, either sex, any walk of life. Common. Started by hang-nail, pinprick, or careless manicure.

Identification: Pain, redness, swelling around side and base of nail. White appearance at cuticle edge later due to pus, which may ooze out but not usually completely, so the infection continues.

Treatment: Go to doctor promptly, because penicillin given before pus collects clears the trouble rapidly. In later stages an operation (local anesthetic) is usually needed.

CHRONIC [Ch: 48, 1]

Housewives who wash dishes are particularly prone to this.

Identification: Gradual onset of the same symptoms as occur in acute paronychia, often affecting several fingers.

Treatment: Gentian violet 1% pushed right under the nail fold, two or three times a day, on an orange stick. If it does not begin to get better in a day or two, see doctor.

Prevention: Automatic dishwasher; rubber gloves so long as they are not worn for long and the hands are thoroughly dried after. Thorough drying every time hands are wet. Keep them warm, as the infection gets worse if the hands are cold and bloodless.

Operation should not be necessary, but some doctors use different antiseptics.

Whitlow, Felon, or Pulp Abscess [A: U, 1]

An acute infection of the tips of the fingers, usually through a prick. Symptoms come on 12 to 24 hours after the injury.

Identification: Intense, throbbing pain in the finger tip. It is tender, hot, swollen, and tense. Fever sometimes.

Treatment: If caught very early, rest in a sling; use a big soft dressing of cotton; antibiotics. If an abscess has formed, an operation to let the pus out is needed.

Under Nail Infection   [A: S, 1]

From prick or splinter under the nail.

Identification: Agonizing tenderness just beneath free edge of nail, but not much swelling. Pus may ooze out, anywhere around nail.

Treatment: Pus must be let out, by doctor.

Infection Deep in the Hand   [A: U]

Puncture wounds, pricks, or cracks in the skin may introduce organisms deep in the hand, in the paomar and web spaces particularly.

Most frequent in housewives, manual workers, and fishermen.

Identification: Throbbing pain, worse when the hand is hanging down, often interfering with sleep, and having started, usually, within twenty-four hours of prick. Swelling of hand, usually most noticeable on the back even if the palm is the site of infection. Tenderness, worse in one place; feel with a matchstick to locate the spot accurately.

Treatment: URGENT. This is an emergency. Meanwhile keep the hand up. Antibiotics may be successful, early enough, otherwise a drainage operation must be performed to release the pus.

THE LOWER EXTREMITIES

Hip and Thigh

THE LOWER LIMB: WALKING

Walking erect is a fantastic complex of nervous, muscular and mental co-ordination, and how you walk is as highly individual as how you talk.

Nevertheless, there are some limps and unusual gaits that are characteristic not of people, but of various disorders. Since walking is so complicated, a limp may result from trouble in one of many parts: foot, ankle, calf, knee joint, thigh, hip joint, groin, pelvis, spine, the nerves supplying them, or the brain controlling them.

Limps and Abnormal Gaits

Pain, weakness, or deformity are the three basic causes of limp, except for those associated with psychological aberration.

Unsteady gait, often worse at corners, over uneven ground, and in the dark.

Reeling: Ménière's disease, alcoholic incoordination; nerve disorders, weakness from age or in convalescence.

Waddling or lurching: muscular weakness (unrecognized), congenital hip abnormality.

Stiff hip: leg and trunk on affected side swing around in one piece.

Shuffling and leaning forward, with arms not swinging: Parkinson's disease.

High steps, usually because foot tends to drop at the toe: nerve disorder (sometimes from a slipped disc), paralysis. Uncommon.

Dragging toe: after poliomyelitis; stroke; spastics (from childhood); multiple sclerosis, and other nerve disorders.

Circulatory disorders: limp due to pain in calf, goes off with rest; arteriosclerosis.

Very peculiar and exaggerated difficulty: clutching for support, dragging bad leg, hopping on "good" side: hysteria, may be the aftermath of an injury, an anxiety, or a disappointment.

Painful disorders, injury or inflammation of hip, knee, or ankle joints or feet. Site of the cause obvious because it hurts.

Children may limp because of minor troubles which they do not mention, such as blisters, uncomfortable shoes, corns, chilblains; or children's heel, which has no outward sign, may be the cause.

HIP AND THIGH

The hip, like the shoulder, works on the ball and socket principle, allowing for the maximum range of movement. Its task is, however, immeasurably more exacting. When you stand on both feet, the load this huge joint bears is comparatively small: half the weight of trunk, head and arms on each side.

Lift one foot, and the muscular pull required to balance is four times your total body weight! Run, and it is considerably more; jump and land on one foot, and the increase is enormous.

No wonder the hip joint is vulnerable to injury, from youth, and tends to show signs of wear in later life. No wonder that so many in old age appreciate the friendly aid of a cane which, properly used, can halve the pressure on the hip.

Limp and pain are symptoms of hip disorders but, as we have seen, limp alone may be due to conditions elsewhere.

Pain in the Hip, and Limp
CHILDREN, COMMONLY AGED 2–7 YEARS
Inflamed joint lining, sometimes after a slight sprain. Movements limited compared with other side.
Treatment: Bed rest for two weeks as a safety measure, unless very mild indeed. This is an important joint, and more serious disorders present the same picture in the early stages.
Outlook: Uneventful, complete recovery.
Tuberculosis, nowadays rare.
CHILDREN, COMMONLY AGED 4–9 YEARS
Perthes' disease [Ch: S, 1–2 yrs.]: A softening of the upper end of the thigh bone, in the hip, commoner in boys.
Limp more noticeable than pain.
Limitation of sideways movement of joint, disappearing with rest.

Hip Joints, from the Front

Treatment: Take pressure off hip joint; may mean one year off the feet.

Outlook: Usually better within two years. X-ray will show return to normal.

ADOLESCENTS, OR 8 TO 19 YEARS

Adolescent coxa vara [Ch: S, U]

Gradual slipping of the top of the thigh bone in the hip joint.

Commoner in boys, especially fat ones.

Pain more troublesome than limp.

Treatment: Take weight off hip, as above. Doctor essential. Operation nearly always necessary.

Note: In all these children's hip troubles, it is important to take the weight off the joint, or painful osteoarthritis is likely to develop later.

ADULTS

Osteoarthritis, especially in middle-aged and elderly.

Pain, limp, stiffness, with hip finally permanently slightly bent and turned outwards, and the leg apparently shorter. There is a wide variety of treatments, some markedly successful. Operation should be considered before the hip becomes too stiff, and if pain is severe.

Rheumatoid arthritis, any age from childhood to late middle age. Usually a part of generalized arthritis.

Fracture of the Neck of the Thigh Bone: "Broken Hip"
[A: U, 6–6/12]

A common accident in the elderly.

Identification: Trip or stumble followed by pain in the hip and loss of the power to use it. The foot is usually turned out. Bruising and swelling may also be present. X-ray confirms diagnosis.

Treatment: Usually operation, and results often remarkably good.

Note: Other fractures of the thigh bone do occur, but are so obvious and painful that assistance will certainly be sent for.

Dislocated Hip Joint [Ch: SU]

Usually an abnormality at birth (dislocation from injury in later life could not be overlooked) and if treated within a few days, perfect normality can be obtained. Unrecognized dislocation of

one or both hips can produce a typical, lurching, ungainly walk (above); in middle adulthood backache often develops, and later, painful osteoarthritis of the hip.
Treatment: Varies with age and stage, and is most successful in the young. Operation may greatly help older patients.

Snapping Hip [Ch]
Due to a strap of strong ligamentous tissue slipping over a knob of bone. Not significant: it can sometimes be done at will. No treatment necessary.

Clicking Hip [Ch]
Probably the same mechanism that makes the finger joints "crack" when they are pulled. Not indicative of any abnormality.

Varicose Veins in the Thigh
See Knee and Leg Section.

Knee and Leg

Acute Pain in the Knee: Usually accompanied by swelling [A]
Injury: acute sprain; fractured kneecap or other bone near knee; torn cartilage of the knee.
Locking of the knee.
Inflammation: acute arthritis.
Occasionally trouble in the hip gives rise to pain in the knee (shared nerve).

Injuries to the Knee
SPRAIN [A: U, 1/12], i.e. partial tearing of the ligaments around the joint: that on the inner side is most often subjected to strain, especially in football and skiing.
Identification: Injury, followed by pain, tenderness, and swelling.
Treatment: Elastic strapping from midthigh to midcalf applied as soon as possible, then normal activity, but not sports.
Outlook: If treatment not persisted in, *chronic sprain* may follow.
TORN LIGAMENT [A: SU, 6], i.e. complete or nearly.

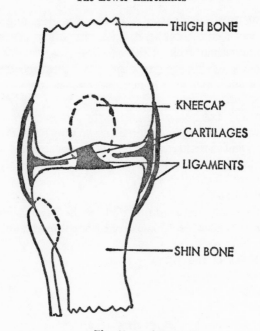

The Knee Joint

Identification: Injury followed by signs as in sprain but more severe; it is impossible, or nearly so, to walk, because the knee gives way usually towards the other leg. The joint may be swollen by fluid inside it, and bruising may show.

Treatment: Operation.

TORN CARTILAGE   [A: U, 6; Ch: S, 2–6]

The knee joint is unique in having washers of gristle, the cartilages, between the joint surfaces. These are injured by twisting accidents, especially if the foot is firmly on the ground and the body swings around as it falls. A common accident for footballers, but may happen to anyone, even a housewife at home. Unusual in those under 16.

Identification: Injury: knee immediately agonizing to move. "Locking" may occur; i.e. the joint cannot be straightened because something is in the way. Someone else may "unlock" the joint by manipulation, and a click may then be heard.

Tenderness, usually front and inner side, along the joint line. Joint soon becomes distended with fluid.

Later symptoms, particularly if original injury not treated seriously. Knee gives or "catches" frequently, without cause—even during sleep. Pain and swelling, but not invariably. Tenderness, always, along joint line.

Treatment:

Immediate: Manipulation, then as for sprain, except that walking should be avoided for 48 hours.

Later: If there are symptoms, only operation is likely to help. Time off work after operation varies from two weeks for an office worker to eight weeks for a professional football player.

BROKEN KNEECAP [A: U]

Due to direct violence: a kick or fall onto the knee. Pain, swelling, bruising.

Treatment: Plaster cast for a week, after which active movements should begin.

Due to sudden muscular pull, with the knee half bent. A snap may be heard and felt. Pain, swelling, bruising. Knee unusable.

Treatment: Operation, without delay.

Note: A piece may be pulled off the leg bone instead of breaking the kneecap.

Chronic Pain and Swelling of Knee

Injury: chronic sprain (below); torn cartilage (above).

Chondromalacia of the kneecap (below).

Loose bodies in knee joint, e.g. tag of torn cartilage, broken fragment of bone.

Chronic arthritis: osteoarthritis, rheumatoid arthritis.

Rare and uncommon diseases, e.g. tuberculosis, syphilis, hemophilia.

Note: Pain may be felt in the knee although the trouble is in the hip, due to a shared nerve, but of course the knee will not be swollen in such a case.

Chronic Sprain [Ch: S, 2–6]

Due to incomplete healing of injured ligament, usually the inner one, after an acute sprain.

Identification: Pain, weakness, knee "gives way," may be tender to press in one spot. Movement may be slightly limited, but *no locking* (below). Thigh muscles weaker and may look smaller on bad side. Measure round both thighs to compare.

Treatment: The nub is restoration of muscle strength by exercises performed conscientiously three times a day. See doctor for exercises.

Note: See also Torn cartilage (above).

Slipping Kneecap   [A Ch: SU]

Sex: Usually female.

Age: Usually young adult.

Identification: Repeated "slipping out" of knee on walking or running. Sharply painful, and cannot be straightened except by hand—or help of friends.

Treatment: Operation, good results usual.

Chondromalacia of the Kneecap   [Ch: S]

An important precursor of osteoarthritis. The sliding surface of the kneecap degenerates, becoming rough and cracked, and flakes may come off. Young adults or middle-aged persons mainly affected.

Identification: Pain, swelling, sometimes "catching" of the knee, especially after exercise. Painful to press the kneecap.

Treatment: Avoid overuse: running games, athletics.

Plaster cast or operation may be needed in bad cases, and may prevent the later development of osteoarthritis.

Locking of the Knee

See also Torn cartilage (above).

Movement restricted by mechanical obstruction in the joint, usually straightening. Unlocking occurs with a click, by manipulation or by itself. *Pseudo-locking* occurs when a painful disorder makes the muscles go tight, but there is then no unlocking.

Causes of Locking

Torn cartilage (above). Common in young adults.

Fragment of fractured bone in the joint.

Faulty development of the joint surfaces, in children: osteochondritis dissecans.

Chronic arthritis.

Dislocation of kneecap (above).

Clicking Knees [Ch]

Sometimes, not necessarily, painful.

Types

Vacuum click: Commonest, the same mechanism as when the finger joints are made to snap by pulling them. Can be noisy on going upstairs, or with some particular movement. Annoying. No treatment except to get out of the habit of any causative movement.

Torn cartilage: Deeper note than vacuum click. Operation to remove cartilage.

Clicking tendons, attached near the knee joint. Often painful, and curable by operation.

Grating Knee

Not significant unless painful.

Coarse: osteoarthritis.

Fine: rheumatoid arthritis; chondromalacia of the kneecap; inflammation of the lining of the joint.

Pain in the Calf

Causes

Injury: pulled muscle (below).

Thrombophlebitis of deep veins (below).

Arterial disease [Ch: S, X], including Buerger's disease: narrowed arteries are inadequate to supply muscles with blood during exercise, so pain comes on after walking. It is immediately relieved by rest, even merely pausing to look in a shop window. Feet cold. See Pain in feet.

Treatment: General: stop smoking, particular care of foot hygiene, warmth and well-fitting footwear.

Special: See doctor.

Pulled Calf Muscle   [A: SU, 6]

Identification: Sudden pain in the calf during exercise, with tenderness in one area.

A few muscle fibers have probably been torn.

Treatment: Elastic strapping from knee to foot as soon as possible to prevent a weakening scar in the muscle.

Pain, persisting, may require injection.

Varicose Veins   [Ch: S, X]

These may occur in the thighs and other parts, but most commonly appear, in the first instance at least, in the lower leg.

The veins of the leg consist of three groups: those just under the skin, which are visible if they become distended; those running between the muscles, out of sight; and others which communicate between these two sets.

Varicosity, the twisting and bulging of the veins, occurs when there is too much back pressure from the blood which is returning from the lower limb to the heart. The back pressure may be due to pregnancy or some other lower abdominal swelling or disorder, garters, obesity, and/or incompetence of the valves in the veins. The latter is often a hereditary mild effect.

Identification: There may be no discomfort. Unsightly appearance from tortuous and dilated superficial veins, or discolored skin over them. Fatigue, aching, itching, and a feeling of fullness in the leg may be noticeable before menstrual periods, in hot weather, after a hot bath, after standing. Swelling of the ankle may occur in the evening.

Treatment:

General: Reduce strain on veins by correcting overweight, sitting instead of standing for housework like ironing, checking constipation, and raising the foot of the bed nine inches: not noticeable after a couple of nights. When resting, it is futile to put the feet on a low stool: they must be at least as high as the body.

Stimulate the circulation by "cycling" exercises before rising. Ask doctor for toe and ankle exercises to use at odd times during the day (e.g. while washing dishes or watching television). Cold baths.

Hygiene of the skin over the veins: it is particularly delicate.

Daily wash, careful drying, and powdering. Rub cold cream in overnight.

Support hose: Either nylon or elastic. Put on before getting out of bed, while the veins are empty and flat.

Injection ⎫
Operation ⎬ according to doctor's advice.

Outlook: Care needed, because of the possible complications: Varicose eczema, an infective condition usually started by scratching; varicose ulcers; thrombophlebitis (below).

Thrombophlebitis [A: S]

Clotting and inflammation in a vein.

Identification: Tender, red "cord" under the skin if a superficial vein is involved; deep pain, and swelling of ankle if deep vein affected. Both maybe. General malaise and fever may be present.

Treatment: Anticoagulant medicines through doctor, support bandages or stockings, and general care as for varicose veins (above) for some weeks after. Time to full recovery varies from a week or two to months.

Knock-Knees [Ch: N]

Medical name: Genu valgum.

A slight degree is normal at one stage during childhood, but the deformity is rare among adults, so the majority must correct themselves unaided. See Children's Section.

Identification: Of more than normal degrees of knock-knees: gap of more than 1½ inches between the ankles, when the knees are straight and touching and the kneecaps facing directly forwards.

Causes: Exaggeration of normal.

Due to general diseases, such as rickets. *RARE.*

Treatment: None usually necessary and in any case neither massage, exercises, nor wedged heels have any effect. Overweight should be corrected, however, as this can worsen the condition. In severe cases (more than 3-inch gap at three years) or those due to general diseases, operation or splinting may be needed.

Often associated with flat feet.

Bowlegs [Ch]

Medical name: Tibia vara.

Normal, in babies before they walk. Do not have too bulky a mass of diapers between the legs.

Infantile type [S], noticeable when walking begins. Development continues normally.

Adolescent type [S], gradually develops between eight and thirteen years.

Treatment: Operation.

Rickets [S]: Rare.

Broken Leg [A: U]

Signs of a break are pain, swelling, and bruising; the limb cannot be used, may be out of shape, has *one very tender place over a bone.*

X-ray is essential.

"Bumper fracture": Commonest in elderly people struck by a car bumper just below the knee.

Shin bone break: Easily visible.

Break near ankle: Symptoms as of sprain (above), but there is a very tender spot on the bone. Even stepping off the curb with a jolt can cause this fracture.

Foot and Ankle

The foot is a dual purpose structure, supporting and balancing the body while static, and propelling forwards when required. The outer side is concerned with balance, and the bones are slightly bowed to give springiness. The inner side is a massive arch, its bones cunningly contrived to stay in position and bear the weight with minimal effort while yet providing leverage for the muscles in locomotion. Equally good service can be provided by either a high or a low arch, and a child's or other really supple foot may rest with the inner border touching the ground, and raise the arch for walking.

Flat Feet

Medical name: Pes planus.

Nearly always a fault of posture, but may be compensatory to an abnormality in the leg or ankle, the aftermath of poliomyelitis, due to spasm of the muscles (below), or a congenital structural fault, which is too rare to require more than this mention.

SIMPLE (POSTURAL) FLAT FEET AND ANKLES THAT "ROLL IN"

Bad posture of the feet is a matter of bad posture as a whole: legs, back, even neck; and so foot exercises alone, while useful in increasing the suppleness of the foot, will not cure the fault.

Much flat foot rights itself without treatment, and the general postural ungainliness of adolescents, particularly girls, disappears when the other sex becomes of interest. Occasionally, however, flat feet can cause *pain,* especially after long walks or games: any time from the second decade onwards.

Pain in the feet, particularly in the elderly, is nearly always due to some other cause.

Treatment: Postural re-education, through remedial exercises, probably from a physiotherapist (arranged by doctor). Useless unless you make a sustained co-operative effort.

Arch supports, shoes of a special shape, and wedged or elongated heels are more hindrance than help.

Operation may be necessary in severe cases.

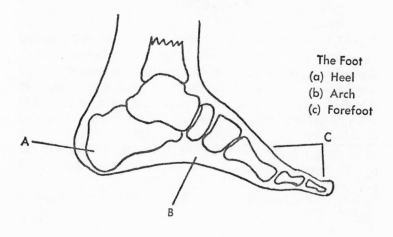

The Foot
(a) Heel
(b) Arch
(c) Forefoot

Outlook: Even if the foot remains flat it usually gives no trouble.

SPASMODIC FLAT FOOT   [Ch: S, 6/12]

"Apprentice's foot"

Commonest in boys starting work, from 15–17 years.

Identification: Pain, at first only in the evening, but soon all walking and standing hurts. The foot is pulled up, especially at the outer side, by involuntary spasm of the muscles of the leg. One or both sides.

Treatment: Injection may relieve spasm and pain, otherwise several weeks in a plaster cast, with no weight bearing on affected foot, then exercises. Operation often the best treatment: sometimes a congenital fault can be corrected.

Painful Feet

See also Cramp.

CHILDREN: Usually there is a visible cause:

> Chilblains ⎫
> Warts   ⎬ see Skin Section.
> Corns   ⎭

Occasionally:

> Flat feet, in the second decade (above).
>
> "Apprentice's foot" (above) from 15 to 17.
>
> Kohler's disease, aged four to six years, pain and limping. *Rare.*

ADULTS

Pain in the arch area   [Ch: S]

Identification: Aching of inner side of foot only, and only when tired at first; later, pain spreading all over foot and up calf, and becoming constant. Swelling at end of day, gone in morning.

Causes: Strain on the ligaments from prolonged and unaccustomed standing, such as being in line; after long illnesses and, less often, after short, acute ones; rapid increase in weight, due either to pregnancy or to just getting fat.

Arthritis is a cause from middle age onward.

Note: Deformity, e.g. flat foot, is seldom a cause of pain in this part of the foot.

Treatment

Exercises to strengthen the muscles, thereby relieving ligament strain.

Manipulation and massage may sometimes precede the exercises. Arch supports may be used if other methods fail: defeatist treatment.

PAIN IN THE FOREFOOT

The site of three-quarters of all adult foot pain, but unusual in childhood and adolescence.

Outer toes: Two common causes: faulty weight distribution, and fatigue fracture.

Faulty weight distribution [Ch: N or S]

Means that too much weight is carried by the outer side of the foot, which is designed for balance, not weight bearing (see above). Reasons for this: inefficiently pulling muscles, because of weakness after an illness, or working at a disadvantage because of such deformities as *claw foot* (below), and *bent big toe* (below); painful condition such as bunions, corns, etc., so that the foot is curled awkwardly; *hammer toe* (below); injury, such as stepping heavily onto a stone or spike; unsuitable shoes, too short, too narrow, or sloping down from a high heel.

Contributory: Overweight, and weaker muscles, as may occur in middle age.

Identification: Gradual onset, or on wearing new shoes. Pain in joints of the ball of the foot, later spreading, so that sufferer can bear to walk only on the heel. Tenderness. Ball of foot bulges downwards.

Treatment: Check causes. Rest foot. Pad of chiropodist's felt under foot just on the heel side of the painful joints. *NOT* under them. Exercises, but not allowing the toes to curl. Have an expert show you.

FATIGUE FRACTURE (Stress fracture, march fracture) [Ch: S, 3–6]

No special injury, but most common in those who walk a lot, such as nurses and soldiers.

Identification: Pain in the forefoot, tenderness in one place usually of one of the middle bones. X-ray makes sure.

Treatment: If severe, keep off the foot for one to two weeks; but usually firm strapping and moderation in walking is sufficient. Full activity may be resumed in three to six weeks, when the pain has gone.

PAIN UNDER BIG TOE   [Ch: S]

Causes

Commonest is osteoarthritis of the joints, due to deformity of big toe, hallux valgus (below) or hallux rigidus (below).

Minor injury: stepping hard on a stone.

Callus (hard skin) under joint if big toe is clawed (see Claw Foot, below).

Treatment: Of deformity, and/or sorbo pad or insole.

PAIN IN THE FOREFOOT AND TOES   [Ch]

Especially at night, usually associated with pain in the calf on walking: arterial disorder.

Pain under the Heel

A common complaint.

PLANTAR FASCITIS   [Ch: S or N, 6/12]

In the middle-aged and over, possibly due to inflammation of muscles and connective tissues attached to the heel bone. Deep tenderness in one spot immediately in front of the heel pad.

Treatment: Injections into tender area are worth trying. Pad under the heel, with a gap cut in it opposite the tender spot.

Outlook: Often difficult to cure rapidly, but usually gets better in nine months whatever the treatment.

STRESS OR FATIGUE FRACTURE OF THE HEEL BONE   [Ch: S, 6–10]

In young adults. Pain comes on gradually, worse on walking, and may extend all around heel.

Treatment: Rest for ten days by using crutches if severe; if not severe, and in any case later, thick pad under heel and much reduced activity for six to ten weeks.

Outlook: Complete recovery is the rule.

Pain behind Heel

SUPERFICIAL INFLAMMATION   [A Ch: N, 2]

Red, swollen, tender area like a chilblain, especially in cold weather. Usually in females of under 25, partly due to deficient circulation, partly due to rubbing by shoe.

Treatment: "Heel protectors."

INFLAMMATION OF THE TENDON SHEATH   [A Ch: S, 6]

Pain, tenderness, and creaking that may be felt on movement, in the big tendon (Achilles) like a section of rope, joining calf muscles to heel bone. Due to overuse, as in athletes and dancers.

Treatment: Rest. Foot must be strapped in toe pointed position.

CHILDREN'S HEEL   [A Ch: N, 2]

Children aged 8–14, especially boys. Pain, swelling, tenderness at low back of heel. Limping at end of day.

Treatment: Child may do anything he likes so long as he does not complain afterwards; if he does complain, he is doing too much and should stop. Tell him this. Recovery rapid.

TORN TENDON   [A: S, 6–6/12]

Commonly in middle-aged men—classically on playing baseball or football with sons, after years without practice.

Sudden pain behind ankle when running. Falls down. Unable to stand on tiptoe on affected side. Lump in the tendon (blood clot fills the gap).

Treatment: Operation, better in six weeks; or, strapping in toe down position, and raised heel for six to eight weeks.

Outlook: Perfect recovery after operation, but ability to stand on tiptoe may be lost after simpler treatment.

Bent Big Toe, Bunion   [Ch: N or S]

Medical name: Hallux valgus.

The commonest of all foot deformities, occurring more in women. There is a familial tendency. Shoes are usually blamed, but their effect may not be as great as supposed.

Identification: Prominent big toe joint, because the big toe turns, deflecting outwards, and the bone to which it is attached is deflected inwards.

Secondary effects: Bunion, a bag of gelatinous material which can become inflamed over the joint; corns and calluses; big toe may ride over or under other toes, and hammer toe or mallet toe may result; big toenail tends to face towards other foot, not up. The ball of the foot bulges downwards; there is pain in the forefoot and in the bunion and corns, etc., so that the step loses its spring, and the gait becomes a painful hobble.

Treatment: Many cases do not progress, and need no treatment. X-rays at intervals can reveal any progress, for certain. Operation helps severe or rapidly progressing cases: results good. Two to three months before completely painless. If bunion only is causing trouble, "bunion protectors" and well-chosen shoes may be adequate.

Stiff Big Toe

Medical name: Hallux rigidus.

ACUTE   [A: S, 6]

Uncommon. Mainly adolescent boys with long, narrow feet.

Identification: Pain and stiffness of big toe, coming on suddenly. Walking difficult. Tenderness of joint.

Treatment: Do not delay: a permanently stiff joint could result. Rest in plaster cast, via doctor, for six weeks. Bar under the sole of the shoe for a few months afterward.

Outlook: Good, if treated thoroughly.

CHRONIC   [Ch: S]

Common form: mainly in men. It may follow a single, noticeable injury or such repeated insults as playing football in tight boots; or come after acute stiff toe.

Identification: Pain and stiffness. Latter comes gradually, and sufferer learns trick of rolling on the outer edge of the foot when walking.

Treatment: Bar under shoe, to provide a rocker and replace the movement of the joint.

Operation may be only effective method of curing pain.

Hammer Toe and Mallet Toe   [Ch: N or S]

Bent at a right angle at the first joint (hammer) or the last joint (mallet). Painless apart from corn on the top of the joint, or aching forefoot if the ball of the foot is disturbed. Awkward to find comfortably fitting shoes.

Treatment: Conservative, by regular chiropody; or operation.

Curly Toes

Seen in babies, are not significant; they get into line without treatment. Strapping or other maneuver is uncomfortable, unhygienic, and unnecessary.

Claw Foot [Ch: S]

Medical name: Pes cavus.

There is a familial tendency to claw foot and claw toes, and they usually begin before the age of 10.

Identification: Unusually high arch; shoes worn out unduly fast. Later, heel cannot touch ground when standing, and there is pain under the joints of the forefoot, with corns and calluses above and below.

Treatment: Very early: exercises, and heelless shoes. Later: surgical shoes with insoles at the heel, which give relief but neither cure nor stop progress of the trouble. Operation.

Ingrowing Toenail [Ch: N or S, X]

Causes: Tight shoes, overlapping toe, or just a naturally occurring, extra curved nail. Well-kept, well-washed feet produce fewer symptoms even with ingrowing nails.

Identification: Pain, from infection where the thick curved nail has dug into the grooves in the soft tissues on each side.

Treatment: Deal with infection first: Gentian violet, 1%, in grooves and under edge of nail, by orange stick. File top of nail thin or cut a groove in it, so that it is not so strong in pressing in. Cut end concavely forwards, or straight. Scrupulous cleanliness.

Club Foot [Ch: SU]

Medical term: Talipes.

This condition is congenital, but mild cases may not be recognized until later childhood or adult life. Hippocrates' view of the cause is still current: an abnormal position in the womb before birth, pressing the feet out of position, but there is also a hereditary disposition.

Identification: Small, raised heel, broad forefoot, twisted downwards and inwards so that the two sets of toes face each other. Usually both sides affected. Movements of foot upwards much restricted.

Treatment: Ideally it starts on the *DAY OF BIRTH,* while the tissues are still pliable. Manipulation, splints, or operation, as necessary: in any case a first-class surgeon is essential.

Outlook: Other types of clubfoot occur but are less common. Management is the same.

Pain in the Ankle

ACUTE SPRAIN   [A: SU, 2]

Injury of the ligaments when the foot twists while walking, running, or jumping on uneven ground, and the muscles are caught unprepared.

Identification: Accident as above, quickly followed by pain and swelling. Bruising may show. Tenderness, but not as localized as in a fracture.

Treatment: NOT rest. Elastic strapping as soon as possible (preferably before swelling occurs) from knee to toes: then normal life except that competitive sport should be suspended. Try not to limp. Two weeks usually sufficient in strapping.

Injection and massage may help if pain persists.

CHRONIC SPRAIN   [Ch: S, 2]

Identification: Acute sprain in the past inadequately treated; pain on walking on uneven ground, running, or jumping; and attacks of swelling and pain after the slightest injury.

Treatment: Manipulation, massage, and exercises.

TORN LIGAMENT   [A: SU, 3/12], i.e. a more complete injury than a sprain.

Identification: Severe sprain, with much swelling and bruising. Tenderness in upper part of ligament. X-ray confirms.

Treatment: Important or ankle will be permanently unsteady. Plaster cast from knee to toes; massage and exercises afterward.

STRESS FRACTURE, FATIGUE FRACTURE   [Ch: S, 6–6/12]

See also Stress Fractures of heel and forefoot bones (above). The outer bone of the leg (the fibula) is commonly affected in athletes and ballet dancers. There is no particular accident, but a crack appears in the bone, seen by X-ray.

Identification: Pain above and behind outer side of ankle, coming on gradually, especially after exercise. Running and going upstairs become difficult. Tender in one spot.

Treatment: Do not delay. Elastic strapping from knee to toes, minimal activity for six to eight weeks.

Pain behind and above heel in torn tendon (above).

General bone and joint disorder, e.g. tuberculosis, osteoarthritis.

Swelling of the Foot and Ankle

The commonest type is due to fluid accumulating in the tissues: *edema.*

Causes of Edema

Normal: Standing for long periods, especially if overweight or pregnant, or the weather is hot.

Convalescence after some time in bed.

Advancing years, due to less efficient circulatory system.

Injury: Fracture, acute or chronic sprain.

A sign that the injury has not completely resolved, especially when an acute sprain becomes chronic. The swelling gets better overnight, or if the foot is raised, but increases during the day. It is sharply defined by the edge of the shoe.

Injuries high in the limb can cause edema of the ankle, because fluid gravitates downwards, and there is very little muscle in this area to massage it away.

OBSTRUCTION TO THE RETURN OF BLOOD THROUGH THE VEINS

This type is characterized by "pitting": if a finger is pressed into the swollen area, a little depression remains for some minutes. It may be due to:

Varicose veins.

Thrombosis: clotting in a vein, thrombophlebitis.

Tumor, for instance, or pregnant womb, pressing on the veins.

Heart difficulties.

Type without apparent cause, in some young women: perhaps due to a fault in the body's mechanism for dealing with water, and sometimes helped by large doses of alkali, say, bicarbonate.

Cirrhosis of the liver.

Lymphatic edema: Obstruction of the lymph channels to the glands in the groin. The whole leg may become very large and solid.

Congenital defect: present from birth, or appearing later.

Tropical disorders, and other infections involving the groin glands.

X-ray or radium treatment in this area.

Tumor.

Kidney trouble: Acute or chronic nephritis. Puffy appearance around the eyes also common; worse in the morning.

Angioneurotic edema: Giant hives. A symptom of allergy, special sensitivity to certain drugs and foods.

Chronic lung trouble.

Severe anemia.

Thyroid gland disorders.

Snakebite.

GROSS OBESITY: the fat may hang in rolls over the shoe.

DISORDERS OR TUMORS OF BONE OR JOINT: e.g. rheumatoid or other arthritis.

Heart, kidney, lung, or general troubles like anemia, standing too long, or angioneurotic edema usually produce swelling on both sides, but injuries and vein disorders are likely to be confined to one.

"GIVING WAY" OF ANKLE

Usually, but not necessarily, it gives so that the sole faces inwards. Pain and swelling (slight sprain, above) may follow.

Often, but not always, when walking on rough ground, or with spike heels. Women more than men.

There is usually no special reason and no special treatment, but occasionally it may be due to an unrecognized, untreated tear of the lateral ligament of the ankle, which calls for an operation.

Ringworm of the Feet

Athlete's Foot

Identification: Redness, itching, and peeling between the toes: patches of soft white skin come off, leaving sore, raw areas.

Due to a fungus, but sometimes eczema gives a similar appearance and is dealt with in the same way.

Treatment: Daily ten-minute foot soak with potassium permanganate: enough just to color the water. Whitfield's ointment or anti-fungal cream.

Allow the air to reach the feet: go artistic with sandals and no socks whenever possible. Long term: dry the feet well after bathing and dust with powder between the toes. Have roomier shoes, thinner hose.

Gout   [A: S, R, I; Ch: S, X]

Medical name: Podagra.

Likeliest at 45 plus. Becoming less common. Unusual in women.

Identification: Acute attack: waked up from good health one night by acute pain in big toe joint, which is shiny, swollen, red, and agonizingly tender to touch. Wrist, ankle, or thumb joints may be affected. Temperature 100°–103°F. Irritability. Urine less in volume and of higher color than normally.

Chronic: more frequent acute attacks, and recovery incomplete between them. "Prickling" in joints; flatulence; testy temper. Lumps on ears occasionally: gouty tophi.

Treatment: Bed; cotton wrapping and cradle over affected joint to keep bedclothes off. Medicine relieves pain in 24–48 hours. Back to good health, from an acute attack, in a week. Drink five pints daily—fruit juice, weak tea and coffee, water.

Chronic: medicines, diet.

Outlook and prevention: With care, the gouty tendency should cause you very little trouble. Medicines now available are very effective in acute attacks and in chronic gout. Gout is associated with drinking beer and wine, and eating certain nucleo-protein foods. Shift to a diet based on vegetables, cheese, and fish (not sardines), bread, butter, and fresh fruit. Keep the weight somewhere *below* the average.

This, if it is any consolation, is not a disorder that failures in life suffer from.

THE BACK

The spinal column—composed of many small interconnecting bones, the vertebrae, cushioned by discs of gristle between them —although shaped like an S-spring standing on end, acts as a rod to hold the trunk upright; threaded through each bone is the spinal cord, the vital bundle of nerves by which all sensation and all movement is possible, from feeling a stone in your shoe to breathing.

The Bones of the Back
Top seven: neck or cervical vertebrae.
Middle twelve: thoracic or dorsal vertebrae.
Lower five: lumbar vertebrae. Sacrum. Coccyx or tailpiece.

Imagine a vertical tower of blocks of unequal size and shape, held together by a system of elastic bands and ropes, having to move, twist, and bend while supporting a substantial weight: 140 pounds or more. This is the fantastic feat of standing and walking erect, which no other animal has mastered: the hunched and awkward shuffle of the ape is the nearest approach. But our proud posture has its price.

The spine is subject to severe stresses: for instance if a 200-lb. weight is lifted from the floor, a force of over 2,000 lb. is exerted on the lowest intervertebral disc. Nor is the spine normally at rest: when upright, the body is never still, but in a continuous slight sway from ankles up. Even so small a movement as raising a hand causes the great muscles each side of the spinal column to adjust their tension.

Such a delicately balanced and sensitive structure as the human back deserves its possessor's consideration: standing, sitting and lying straight and unstrained; keeping supple by such exercises as swimming and walking; not making unfair demands by routine use of spike heeled shoes, sudden or unaccustomed muscular efforts, or the continual burden of obesity.

Injuries to the Spine
SPRAINED BACK   [A: 48, R, 1]

Injury of the muscles and ligaments. Common, as a result of lifting, straining, or a direct injury.

Identification: Severe, localized pain after injury, worse on movement; tender, and maybe boggy to touch, if blood has leaked into the tissues (deep bruising).

X-ray may be required to make certain there is no bone injury.

Treatment: Rest, best in bed on a hard mattress, for 2–3 days. Cold applications. Injection at the site of maximum tenderness is useful in some cases, to relieve pain.

Massage and exercises should follow.

Outlook: Chronic backache may drag on if the original injury is neglected, i.e. not rested sufficiently at first, nor the back rehabilitated and strengthened by graduated exercise later.

DISLOCATION   [A: U]

Often accompanied by a fracture. Dislocation can occur only in the neck region of the spine: *"Broken Neck."*

Dislocation between the top two vertebrae is the end result of judicial hanging, but has also caused accidental death in children who have been lifted up from behind by head or neck, as a joke.

Dislocation lower in the neck results from falls on the head, diving into shallow water, or the whiplash effect of a sudden stop in a car.

Identification: If spinal cord is injured, paralysis and loss of sensation from neck down or, in luckier cases, merely severe pain in neck and arm or arms. Head in unnatural posture.

Treatment: Do not move patient. Cover. Ambulance to hospital *urgently.*

Medical dislocation: Rarely, the neck bones may slide out of position when the ligaments are softened by severe infection around the tonsils. Head and neck are bent forwards.

Treatment: Hospital.

FRACTURE: BROKEN BACK

Incomplete Fracture   [A: S]

A break that does not interfere with the continuity of the spinal column, as when the knobs of the vertebrae are snapped, e.g. *"shoveler's fracture,"* which occurs in men of poor physique working too hard with a shovel.

Or the body of a vertebra may be crushed slightly wedgeshaped.

Identification: Pain, usually in the lower part of the back, and inability to straighten up perfectly. X-ray confirms the diagnosis.

Treatment: Varies with injury. Bone-graft or support for many months may be necessary.

Complete Fracture   [A: U]

One in which the continuity of the spine is interrupted.

Cause and site: Direct violence, e.g. car running into victim, can cause a fracture at any level. More commonly, indirect injury by overbending the spine occurs, and in this case the most mobile parts, in the neck and below the waist, are most likely to be affected. Falls, crushing, and traffic accidents can be responsible.

Identification: Severe pain in back, along limbs, or encircling body, or "feeling dead" below the site of injury.

Treatment: Utmost gentleness vital; as for Dislocation (above).

Outlook: Recovery may be complete, or to any degree between this and permanent paralysis.

Chronic backache is a common sequel to any form of injury to the back. See discussion above.

Postural Defects [Ch: S]

The way in which we stand depends upon the position of the joints, which is in turn determined by the pull of the muscles, acting automatically. The automatic actions are called *reflexes*. The strength required for them is so slight that muscular weakness is very *rarely* the primary cause of bad posture.

The habitual bodily attitude is a reflection of habitual mental attitude, or personality, for instance aggressive or timorous.

Anxiety: tense, hunched shoulders—the attitude of a frightened bird.

Discouragement, depression: general sag; round shoulders; abdomen bulging forwards; flat feet, flabbiness.

Perfectionist, obsessional: odd ways of holding body and of

Types of Fault   **STANCE**

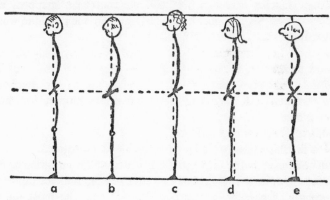

(*a*) Normal
(*b*) Round back
(*c*) Flat back
(*d*) Sway back

(*e*) Lordosis (small of back too hollow, so stomach sticks out, shoulders round)
(*f*) Lateral curvature (see page 261)

gait, often asymmetrical, e.g. one shoulder high, the other drooping.

Heavy involvement in other interests may make you neglect the way you stand. Children, who have such exciting things to see and hear and do; students, who have much to learn; adults with absorbing work—all may stand badly. An interest in games or the other sex, on the other hand, is a great natural improver to posture.

Fatigue: from mental causes, chronic illness, or the aftereffects of an acute disorder, also prints its pattern on posture.

Naturally enough, faults of posture tend to arise during periods of rapid growth, for instance the adolescent shooting up; in adolescence also, commonly there is emotional uncertainty, which shows in the posture.

Treatment

Check physical health, and review habits for adequacy of exercise; stimulation, indoor and out, rest. Cultivate mental poise.

Exercises to make the back supple, and then to inculcate by repetition the habit of new improved posture, getting into the position and holding it. Do exercises in your normal footwear, when possible, because it is in that that you want to stand well.

Ballet dancing exercises are good and make for grace as well as correct posture, and may help a girl, if other teaching of exercises is not available.

Round Shoulders, Stoop

Medical term: Kyphosis.

BAD POSTURE [Ch: X]: Any age from school child up. A habit to eradicate.

ADOLESCENT KYPHOSIS　　[Ch: S]

Age: 12–15 years at onset.

Identification: Smooth curve in the middle and lower chest regions. Later, pain or ache at end of day or after strenuous sport. "Apprentice's back."

Treatment: Exercises to strengthen back muscles, but avoidance of really fatiguing games. Swimming is ideal.

Flat, firm mattress.

Outlook: Better in a year, or when growth stops.

SENILE KYPHOSIS　　[Ch: S]

Age: 60 plus, especially manual workers.
Identification: Bent back, middle of chest area (higher than in younger people). Pain, worse at night, disturbing sleep.
Treatment and outlook: Analgesics. Later the back becomes stiff but painless, a condition sometimes called *poker back*. This term is also commonly applied to:

Rheumatic Arthritis of the Spine [Ch: S, 6/12]
Sex: Men nine times more often affected than women.
Age: Third and fourth decades. Usually persons of spare build.
Identification: Constant ache in low back, made worse by exertion, and not completely relieved by rest. Increasing stiffness of lower back then upper, and difficulty in expanding the chest completely. Head bent forwards, chest drawn in, back curved, gradually getting worse.
Treatment: X-ray treatment may help, but carries certain risks and is avoided if possible. Exercises. Operation in severe cases.
Outlook: The disease may burn out at any time and stage; the pain can always be stopped by treatment. It does not usually recur.

Tuberculosis of the Spine [Ch: S]
Now very *rare*. A sharp bend in the upper part of the back is characteristic.

Lateral Curvature of the Spine
Medical name: Scoliosis.
Although viewed from the side the spine is normally curved, seen from the back it should be straight. Most people have a slight deviation: a noticeable one is called scoliosis.
IDIOPATHIC LATERAL SCOLIOSIS [Ch: S, X]
This type is commonest in adolescence, and is usually noticed between 10 and 18 years, in girls 9 times as often as in boys. It probably starts earlier. The vertebrae (spine bones) grow faster on one side than the other: no one knows why.
Identification: The curvature is usually the only symptom, frequently noticed at a school physical check-up or by a dressmaker, originally. Pain or aching is not common before middle age.

Treatment: There is controversy: some authorities advise against treatment except in cases of very severe deformity; for this, an operation which leaves the back straighter but rigid is performed. Some advise exercises, braces, and plaster casts. *Exercises* are always useful, for strength and suppleness. *Outlook:* The curvature gradually increases until growth stops (girls: 15, boys: 17). So long as the back remains supple, however, it need be no hindrance to ordinary activity.

More of a worry to the parents than the patient.

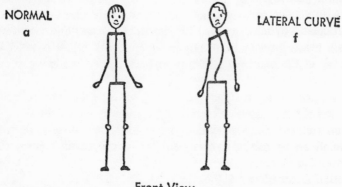

NORMAL
a

LATERAL CURVE
f

Front View

Postural Lateral Curvature   [Ch: S, 6/12]

Also affects chiefly adolescents, and chiefly girls, usually bulging to the left. There is no structural change, so the back can always be straightened, for instance in swimming or lying down, unlike the permanent curvature of idiopathic scoliosis (above). It may just be a bad habit, like some forms of round shoulders, or may be to compensate for one leg being shorter than the other.
Treatment: Exercises, and establishing a new habit of posture. Any underlying cause must be dealt with.

High Back Pain above the Waist.
See Head and Neck Section for neck part of spine.
Acute   [A: S, 1]
Identification: May start abruptly after coughing or sneezing or stretching arms above head, or come on gradually. Pain may

radiate to front of chest or breast, and breathing may be painful, also neck movements.

Treatment: Usually recovers in a few days without treatment, but injection or manipulation may work immediately.

CHRONIC

Any age.

Causes, on which treatment depends:

Adolescent kyphosis, senile kyphosis, scoliosis and other deformities, rheumatoid arthritis of the spine: all dealt with in this section (above).

Also tender areas of muscles and ligaments, usually helped particularly by massage; and pain from structures inside the chest: lung, heart, bronchi, esophagus; or pleurisy or an aneurysm may be felt in the back. Old injury.

Low Back Pain: Lumbago (see also Sciatica)

One of the commonest of all complaints, and one for which there is no panacea. Each individual case of backache needs to be considered on its merits not only for temporary relief, but for the prevention of recurrence.

ACUTE LUMBAGO [A: 48, An, 1]

Young adults and those of early middle age are especially susceptible to this group of disorders.

Identification: Wide variation in severity from:

(1) Stiffness noticed first on waking in the morning, or coming on gradually during the day, following unaccustomed exercise often, but not necessarily. Difficulty in rising from a chair, and discomfort on sitting for long, especially in a car.

(2) Sudden loin pain while golfing or gardening, for instance; unable to move or stand upright. Pain starts in one place but then extends widely, sometimes to the groin and back of the thigh. Tenderness if one area is pressed; later this area enlarges. Movement much limited, usually one side worse than the other.

Causes

Strain of ligaments and muscles.

Partial slipping of a disc, the most likely explanation for very severe attacks.

Tearing of a ligament between two vertebrae, usually only after a major strain, injury, or fall.

Strain of the joints between the spine and the hip girdle. Not common.

Treatment: Minor attacks recover spontaneously in a few days with no treatment; most get better by themselves within a week or two, but the sufferer may have to go to bed. Analgesics are useful, and a hot water bottle on the back may give relief—or massage. Injections or manipulation by doctor may bring about rapid, dramatic cure. Some victims can put things right for themselves by hanging by their hands from a beam, and letting the trunk muscles relax.

CHRONIC LUMBAGO

Chronic backache always has a psychological aspect as well as a physical one. Sometimes anxiety or depression keeps the symptoms going when the original cause no longer applies: sometimes the backache itself is the cause of depression or anxiety.

Identification: Varies with the cause.

Spondylosis: Thinning or loss of elasticity of the discs which cushion the bones of the spine, an aging process that begins early, producing the commonest low back pain in the middle-aged and elderly.

Identification: No pain on waking; it comes on during the day. Felt in the midline, and is made worse by bending, lifting, a long car or train ride, or working in a stooping position. Eased by lying down, a cushion in the small of the back.

Treatment: As in general for chronic lumbago, but recurrence is so common that particular care must be taken to avoid strain. See below.

Slipped Disc: Also likely to cause *Sciatica* or *Acute Lumbago*. Recurrent attacks rather than constant pain.

Deformities: From poor posture, congenital variations from normal, and those acquired later. Slight deviations from the normal curves are especially likely to cause backache in middle age: see Idiopathic Scoliosis for instance. Obesity may be a factor in bed posture and strain, also hip and knee conditions, or shortening of one leg.

Osteoarthritis (*osteoarthrosis*): Common after middle age, and particularly in spines which are slightly out of alignment (above) or if there has been a back injury earlier in life.

Identification: Pain and stiffness, worse on movement and after exercise, but worst of all when first getting up after resting. Movements limited. Diagnosis made certain only by X-ray.

Tendon and muscle pain: Bones and joints not involved.

Identification: Back pain, but also often felt in the buttocks or down the thigh. Tender spots, if you feel carefully for them.

Treatment: Rubbing or massage, and injections, which temporarily make the pain worse if they are in the right place, are particularly successful.

Unrecognized fracture: Or the aftermath of one that has been treated by too long an immobilization. The vertebrae are sometimes cracked by being slightly squashed, which alters the alignment of the spine, or one of the knobbly processes of a vertebra may be partly torn.

Identification: History of injury in the recent or far past: often there is a psychological aspect, e.g. a worry about compensation.

Treatment: Exercises are especially helpful, strengthening the spine.

Two conditions not recognized by all authorities:

"Sprung back": Partly torn ligaments between the spines of the vertebrae, which may have healed leaving a weak place; women are more often affected than men, ages 15–35 most commonly.

Identification: Dull, nagging, low backache, not severe but recurrent; made worse by stooping, sitting with the back unsupported, or driving for long. Relieved by rest or massage, but readily comes back.

Unstable vertebrae: i.e. the small bones of the back tending to slide on one another slightly, causing chronic low backache with acute episodes; movement not limited. Massage does not help, but exercises to strengthen the supporting muscles may.

Treatment of Chronic Backache

Rest: A few weeks' change from the occupation that has caused or allowed the back pain to come on, whether housework, engineering, or truck-driving.

Active measures: (These alone are usually sufficient in young adults, or after childbirth; see Women's Section).

Heat, from hot water bottle to radiant heat, by the fire, or at hospital, or diathermy. Often a useful preparation for: Massage, amateur or by physiotherapist.

Manipulation, by expert.

Exercises.

If all these fail

Spinal support, somewhat irksome, and makes back stiffer even if less painful.

Operation: no pain, but a permanently stiff back in the affected area.

Prevention

Alteration of habits: not easy, as smokers and overeaters can testify.

Avoid long standing.

Modify jobs which require stooping, by raising level of work surface or sitting down to it.

Bending to the ground should be done by bending the knees, not just the back.

Keep back hollow when lifting a weight.

Use a back rest with your car seat or a cushion in your favorite chair, to keep back hollow.

Exercises: Regularly, and for an indefinite period, to strengthen spinal and abdominal muscles, and keep large range of mobility. Really useful in preventing attacks.

Note: If, despite all, back pain recurs, get treatment started that very day. Delay will only waste more time of yours, the doctor's and the physiotherapist's.

Causes of Low Backache Not Due to Back Trouble

In acute illnesses, like influenza: temporary.

Shingles before the rash comes out. Superficial, temporary.

Trouble in an organ inside the abdomen: kidney, womb, ovary, pancreas, colon, rectum, appendix, bladder, gall bladder. Uncommon.

Secondary to a tumor at a distant site. Usually the original trouble has been discovered long before.

Aneurysm: a weakening in the wall of the large artery just in front of the spine.

Pain at Lower End of Back   [Ch: S]
Medical name: Coccydynia.

See also Ano-Rectal Section, Pain on sitting down.

Commoner in women than in men, and often in nervous types.

Identification: Pain worse on sitting, and sometimes on going up-stairs. Sometimes only a burning or pricking sensation, not brought on by anything apparent.

Causes

Commonest: Slipped disc in lumbar (below rib level) area of back, pressing on nerve to sitting region.

Cracked bone, due to fall or kick: diagnosed by X-ray.

Strain of tail joint: doctor can detect this.

Muscle or ligament strain: tender spots if pressed.

Burning type pain (above): not due to any local trouble.

Treatment: Of disc or other clear physical trouble; otherwise iron-ing out of anxieties, injection, manipulation, or very occasionally —operation.

Sciatica   [A: S, B, 6; Ch: S, X, 6]
Sciatica, i.e. pain in the back and down the leg, is a symptom, and not in itself a disease. See Lumbago. Sciatica is nearly al-ways due to pressure on the nerves as they emerge from the spinal cord through the special gaps between the spinal bones. The commonest cause is protrusion of one of the gristly discs which form little pads between the vertebrae: *slipped disc.* Men are more often affected than women, perhaps because they are more liable to the slight injuries that often precede an attack, e.g. garden-ing, golfing, lifting, twisting.

Identification: Pain, either dull or stabbing, starting in the back, later radiating down the leg, coming on suddenly, or working up; attacks of lumbago may precede the sciatica; pins-and-needles, tingling, burning, or numbness in the leg; maybe weakening buttock and calf muscles; limited movement noticeable on sit-ting, lying, rising, dressing; tenderness over the knobs of the lower

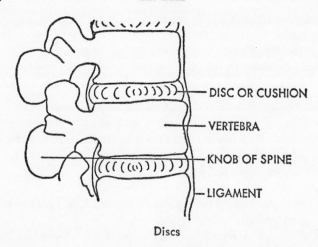

Discs

spine. Worse: on walking, coughing, sneezing, straining. Better: on resting, and sometimes by an individual trick movement. *Treatment:* Bed usually necessary to take the weight off the disc; should be very flat (board under mattress ideal) with not more than two pillows. Sedatives via doctor for night's rest. Injections sometimes help. Operation *rarely* necessary.

Outlook: Pain usually gone in three weeks. However, care as described in prevention of lumbago is needed indefinitely.

Note. Sciatica can occasionally be caused by tumors or inflammations in the pelvis pressing upon the nerves.

Pseudo-sciatica

Pain in leg or thigh from tender spot in muscles in the back, made worse by pressing the "trigger" spot, but not made worse by coughing, etc. Injection of the tender spot cures these cases.

Stiff Back

All the causes of low back pain except those not due to trouble in the back itself.

Spondylosis.

Senile kyphosis.

Arthritis.

Rheumatoid arthritis of the spine.
Poker back.
Local troubles: abscess, injury, infected wound.
Normal: Overuse or unaccustomed use, as with any muscles.

SYMPTOMS AFFECTING
THE WHOLE BODY

Allergy

(See Asthma, Eczema, Hay Fever, Hives.)

Allergic, like neurotic, is a much abused word. Although it may be loosely applied in ordinary conversation to mean dislike or intolerance—"I'm allergic to women with big feet"—medically it has a more restricted meaning.

Allergy is a condition of sensitivity to some substance, chemically a protein usually, which is called an *allergen*. The allergic person reacts in a way that others do not when they eat, inhale, or touch the allergen. Allergy is a normal protective mechanism that has gone off the rails. It is a useful defense for the nose to pour forth its watery secretion to wash out a harmful irritant or bacterial toxin, but plain maddening if it does the same thing for a grain of timothy grass pollen.

Why some and not others should react in this violent way is still a mystery. Hereditary disposition is of indisputable importance in many cases, but the form the allergy takes may vary from parent to child; e.g., an asthmatic father may have a daughter who is allergic to bee stings. A common story in an allergic person is of eczema in infancy, hay fever or rhinorrhea in later childhood, and asthma as an adult.

Yet allergens are not the whole story: why should a dazzling sky, or the feeling of cold linoleum underfoot set off, as it may, the characteristic pouring from the nose of hay fever, which is usually due to pollen? The part played by stress must be evaluated in each case. The trigger that sets off an attack of asthma, for instance, may be an allergen in the house dust, or a pollen, or it may be an emotional factor, anxiety, or grief.

Disorders which usually have an allergic element:
Hay fever; hives; allergic rhinitis.

Disorders which may sometimes have an allergic element:
Asthma; eczema; dermatitis; drug rashes; serum sickness; Ménière's disease; ulcerative colitis; diarrhea and vomiting; nasal polyps.

Treatment: See under separate disorders.

General: If allergy seems probable from the history of your trouble, your doctor will be able to help you in several ways.

Skin tests, using minute amounts of possible allergens, will help to discover substances to which you are especially sensitive, and of which you may not have been aware. If the skin tests show positive results, it may then be possible to give you a desensitizing course on the Mithridates principle: first a little of the noxious material, then more, until finally you do not react even to large quantities of, say, the pollen.

Medicines which help if you are sensitive are the *antithistamines,* which have the disadvantage of making some people drowsy—important if you are driving—and the *steroids,* which are powerful but, if used continuously, can have other effects which are dangerous. All right under supervision.

Precautions you may take for yourself:

Avoid the substances which you know affect you, as far as consistent with normal life and happiness.

For instance, do not sacrifice the family pet, but do not, on the other hand, replace him.

Foods that may upset you include shellfish, strawberries, pork, cheese, chocolate, wheat, eggs, tomatoes, milk. Avoid those that have upset you before.

Drugs, especially penicillin, aspirin, sleeping tablets and serum injections. Warn any doctor treating you.

Contact may upset you with silk, wool, kapok, chrysanthemums, marigolds, bulbs, etc. Avoid what is the culprit for you.

Inhaled allergens are more difficult to side-step, but are particularly important. Common ones are house dust; pollens, especially of grasses, or ragweed in the U.S.; wool; feathers; dandruff, animal or human.

If you are allergic to house dust, concentrate on making your bedroom as dust-free as possible, since this is the most important room for you—you spend longer in this room than in any other during the 24 hours. Hay fever sufferers who are sensitive to pollens must not have flowers in their bedrooms, and they should avoid grassy fields—the seaside is often better for their summer vacations.

The bedroom should be as bare as possible. Remove all orna-
ments, pictures, and other dust-catchers. Have light chintz or
plastic curtains, vinyl floor covering, no thick carpets, but perhaps
a washable rug.

Furniture should be plain—wooden or iron—sponged weekly. No
cloth-covered box springs. Wash woodwork, floors, radiators. Clean
picture moldings with an oiled cloth, and don't allow bedsprings
and the rear of closets to harbor fluff and dust.

Blankets should be made of a synthetic material or cotton. Sew
an extra half-length of sheet to your top sheet, or buy larger sheets
which can be turned over the bed to cover the blankets.

Have a vacuum cleaner to clean the house, used preferably by
someone else, and certainly emptied by another person. Dispos-
able bags removed out-of-doors are recommended. Oil-impreg-
nated mops and dusters are advised.

Pillows: No feather pillows, bolsters, eiderdowns, or mattresses.
Use rubber or plastic foam. Use plastic bags sealed with tape to
cover feather pillows, etc., until you can change them.

Animals: No animals in the house, certainly never in the bedrooms.
Better outdoors.

Go on vacation while the house is being redecorated. Dry rot,
damp wallpaper, and damp furniture may bring on symptoms. Do
not use an electric razor, because fine hairs get in the nose. Treat
dandruff energetically with medicated shampoos (your wife or
husband should, too).

Anemia

This means, literally, lack of blood, but the use of the word is restricted to a lower than normal concentration of hemoglobin in the
blood. Hemoglobin is the iron-containing red pigment of the
blood, which conveys oxygen to the brain, muscles, and other
organs.

Lack of it causes the characteristic *symptoms of anemia,* from
whatever cause: lassitude, palpitations, breathlessness, swelling of
the ankles, and, of course, pallor.

However, there are other factors, for instance, work under-
ground or at night, or a naturally small number of blood vessels

in the skin itself, which can cause a *pale face*. (See Face in Head and Neck Section.)

Causes

Loss of blood from severe bleeding, or a chronic loss as from piles or heavy menstrual periods.

Destruction of the red cells, which contain the hemoglobin, from hereditary disorders, poisons, incompatible transfusions, Rh factor in babies.

Not enough blood being manufactured because of lack of iron, either by inadequate diet or loss of iron through bleeding; lack of Vitamin B_{12}; lack of folic acid.

General illnesses, particularly rheumatoid arthritis, cancer, rheumatic fever, and some infections. Leukemia, a cancer of the blood.

Those in the third group are common and important.

IRON DEFICIENCY ANEMIA

Sex: Mainly women.

Age: Any, from adolescence up, but commonly in middle age.

Identification: As for anemia generally (above), and sometimes also spoon-shaped nails; smooth, shiny tongue, not sore; cracks at the corners of the mouth; dyspepsia and diarrhea.

Blood examination by doctor makes the diagnosis sure, and is a check on progress during treatment.

Treatment: Iron, usually in tablet form, with Vitamin C to help absorption and, if advised, extra acid. It should be continued indefinitely (unless the cause was blood loss which has stopped). Foods high in iron content should be taken, e.g. sardines, chocolate, liver, egg yolk, nuts, figs, apricots, brown bread, watercress, lentils, spinach and the water it is cooked in. Red meat is valuable because the protein it contains makes hemoglobin.

Outlook: A tendency to anemia, once recognized, needs care, or you will slip from top energy and efficiency unnecessarily.

Well treated, it is no handicap.

PERNICIOUS ANEMIA

No longer pernicious, since the cure is easily available.

Sex: Equal distribution.

Age: Commoner over 40, often in plump people, prematurely gray.

Identification: As for anemia generally (above), and also sometimes tingling in the limbs; unsteadiness; beefy, red, sore tongue; smooth, yellowish, pale skin; dyspepsia; diarrhea; depression. Blood examination clinches the diagnosis and is a check during treatment.

Treatment: Vitamin B_{12}, by injection.

Extra iron or hydrochloric acid are needed in some cases.

Diet is not important in this type of anemia, but plenty of vitamins, liver, kidney, apricots, grapes, and apples should be eaten and not too much in the way of potatoes and pastries, which spoil the appetite for more valuable nutrients.

Outlook: Practically normal, with treatment. Take extra care of infections, which may call for increased dosage of Vitamin B_{12}.

ANEMIA IN PREGNANCY

See Women's Section.

Any anemia is made worse by the demands of the unborn baby, who is particularly greedy for iron, or anemia may occur for the first time in pregnancy.

Two types are common

Simple iron deficiency, treated as above.

Folic acid lack, rapidly put right by taking folic acid tablets. Folic acid is present in asparagus and lettuce. The anemia of pregnancy is looked for and dealt with as part of the routine of prenatal care.

Arteriosclerosis, "Hardening of the Arteries,"
Atheroma [Ch: S]

Loss of elasticity of the tissues, including the arteries, occurs to a certain extent in all of us past middle age, though some are affected more noticeably or sooner than others. Patches of the linings of the arteries become weakened, and fatty material from the blood may be deposited on them or clots form on the irregular surfaces, so that the vessels are narrowed and do not convey such a good supply of blood to the parts.

Here again the condition is patchy, some arteries remaining unaffected, often those to the lungs, for instance, while one or two others may cause symptoms.

Identification: Depends upon which arteries are narrowed. You may notice *a few* of these effects:

ARTERIES TO THE BRAIN

Intellectual: Slower thinking and grasp of new ideas; difficulty in concentrating for long—harder to work out the change; some slips at work; memory less trustworthy, particularly for what has happened lately: this leads to repeating oneself without realizing it.

Mood: Testiness, even petulance, good humor, too, is freely expressed with less inhibition than formerly; tendency to carelessness, over dress or other people's feelings, which earns some old people a reputation for selfishness that they cannot altogether help.

General: Headache; dizziness; tremor; unsteadiness in walking; easier fatigue; diminution of the very fine co-ordination required for such activities as playing the piano.

Stroke, apoplexy.

Parkinson's disease.

ARTERIES TO THE HEART (coronary arteries).

Angina of effort, i.e. pain in the chest after exertion.

Coronary disorders. (See Chest Section.)

ARTERIES TO KIDNEYS. If these are narrowed, the kidneys cannot concentrate the waste materials in the urine quite so well, so *more water is passed* to make up. Can cause high blood pressure.

AORTA, THE MAIN ARTERY: Stiffness of this may be a factor in high blood pressure, or there may be abdominal pain going through to the back, due to disease of the aorta or of the abdominal arteries.

ARTERIES TO THE LOWER LIMB

See Pain in the calf. Pain in the buttocks may come on—and pass off—similarly, in association with exercise, if the vessels higher up are involved.

ARTERIES TO GLANDS: e.g. to the pancreas, may cause mild diabetes; to the thyroid, mild hypothyroidism and feeling cold.

Treatment: There is no general answer to the problems of arteriosclerosis, but some "furred-up" arteries are nowadays replaceable with synthetic tubing, and for the rest, a deliberate slowing of the tempo keeps in step with the slower blood flow. You can usually go for that favorite walk if you take your time, work a problem out, or keep your temper if you do not allow yourself to become hustled or flustered. Let your pace be dignified, in everything.

Parkinson's Disease [Ch: S]

One of the effects of arteriosclerosis involving a particular part of the brain. Men get it far more often than women.

Identification: Stiffness and weakness of the muscles including those of the face, giving a characteristic mask-like look; coarse tremor when at rest, particularly of the hands, with the fingers going one way and the thumb the other as though crumbling a piece of bread—or rolling a pill. There is a tendency to lean forward and walk with short hurrying steps, and rise from a chair in a characteristic way. Most of us put our feet a little way under the chair as we rise; someone with Parkinson's disease stands up directly. Tendency for the mouth to stay open, and for saliva to be extra copious.

Treatment: Medicines help the stiffness and the trembling, and surgery is now hastening to the aid of the sufferers, and is particularly successful in one-sided cases.

Exercising as much as possible does good, not harm, and physiotherapy can help also.

Stroke, Apoplexy [A: U, B, 2, 6/12]

Medical name: Cerebral hemorrhage; cerebral thrombosis.

There are two kinds of stroke: in cerebral hemorrhage a weak place in a blood vessel in the brain gives way, and although it can happen to anyone, it is likelier in those with high blood pressure and old arteries. No one can tell in advance whether there is a weak place in any of his arteries, so there is no point in worrying about it.

The other type of stroke, cerebral thrombosis, is due to a clot or other blockage (possibly a result of arteriosclerosis) in a blood vessel in the brain, and may happen in the 40's and 50's, as well as among the elderly, and in those with normal blood pressures. There can be very mild attacks of this form of stroke, and even a severe one is likely to be less dramatic than the first type.

Identification

Mild attack: Temporary confusion or giddiness; difficulty in speaking clearly; weakness of one part, say a hand; dimming of vision, lasting a week or two.

Severe attack: Headache, vomiting, confusion, unintelligible speech, sudden or gradual loss or blurring of consciousness. Later: a difficulty in using the limbs on one side, e.g., stiff leg, weak grasp, or difficulty in speaking, finding the right word, or understanding words. Tendency to laugh or cry too easily.

Treatment: Call a doctor urgently. Meanwhile, leave unconscious patient on the floor, but put a pillow under his head. Remove dental plate so that it cannot obstruct breathing.

In a mild attack, call doctor; have patient rest until he comes.

Outlook: Good, in most cases: the immediate effects usually pass off in a few weeks, after which gradual recovery takes place, not to the 100% point perhaps, but so that in six months to a year the sufferer can do most of what he could before, although driving a car may not be possible because of insurance difficulties. Speech difficulties may be improved by a speech therapist, and physiotherapy helps the weakened limbs; but it is persistence, confidence, and determination that enable the stroke patient to get about, with a stick if necessary, manage knife and fork, and toilet care, unaided, and restore his health, independence, and self-confidence.

Blood Groups

The existence of different types of human blood was discovered by Landsteiner in 1901, and we now have an International (A, B, O) Classification.

The red blood corpuscles, which are the body's oxygen-bearing messengers and also give the blood its characteristic color, contain *agglutinogens,* which can clash with substances in the blood of another person not in the same group.

The groups are named according to their agglutinogens: AB, A, B, and O. There are finer subdivisions and other factors, but the only one of importance is the *Rhesus factor.* Eighty-five percent of us have this agglutinogen, and are called Rh positive; but the others, Rh negative, may be upset if they have more than one transfusion of Rh positive blood, or, in the case of women, more than one baby if the father is Rh positive.

It is therefore useful to know your A, B, O blood type, and whether or not you are Rh negative, as in case you need a transfusion, it should match.

Blood groups are also useful in police work. Could the blood have been Y's, or was it X's group? It can also help up to a point in disputed paternity: a child cannot have in his blood agglutinogens other than those contained in his mother's and his (genuine) father's.

Blood Disorders
Anemia
Polycythemia: A condition in which there are too many red blood corpuscles, often in later life, causing a bluish-red color, headache, and breathlessness.
Purpura: A nonhereditary bleeding disease: acute or chronic.
Hemophilia: A hereditary disease of males in which the blood fails to clot in the normal time.
Leukemia: A cancer of the blood: either acute, most commonly in children, with a sudden onset of fever and sore throat; or chronic, with fatigue and symptoms of anemia.

Big Appetite
(See Obesity.)
Normal: exercise; growth, especially in boys of 13 to 17; pregnancy.
Habit: the more you eat one day the more you will feel like the next.
Diabetes: loss of weight despite large meals.
Unhappiness or anxiety: consolation by food.
Some types of ulcer and dyspepsia are relieved by food, so there is a constant wish to eat.
Hysteria: in adolescent girls.
Worms in the intestine: traditional but doubtful cause.

Loss of Appetite
Early stages of an infection.
Common cold, because of impaired taste.
Disorders of the stomach: any from acute gastritis to cancer.
Kidney, heart, and liver disorders.
Children: Normally have a falling-off in appetite at the end of the first year, when growth slows down. Frequently at toddler stage

they refuse food as part of their expression of independence. A passing phase that has no ill effects.

Psychological troubles: Fright or shock, anxiety (but this can work the other way); anorexia nervosa in young girls, associated with absence of periods; hysteria; depression, or serious psychosis coming on.

Loss of Weight [Ch: S or N, R]

(See Loss of Appetite, above.)

Loss of weight occurs in many chronic disorders and nearly all acute illnesses, rapidly if there is fever, vomiting or diarrhea. It is normal in advancing years; the loss of fat from beneath the skin causes the characteristic wrinkling. Much increased muscular activity without a corresponding increase in eating is also a normal cause of weight loss. Older children are naturally less chubby than toddlers, but since they are growing in stature there is not usually any actual weight loss.

Special Causes

Infections of the digestive system.

Bad teeth or inefficient dentures.

Peptic ulcer.

Fad diets.

Difficulty in swallowing, from any cause, tonsillitis to cancer of the gullet.

Diabetes mellitus: enormous meals make no difference.

Thyroid disorder: nervousness, sweating tremor.

Tuberculosis: uncommon.

Cancer of stomach, or elsewhere, after middle age.

Liver disorder, after middle age.

Kidney disorder, after middle age.

Disorders of the nervous system, e.g. Parkinson's disease.

Sleeplessness or pain from any cause.

Treatment: Attend to cause.

Allow plenty of time for meals. Eat in a relaxed atmosphere. Do not allow more than two hours to elapse without having either a snack, drink, or meal. Take more rest.

Special diet: Fresh air, exercise, new interests, and sociability are the best appetite stimulants: bottled or tablet tonics have little effect.

Obesity

Obesity is the price of success: a disease of the Western civilizations. In the U.S. alone 1 in 5 adult males is just too fat, weighing 10% more than he should.

Success means prosperity, means overnutrition. It provides money to buy more food than the body can utilize, so the surplus is stored as fat; it provides money to pay for transport that requires no muscle power; it steals time, so that not enough is left for long, regular periods of exercise. The snag is, mental work and traveling around in the sitting posture use no more fuel than lying in bed all day, yet they make you feel tired out and in need of something. What your mind and body really require are a change of scene and activity: a short brisk walk, for instance. But it is easier and quicker to eat something or have a drink, which comes to the same thing.

Emotional factors come in, too. If you are anxious, heart-broken, or bored, you may turn to food for consolation. A full stomach has a sedative effect, and the mechanical action of eating is soothing in itself. Eating on one's own, like drinking, is the most likely to become excessive.

Families in which the members tend to run to fat are common, perhaps because of a hereditary factor, but it is as likely to be because they share the same eating habits.

Other uncommon factors in fatness are thyroid and other glandular deficiency. The middle-aged spread that so often develops at the menopause is more likely to be due to having less to do now that the children are physically independent, and eating more instead, than to the glandular changes. Kidney trouble and heart disorders can cause fluid to be held in the tissues; this makes the weight increase, and may produce a puffiness which is not true fat.

Outlook for Fat People

Overnutrition is as much malnutrition (bad feeding) as under-nutrition. The fat man, and to a slightly lesser extent, the fat woman, is more likely to suffer from: high blood pressure, coronary disease, diabetes, and arteriosclerosis—and pity their poor feet, and joints!

A major operation means more than double the risk if you are too fat, and your expectation of life is considerably diminished. Fat young adults are the worst insurance risks of all.

Short-term snags: Fatigue and shortness of breath, due to having to carry the weight around all day; embarrassment, especially in a clothing store.

Treatment: There is no easy way.

Simple: yes. Easy: no.

There are only two ways of reducing fat accumulation:

(1) Eat less, and differently.

(2) Burn up more: this is a slow method. Walking an extra 1½ miles a day would bring you down 14 lb. by this time next year, provided you ate no more than you do at present.

Plan of Campaign

Medical check, if you have any doubts about your health.

Try to deal with your anxieties, frustrations or lack of occupation. Get your husband's or wife's co-operation.

Keep a weight record somewhere visible, to encourage or shame yourself.

Reward yourself for success but not with food.

Fit into your day an extra quarter-hour of brisk walking. If you do not find you have time, have your exercise instead of lunch, or get up that much earlier.

Start eating: Sensibly.

Cut your calorie intake. Food is what you eat, but the energy it can produce is measured as for other fuel in *calories*. It is not too much bulk, but too much potential energy that is stockpiled as fat if it is surplus to immediate requirements. Different foods vary widely in their calorie value: energy or fat-producing. Compare, for instance, butter at 226 calories per ounce, with grapefruit at 3.

Cancer   [Ch: SU]

Every thinking person who has reached maturity will have considered the possibility of cancer, and it is right to do so.

A cancer is like a weed in an orderly garden: it does little harm, and can be easily rooted out to start with, but it may interfere with the health of the other plants and be far more difficult to eradicate if it has been allowed to get a hold.

You do not want to be afraid of something that may never happen—only a minority are affected—but equally you should not neglect pointers to possible trouble. To seek advice when certain unusual symptoms show themselves is sound sense and the safest course, although in most cases all you will receive, and require, is reassurance.

Identification: Of course this depends on the site of the trouble, but it is worth seeing your doctor for:

Bleeding, or discharge from the vagina, if you are a woman past the menopause. A slight whitish discharge is normal.

Blood in the urine.

Lump in the breast; discharge from the nipple.

Ulcer which does not heal, or warty growth that is becoming larger on the skin, lip, or tongue.

Persistent stomach discomfort, loss of appetite and of weight.

Change in bowel habit, especially constipation alternating with diarrhea.

Slow-starting, dribbling stream of urine in men, usually due to the common enlargement of the prostate gland, but occasionally more serious.

Hoarseness lasting several weeks. Cough.

Difficulty in swallowing.

Unexplained swellings.

General symptoms which are usually not noticeable in the early stages are fatigue and loss of weight.

Note: None of these signs means that there is cancer; the most they indicate is the bare possibility. Other conditions could account for any one of them. There are numerous completely harmless tumors, for instance adenomata of the breast and prostate gland, lipomata and papillomata under and on the skin.

So if your doctor assures you that there is nothing to worry about, believe him, and don't.

Treatment: Operation: with modern anesthetics and techniques this need hold no terrors.

X-rays and radium: particularly good on the skin.

Hormones: Particularly useful for breast and prostate.

Outlook: MANY CANCERS ARE COMPLETELY CURABLE, TAKEN IN REASONABLE TIME; all can be helped by treatment; and at worst, if there is pain, there are powerful drugs to relieve it. Meanwhile, active research proceeds towards the conquering of this, like so many other diseases.

Coma [A: U]

(See also Fainting, and Diabetes.)

Loss of consciousness, gradually deepening, often accompanied by slow, stertorous breathing; prolonged, unlike the transience of a faint.

Causes

Head injury: causing concussion, fractured skull, pressure on the brain from bleeding.

Stroke, brain tumor, or brain abscess.

Poisoning, for instance by alcohol, opium derivatives, heroin, coal gas, gasoline fumes, fire-damp or sewer gas—acutely; lead—chronically.

Diabetes mellitus.

Lack of sugar, insulin coma.

Epilepsy after a fit.

Meningitis and other severe fevers, e.g. smallpox, pneumonia, etc.

Severe blood loss.

Extremes of temperature: heatstroke (sunstroke), or cold.

Hysterical trance. *Rare.*

Coma can be the final state in almost any condition before death, a merciful arrangement.

Cramp [A: N]

Identification: Involuntary tightening of a muscle or muscles, with sharp pain, and usually temporary inability to move. Frequently in the foot or calf.

Causes

Over-exertion: as in swimming, rowing, ballet dancing.

Loss of body chemicals: as in severe vomiting, diarrhea, sweating (heat-cramps are due to this), or overbreathing, and in breast feeding if the calcium balance is deranged.

Arterial disorders: "furring up" due to arteriosclerosis or Buerger's disease. (See Pain in the calf.)

Pressure on an artery from an awkward posture may bring on cramp also.

Varicose veins in the leg.

Common cramp without apparent cause: some people are prone to cramps especially in the night, perhaps through sleeping in a particular position.

Certain postures may set off cramps in the day also. No ill effects; no significance.

Occupational cramps, e.g. writers', pianists', compositors'. In this type there is usually a highly important psychological element: anxiety added to a neurotic temperament, as well as much use of the small muscles. Fear may precipitate swimmer's cramp.

Treatment: Massage the painful muscle, and put it at the stretch, e.g. straighten your knee and press your toes upwards to relax cramped calf muscle.

In cases of vomiting and other fluid loss, take a salty drink, one teaspoon to the pint.

Daily quinine helps night cramps.

Occupational cramps call for discussion with as well as physical treatment from the doctor.

Epilepsy   [Ch: U or S, X]

Dramatic disturbances of brain function manifested by *fits,* and also by a characteristic pattern of electrical discharges as recorded by an electroencephalograph.

Epileptic attacks can be caused if the brain is irritated by injury, inflammation, tumor, or hemorrhage, but true or *idiopathic epilepsy* is not associated with any apparent abnormality in the brain. A common and important illness.

Age: Onset most commonly before 5, often at puberty, but rarely starting after 30.

Sex: Even in childhood, males predominate among adults. Heredity plays a part, but epilepsy is so widespread that there are few families without some in their ancestry, and 1 in 10 of us carry the genes.

Identification: Two forms.

Grand mal: Attacks of unconsciousness and convulsions, very variable in severity. Stages which are typically present: a few seconds' aura or warning, with strange bodily and mental sensations, and flashes of light, noises, tastes or smells; sudden loss of consciousness and falling down with a cry, but no attempt to save oneself; a few seconds' rigidity and holding the breath then twitchings that last for a minute or two. The bladder may be emptied, and foamy saliva froth from the mouth. Coma, deep breathing, and flaccidity follow; after an hour or two the patient may pass into normal sleep, or wake up confused.

Headache usually follows.

Fits recur unless treatment is given, often at the same time of day or in the same circumstances, e.g. with a menstrual period, in women, or when the mind is unoccupied at the end of the day.

Petit mal (minor epilepsy): The attacks are transient and slight, e.g. a sudden, momentary stop in the middle of a conversation, in which the face looks blank and pale, and of which the sufferer is quite unaware. At worst, he falls, but immediately gets up. These minor fits can occur several times a day.

Automatism: That is continuing the day's work apparently normally after an attack but without remembering it later; in some cases there is abnormal behavior which is also done without recollection. These automatic actions are more common after *petit mal* attacks than *grand mal*.

Focal fits: Spasms which start in one group of muscles, for instance, at the corner of the mouth, and then gradually advance to include other groups. No loss of consciousness. Usually due to some weal irritation, or to injury or tumor in the brain.

Treatment

Of a fit: lay a patient on back with pillow, put rolled-up handkerchief or pencil between his teeth to prevent biting his tongue, loosen clothing. Nothing shortens the attack.

General: avoid over-excitement and any known precipitating cause of attack. Avoid situations in which an attack could be disastrous, for instance, working with machinery, swimming, cycling in traffic, or driving a car.

Drugs: such as phenobarbital and dilantin prevent or diminish the frequency of fits.

Outlook: Meticulous and persistent treatment offers a good chance of completely suppressing the attacks, and after two to three years without one, the tablets may gradually be dispensed with. Presumably the cortex of the brain has become less irritable by that time. Marriage and having children are matters for individual discussion and decision, with your doctor's help, but 1 in 10 of us has the gene for epilepsy in his make-up, without its necessarily causing symptoms.

It has been said, "Epilepsy is the only disorder where the sufferer is more handicapped by the attitude of society than by his disability," and it is unfortunate that social and employers' prejudices can mar the life of an epileptic whose disorder is as well controlled by his drugs as a diabetic's by his insulin. Anyone will have a fit if given an electric shock, many others will have them in unusual circumstances, e.g. lack of oxygen, lack of sugar, or odd lighting effects. The epileptic merely has a lower threshold, and his fits follow tiny precipitating events.

Fatigue, Lassitude, Weakness
Identification: Disinclination for muscular exertion and inability to concentrate so that a full day's work is difficult to achieve. Headache, backache, dyspepsia, a run of colds or similar troubles, bad temper, and no pleasurable looking forwards may all be indications of fatigue.
Causes
Normal: A healthy desire for relaxation should follow exertion. There is a wide individual variation in this: for instance, after the emotional strain and physical effort of childbirth, one woman may fall into the sleep of exhaustion for hours, while another will sit up as bright as a button. Then there are individual differences about which part of the day is the best. Some people wake up alertly; others take till noon to get going. Some begin to fold up their energies at sundown; others are at their most vital at that time.

There is a natural, normal diminution of energy when there are great bodily changes, for instance in adolescence (which brings parental complaints of laziness), pregnancy and breast feeding, at the menopause, and in old age.

Plenty of sleep, 9–10 hours at night, helps the adolescent; expectant and lactating mothers need 8 hours at night and an hour after lunch, ideally; menopausals need changes of occupation more than anything; and the older man or woman paradoxically needs more rest, but less actual sleep (5 hours of sleep, but 9–10 hours in bed). A normal adult needs an *average* 8 hours in bed, and sleep most of that time.

Abnormal fatigue can be due to physical disorder or, far more frequently, emotional factors, stress.

Physical Disorders

Fatigue and washed-out appearance: Anemia; blood loss as from piles or excessive periods, vitamin deficiency or other malnutrition, especially in infancy; some heart disorders; chronic liver or kidney disease; colitis and other troubles in the digestive system of any type; pocket of infection in ear, sinus, appendix, etc.; malaria, worms, and other tropical troubles.

Fatigue with loss of weight: Diabetes mellitus; overactive thyroid gland; cancer of any part, especially stomach or gullet; old age and underfeeding; tuberculosis. See also Loss of weight, above.

Fatigue and weakness only:

Old age; chronic dyspepsia; underactive thyroid gland; heavy drinking; obesity: a simple matter of carrying the weight around all day.

Psychological Causes

By far the commonest.

Any of the main psychological disorders may give a picture of fatigue, sometimes so profound that the sufferer just sits and stares, or may not even get up, e.g., depression; schizophrenia; anxiety state; hysteria.

Most common of all is fatigue due to emotional factors, without actual psychological illness. Boredom, loneliness, and frustration, particularly likely among women in their homes, are potent causes of fatigue.

Tension from the noise, speed and competition of modern life, problems about money, work, or children, and shift work may also cause fatigue.

Overweight, in itself tiring, may be the result of over-eating as a reaction to an emotional state, either boredom or anxiety.

Fatigue from fear—commonly a fear of failure. Business executives as well as creative artists are frequently affected this way, and feel too exhausted to go on with their work.

Fatigue to avoid doing something one does not want is exemplified by the wife who is too tired for intercourse. It is more likely that she is unconsciously resentful of, or bored with, her husband.

It is seldom that work itself is too hard, except possibly in the case of a single-handed mother with 3 or 4 children under school age. She is likely to be physically tired as well as strained by the constant demands and need for supervision of her children.

In all the other cases of common, emotion-based fatigue, neither rest, sleep, nor a vacation puts matters right alone.

Treatment

Shorts cuts to vitality: there are none.

Coffee, tea, and cola drinks contain stimulants which postpone fatigue and are harmless in themselves. However, the greatest benefit is stopping one's activity to drink the coffee, and perhaps the refreshment of a chat.

Drugs such as amphetamines also postpone fatigue, but they have undesirable side effects and are habit-forming. To be used only on doctor's orders.

Alcoholic pick-me-ups suppress the feeling of fatigue temporarily in some people (they make others drowsier) by relieving tension. Large quantities act as a depressant.

Cigarettes, if the smoke is inhaled and the nicotine absorbed, may increase the pulse rate, and thus the blood flow through the brain, but this is counterbalanced by the deleterious effect of the carbon monoxide in the smoke. Cigarettes may assist relaxation by making a break in activity.

None of these short cuts has any long-term beneficial effect, and most are harmful to the health.

Radical Treatment

Get your emotional life straight, and decide on the goal in your life, so that you do not chase the impossible. Reorganize your day so that the main activity coincides with your most alert period, when possible. Allow for rest periods or changes of occupation at intervals in the day. Allow time for adequate but not excessive sleep (above). See discussions on Insomnia.

Make each day's plan in the morning. Get up 15 minutes earlier if normally you have to have breakfast at the gallop. Take small, frequent meals, but do not allow yourself to get fat. If you are already overweight, reduce.

Take exercise consistently.

When you are too tired to think, take a walk.

When you are tired in the muscles, listen to some music, read.

Fits, or Convulsions [A: U]

Involuntary paroxysms of muscular contraction: jerks, twitches, or spasms of tightening, either generalized or in one area only.

GENERALIZED

Chills: Bouts of shivering cold and teeth-chattering wretchedness, lasting minutes to hours. Hands and feet cold to touch but body temperature raised. Gives way to warm, then overhot sensation, as temperature rises still higher. Thirst.

A single chill may usher in a feverish illness such as pneumonia, influenza, blood poisoning, tonsillitis, poliomyelitis.

A series of chills, more serious, may occur in mononucleosis, pyelitis, abscess formation, puerperal infection (childbed fever), malaria, etc.

Convulsions in children: Occur in the conditions which would cause chills in an adult; also due to birth injuries in the first few weeks, and digestive disorder, ear infections, whooping cough, rickets, or worms, later. (See Convulsions in Children's Section.)

Convulsions in adults: Sudden onset: seizure; may fall down; clenched jaws may make breathing noisy and labored; muscles jerking or rigid; control of bladder and bowels may be lost; saliva may bubble at the mouth; unconsciousness.

Causes: Epilepsy, stroke, meningitis, brain injury from any cause; uremia with failing kidneys; hysteria; eclampsia, the end-result of untreated toxemia of pregnancy; alcoholism; sunstroke; heart disease; lockjaw.

LOCAL: SPASMS AND TWITCHINGS

Fatigue: violent involuntary twitching in a normal person, usually just as he is going to sleep. In nervous or excitable people such spasms can occur frequently, often following a surprise.

Chorea (St. Vitus' dance) }
Thyroid disease   may all produce a similar jumpiness
Hysteria   of the muscles at their onset.
Early epilepsy.

Petit mal (minor epilepsy).
Tetanus (lockjaw): stiffness or twitching may first occur round the wound where the infection gained entry.
Brain irritation: by tumor, bleeding, infection, or injury, confined to one part.
Habit spasms or tics: although automatic, such movements usually begin as purposive actions, e.g. shrugging a shoulder because it is itching. Unconsciousness does not occur with local convulsions, except sometimes with petit mal.

Insomnia, Bad Sleep

Sleep is truly "Tired nature's sweet restorer," and oddly, although we are unconscious for it, we all feel that we enjoy a good sleep. Its effects are widespread: heart rate and breathing both slow down, temperature falls by about ½° F., the blood pressure becomes lower, the kidneys almost stop secreting urine. The electrical waves passing through the brain alter, but do not cease, and unexpectedly, the blood supply to it is not diminished. The hands become colder but the feet warmer in sleep, and the sweat glands are more active. It is marvelous, mysterious, and something we are miserable about when it goes wrong.

Insomnia may be inability to get off to sleep, early waking, broken or restless sleep. It is the price of human intelligence. Animals, idiots, and new born babies have no sleep problems.

Identification: Effects of too little sleep: irritability or plain bad temper. Animals become vicious if deprived of sleep, and just as hunger makes a dieter cross and difficult to live with, so does lack of sleep make the sleepless one. Children become particularly unreasonable when sleepy. Efficiency at work (Medical Research Council Report, Britain, 1965) however, is *not* impaired unless a complete night's sleep is lost. Dull, unstimulating work is most likely to suffer.

Hallucinations: seeing, hearing, or feeling what exists only in the mind, so vividly that you behave as though it were real, can occur after prolonged lack of sleep.

Causes of Insomnia
Physical
Pain.

Fever.

Pregnancy.

Difficulty in breathing which starts on lying down, as in heart disorder and lung troubles.

(See Chest Section.)

Full bladder, particularly in men past middle age, is the commonest cause of broken sleep.

Arteriosclerosis: typically causes early waking.

Old age: there is a normal falling off in the hours of sleep, to around 5.

Menopause.

Discomfort from cold, wind in the abdomen, itching, overfull stomach, etc.

Children: Babies: colic, hunger, ear or other infection. Older: cold in the nose, indigestion, perhaps.

Rare: "Sleepy sickness," lethargy by day, wakefulness at night.

Psychological

Far commoner.

Forerunner of nervous breakdown; whether cause or effect, it often is part of the process. The triad of anxiety, social isolation, and sleeplessness could mean trouble. Advice from doctor should be sought.

Depression: Typically the sleep fault is early morning or middle of the night waking.

Anxiety: Typically the difficulty is in getting off to sleep.

Bad habits: Worrying and preoccupation with the affairs of the day; exciting television, radio, or book at bedtime; quarrels (usually due to tiredness anyway); tea or coffee in late evening; too full or too empty a stomach; over-use of tobacco; noisy, airless, or over-heated bedroom.

Change in routine: Of all the causes of poor sleep, *anxiety* comes top, either severe to the point of psychological illness, or common or garden worrying. Even worry lest you do not get off to sleep can build an endless chain of anxiety: no sleep; anxiety; therefore no sleep.

Treatment: See doctor to eliminate physical disorders. Breathing difficulty at night may be relieved by propping yourself up with 4 or 5 pillows, or it may be an allergy situation, in which case getting rid of feather pillows may help. Some forms of foot and leg pain are better if the feet hang down over the edge of the bed. Severe psychological disorders (e.g. a feeling of anxiety that you cannot account for) also need a doctor's skill and care.

COMMON INSOMNIA

Start tackling it in the day, by getting a modicum of fresh air and enough exercise to feel muscle tired by evening.

Get your interpersonal relations tranquil by sundown.

Do not wait to go to bed until you are already too tired, but on the other hand do not expect early sleep if you have been snoozing in the day.

Stop worrying, especially about losing your sleep. Insomnia does not do nearly as much harm as anxiety, and you do not have to be asleep to be at rest. Do not feel that you necessarily need the same amount of sleep as, say, your spouse. People vary. Some find 4 or 5 hours enough. They have developed to a high degree the power of *micro sleeping:* taking short naps during gaps of activity, e.g. traveling, even waiting at the telephone, in the day. You may be one of the fortunate ones, usually intellectual, who need only a few hours of sleep. You will, anyway, need a steadily diminishing period from adolescence onwards.

Train your mind and body to accept the idea of sleep at the right time. Cultivate regularity and a leisurely bedtime ritual, preferably an enjoyable one, so that you are not anxious to get it over and done. Women usually sleep better than men because of bedtime beauty routines, whereas the male equivalent, shaving, is a morning affair.

A warm drink and a cracker, a hot bath, tooth brushing, 15 minutes' music, or reading something mild are all suitable steps to lead you to the brink of sleep.

When you are in bed, remember that now, at least, there is no hurry. Let your mind range over things objectively; places, books, gardens, golf courses, pictures, perhaps people, but *not* yourself or your problems. A thermos flask, a light snack, and a non-stimulating book can wait to be your companions should you wake before you need to get up.

Sleeping pills: If necessary, your doctor will prescribe them. They are nothing to be ashamed of, and taking them as directed will do you no harm, or far less than the unhappiness of tossing wakeful in a sleeping world, night after night. Often the use of pills temporarily (weeks or months) may be sufficient to re-educate your mind and body to the habit, so that you can manage without them in due course. Sleeping pills are also valuable in short-lived conditions such as a painful illness, or a passing excitement, anxiety, or grief.

Sleepwalking   [A: N]
Medical name: Somnambulism

A symptom of anxiety or excitement commonest in children, but similarly caused in adults. Talking in sleep is also a sign of being disturbed. (See Sleep problems in Children's Section.)

Multiple Sclerosis

A disease of the nervous system in which the fatty sheath (myelin) present on many nerves disappears. The exact cause is unknown, although suspicion has been cast variously on allergy, viruses, and abnormal blood clotting.

The disease is most common between the ages of 20 and 40, and is slightly more common in women than in men.

The symptoms will be manifest in whichever part of the nervous system is attacked; very likely, an initial attack will clear spontaneously, not to reappear for weeks, months, or years. The onset of the disease may be with sudden blindness, which will clear, or sudden weakness on one side of the body. There may be numbing or tingling sensations in addition to weakness, or even speech disturbances.

Treatment: Physiotherapy and rehabilitative methods are helpful. Specific treatment at present is controversial, including the use of cortisone or anticoagulants.

Muscular Rheumatism, Myalgia, Fibrositis,
"Cold in the Muscles"   [A: 48, An, 1; Ch: S, An]

Very often, painful movements in those over 50 are blamed on the joints, but are actually due to the muscles and ligaments. The trouble often follows getting cold and wet, or some unaccustomed activity.

Identification: Pain, stiffness, and limitation of movement.

In the back it is called lumbago; in the rib muscles which move with breathing, pleurodynia; in the neck, torticollis; but it can be in any part. Health in general unaffected. No fever.

Treatment: Hot water bottles, massage, aspirin, or, if severe, injections and physiotherapy.

Outlook and prevention: Avoid drafts, damp clothes, and exertion you are not used to. Nothing to worry about: your grandparents had this trouble, too.

Osteoarthritis, Osteoarthrosis [Ch: S]

A wear and tear process that happens to everyone over 50, but often causing little or no inconvenience. The gristle lining the joints becomes thin, and the bone round the edges grows knobbly: the knobs may get in the way.

Joints that have been injured, maybe long ago, or have had to work especially hard because of their owner's occupation, or have to carry around an extra heavy body are particularly vulnerable.

Identification: Stiffness; limitation of movement of joint or joints, usually the hip, knee, thumb, or back or the big toe if that is already in a bad position. There may be hard lumps at the joints, particularly the joints of the fingers. Pain is very variable, and by no means always present. When it is, it is worse in damp and cold weather than warm, and can be a nuisance in the night.

A grating noise may accompany movement.

The general health is unaffected.

Treatment: Surgery may be resorted to in some severe cases, for instance to reline the hip joint. Adjusting the alignment may even stimulate the joint to grow a new lining for itself. Sometimes injection into a joint helps. For most, however, *medicines* are used to relieve the pain, and a course of *physiotherapy*. Home *heat* treatment may be done by warming a dish of sand in the oven and then putting the hands in it. Heated paraffin wax may be used similarly but is more dangerous.

Padding the knees with cotton may prevent pain in the night from their being bumped.

If knee or ankle joints are affected, *reduce* any overweight: give them a fair chance!

To *keep moving* is more beneficial than rest.

Osteoarthritis of the Spine [Ch: S]

This may cause lumbago, or sciatica, pain down the leg, from pressure by the bony knobs on the nerves.

Similarly stiff, painful neck, bending forwards, may be accompanied by pain down the arms.

Treatment: Surgery sometimes necessary.

Pains All Over: Limbs and Back

ACUTE

Infections such as: feverish cold, influenza, tonsillitis, pneumonia, measles, etc.

Muscle overstrain, from gardening, etc.

Rheumatic fever.

Tropical fevers such as malaria.

Hysteria, psychological causes.

CHRONIC

Anemia.

Arthritis: osteoarthritis, rheumatoid arthritis.

Gout.

Muscle.

Cancer.

Bronchitis.

Kidney disorders.

Sugar Diabetes, Diabetes Mellitus [Ch: S, X]

The chemical activities of the complex electrochemical concern which is the human body are controlled by minute quantities of substances called hormones in the blood. The butterfly-shaped thyroid gland, for instance, which hugs the windpipe, produces thyroxine, and this directs the rate at which the body processes shall work. The *pancreas,* a soft, pinkish slip of tissue lying in a bend of the intestine, produces *insulin.* Insulin is the chemical controller of the sugar in the blood, a vital nutrient in the right quantities, but a menace in excess. If there is too much sugar circulating, the surplus is normally stored in the liver as glycogen, ready to be remobilized when there is need.

In diabetes there are several disturbances, but the most striking is that the pancreas fails to produce adequate insulin, and the blood sugar rises out of control. Some of the excess spills over into the urine, and physicians 2,000 and 3,000 years ago observed the sweetness of the water of those suffering this malady. Nowadays we estimate the blood sugar level as well as test the urine for sugar: equally easily by dipping a chemically treated sliver into blood or urine, and observing the color change. These tests are of immense value in detecting the disorder and assessing efficacy of treatment.

Age: Rare before five. Particularly common from 40–60 in the overweight.

Sex: Even, except in the fat and middle-aged group, where women predominate.

Heredity: Other members of the family are or have been diabetic in 50% of cases. Jews and East Indians are especially susceptible.

Food habits: Overindulgence in carbohydrates (bread, cakes, potatoes) often starts off the trouble in a predisposed person.

Identification

Mild type of middle age: Gradual onset, usually in a plump person, who has recently had a noticeable increase in weight; itching of the area around the urinary outlet; recurrent infected spots; ulcers on the feet; cramps and nerve pains in the limbs; blurred vision. There may or may not be excessive thirstiness and loss of weight in this group of diabetics.

Sometimes extra hair appears on the (female) face.

Severe type of young people: May come on rapidly, even suddenly. Thirst; large quantities of pale, dilute urine; loss of weight and weakness, despite big appetite and good digestion; constipation; recurrent boils; dry skin with eczematous patches; sore, red, dry tongue; itching near urinary outlet; premature furring of the arteries, causing leg and foot pains at night; blurred vision. Periods may be disturbed or absent in women, potency impaired in men. Pins-and-needles and tingling may occur in the limbs.

Urinary sugar and blood sugar estimations made by doctor make the diagnosis certain.

Treatment

Mild type: Diet alone suffices to control the condition.

Moderate type: Diet in combination with sulphonamide derivative tablets, which stimulate the poorly acting pancreas.

Severe cases: Insulin, to replace what is not being manufactured by the body. The dose needs to be carefully adjusted to the individual, and there are various types of insulin preparations which suit different people.

Periodic checks of the blood sugar, condition of the eyes and arteries, and weight, are made, and the chest X-rayed, since diabetics are extra-susceptible to chest complaints, including tuberculosis.

COMA: A condition of increasing unconsciousness, from which the patient cannot be roused. Two types can occur in diabetics, and it is often a matter of life and death to distinguish between them.

Diabetic Coma

Mainly in the younger diabetics, when they have been slack in taking their insulin, or need more *because of an infection* such as gastroenteritis, influenza, tonsillitis, or boils. It occurs when not only the sugar control but the management of the fats in the body goes awry.

Early indications: loss of appetite, nausea, abdominal discomfort; furred tongue; drowsiness or giddiness. Later: slow, deep breathing, sweet-smelling breath, flushed face, dry skin, the body lacks fluid; unconsciousness.

URGENT: Doctor, insulin, and probably penicillin.

Sugar-lack Coma (Insulin shock)

Medical name: Hypoglycemia.

Occurs if the dose of insulin is too big, or the intake of carbohydrate too small, or vigorous exercise has used up too much. Rapid onset, always, but there is usually time to take a sweetened drink before there is complete unconsciousness.

Early indications: sweating, palpitation; trembling; restlessness; excitability; intense hunger, or a "sinking feeling." Later: confusion; unsteady walk; pins-and-needles or tingling of tongue and lips; drowsiness; convulsions. Headache and nausea may also occur with certain types of insulin.

URGENT: Sugar lump or candy or sugary drink, doctor.

Outlook: A treated diabetic nowadays can live a normal life, for the normal span, and have children. He or she cannot, however, expect ever to be able to relax vigilance, for although treatment is specific, there is as yet no cure.

Sweating, Excessive

Adolescence: there is normally a great increase in the development and activity of the sweat glands at this age, and an alteration in the odor of the sweat, which can be embarrassing. Daily bathing is important. Deodorants should be used and underwear changed daily.

Menopause: associated with hot flushes.

Nervousness.

Fever from any cause: usually causes relief as the temperature falls.

Overheating: especially overclothing in babies.

Thyroid gland disorder.

Rare Causes

    Tuberculosis.

    Rickets ⎫
            ⎬ in infants.
    Scurvy ⎭

Temperature of the Body

A temperature regulating center in the brain receives messages from the body and accordingly makes adjustments by opening or closing blood vessels in the skin, pouring out sweat or making the muscles produce heat by shivering, or if it is really hot, panting. It is remarkable that whether we live on the equator or in Lapland, our body temperature remains constant. It is not, however, spot-on 98.6°F. *Normal is within the range 97.2°–99.5°F.* in the mouth. Equivalent reading under the arm (allow five minutes) is 1° lower, and in the rectum 1° higher.

There is a daily variation of about 1°: The temperature is at its lowest around 4 A.M. and highest in the evening, after the day's main muscular activity and fuel intake. Young babies and old people tend to run at a slightly higher temperature than others, and their regulator is especially sensitive, so that a bout of crying may raise a baby's temperature noticeably, and an old person's body temperature may fall in freezing weather.

RAISED TEMPERATURE, FEVER

    100°F.: slight.

    102°F.: moderate.

    104°F.: high.

Fever is a defense mechanism; hence a large group of infectious illnesses are called fevers. Fever can also occur if the temperature regulating mechanism in the brain is disturbed, as in sunstroke. *Symptoms which may accompany fever:* Chilly sensation; shivering; feeling boiling hot, usually dry, maybe sweating; headache; restlessness; pains all over; no appetite; feeling ill; weakness; furred tongue; constipation; highly colored urine; confusion of thought and speech; delirium, convulsions, or vomiting in children.

Causes of Fever:

Common: Colds, influenza, tonsillitis, sore throat, bronchitis, sinusitis, gastroenteritis, excitement and crying in young children, ear infection, or pyelitis (kidney infection), usually in children.

Most other causes of fever have other more pressing manifestations, but the following are some of the conditions which may start with no other obvious sign or symptom:

Fevers with a rash: In the first four days usually, but may be delayed a week especially in measles, and more in typhoid. In these two fevers also, the onset is gradual, taking 2–3 days to creep up, whereas it is sudden in most. Chicken pox, scarlet fever, German measles, erysipelas, typhoid fever.

Fevers without a rash, continuous (i.e. remaining high throughout the day): influenza; rheumatic fever; pneumonia; whooping cough; mumps; mononucleosis; diphtheria; poliomyelitis; sunstroke; gout; rheumatoid arthritis.

Fevers which rise and fall: Abcess anywhere in the body; blood poisoning; malaria; typhoid.

Prolonged fevers: Often due to a pocket of infection in, for instance, tonsils, glands of neck, boil, sinus, appendix, prostate gland, colon, breast during breast-feeding period, teeth, kidney, heart. Liver disorders; cancer; tuberculosis.

Many of these are uncommon and can be discovered only after careful investigation by your doctor.

Treatment

According to cause: get doctor's instructions. Bed rest and light diet.

SUBNORMAL TEMPERATURE

Medical name: Hypothermia.

That is, 97°F. or below. It is usually discovered by chance; the temperature has generally not been taken because of the patient feeling ill. He may look or feel cold, but not necessarily.

Chronic Causes

Convalescence, especially after illnesses in which there has been high fever, such as pneumonia. Temporary overcompensation.

Chronic illnesses in which there is inefficient oxygen supply to the tissues, such as heart disorders, kidney disorders, diabetes, underactivity of the thyroid, arteriosclerosis.

Residence in the tropics: On returning home after years in a hot climate, the temperature may be found to be running at around 96°F. or less, with normal health.

Lower vitality in old age and privation.

Long illness such as cancer.

Acute Causes

Shock, from injury, especially burns.

Collapse, from loss of fluid by bleeding, vomiting, or diarrhea. The bleeding may be internal.

Exposure or *immersion* in icy cold water. Fat people and women survive these accidents best.

Newborn babies are particularly susceptible to cold; a day and night temperature of 65°F. is required for a young baby.

Poisons such as opium, phenol, phosphorous, alcohol in doses large enough to produce coma.

Raised pressure inside the skull, from hemorrhage, including a form of stroke, abscess, or tumor.

Treatment

An injured person who may be suffering from shock, or one who has collapsed, urgently needs to be kept warm with blankets, and given hot tea if able to swallow, but hot water bottles need using with care; they can cause burns on a semiconscious person.

Warming a person who has suffered exposure must be very gradual, possibly in the hospital.

Cold in itself does little harm to the tissues; blood for transfusion purposes and corneas for eye operations are stored under refrigeration, also sperm for artificial insemination in animals. But *low temperature surgery* is the most remarkable use of cold. The patient's temperature is lowered to 32°F. for heart operations, including those on the coronary arteries. From an appearance as of death, the patient recovers rapidly and dramatically and may be complaining of feeling cold before he leaves the operating room.

Tremor, Trembling
Causes
Normal: After prolonged or violent muscular exercise, a fine movement that becomes noticeable only when you attempt to use a limb.

Fear, excitement, nervousness. Cold.

Parkinson's disease: Characteristic coarse tremor of the hands as though feeling the texture of a material or rolling a pill. At the same time it may be noticed that the writing has become smaller, and few movements are made. This tremor diminishes when the hand is being used.

Intention tremor: The trembling comes when the person starts to do something, unlike the Parkinsonian tremor. Usually due to a disorder of or damage to the nerves.

Senile tremor: Finer than the Parkinsonian type, but in a similar age range. Annoying, but not indicating any ill health.

Thyroid gland disorder: Sweating, nervousness, loss of weight also likely. Fine tremor.

Hysteria: Variable and grotesque.

Familial tremor: Runs in the family and comes on at puberty. Sometimes severe, but seldom disables the person.

Tics, Habit spasms, St. Vitus' dance (*Chorea*): All these are involuntary jerky movements, but not true tremors because not regularly repeated.

Venereal Diseases
Those infections transmitted by sexual intercourse. Syphilis and gonorrhea are the two main disorders of this type, and they are both seriously on the increase. In some countries their incidence has already reached epidemic proportions; young people in big cities and immigrant populations are particularly affected.

SYPHILIS   [A Ch: S, C, 6, X]

Almost always contracted during sexual intercourse, except when transmitted from mother to baby.

In the 16th and 17th centuries, Europe was ravaged by epidemics: the French disease, as the English called it; the Neapolitan disease, according to the French. The infection was thought to have been brought to Europe from the New World by Columbus. Time has changed its character from a savage killer to a deceptively mild disorder, which advances, if untreated, in silence through its three stages.

Identification

First stage: A single, painless sore appears three or four weeks after intercourse with an infected person, usually on the penis, or the entrance to the vagina or inside it, but sometimes on lip, nipple, anus, or finger. The chancre gradually becomes an oozing ulcer with a hard red surrounding, and the glands in the groin may become painlessly enlarged.

Second stage: A month or two later, a mild general illness, with sore throat, sometimes "snail-track" ulcers in the mouth, headache, mild fever, pink non-itchy rash. Voice may become husky, because of laryngitis.

Third stage: Four years or more after. Any organ may be affected, but the arteries, brain, and nerves are commonly and vitally attacked. This stage is nowadays rare.

Treatment

The earlier it is started, the better the outlook. Penicillin usually clears the body of the infection in a few weeks, but two years of periodic checks are necessary before a patient can be pronounced cured. Tests of the blood serum and of the fluid surrounding the brain and spinal cord help in diagnosis and assessment.

CONGENITAL SYPHILIS   [Ch: S, X]

One of the most easily prevented of diseases, and for this reason expectant mothers often have a blood test of unrecognized syphilis.

Sallow, underweight, snuffling syphilitic infants are rare today. Treated with penicillin.

GONORRHEA   [A: S, C, 6/12]

Known familiarly by other names: the clap, etc. This venereal disease is causing public health authorities anxiety, since not only is it on the increase, but the responsible organism, the gonococcus, has a propensity for acquiring a resistance to our medical weapons, first sulpha drugs, then penicillin and streptomycin.

Identification: Three to ten days after infection there is a scalding on passing water, and then a discharge of pus from urinary outlet and vagina. If untreated the discharge becomes less profuse, but appears on and off: the "gleet."

Treatment: Penicillin from choice. If this is not effective the tetracyclines, erythromycin, and newer penicillins can be tried. Checks must be made at monthly intervals for six months, and also a test for syphilis, which may have been contracted simultaneously.

Outlook: It is important to have this illness adequately treated, not only for the sake of others who may be infected, but because of the complication of untreated gonorrhea, e.g. inflammation of the prostate gland in men, or the tubes in women (a cause of sterility); arthritis; inflammation of the heel; infection of the eyes.

Women, in particular, may neglect a slight gonococcal discharge and remain a source of danger to themselves, their sexual partners, and their babies. The gonococcus goes for the eyes of the baby as it is being born.

SOFT SORE, CHANCROID   [A: S, C, 2]

Identification: Five days incubation, then a blister appears in the genital area, which becomes a pustule, then breaks down into a ragged ulcer. It is painful, tender, and bleeds easily. Several other ulcers may arise by infection from the original one, all in the genital region.

Swelling of glands in the groin occurs within a week, the skin over is red and tender.

Treatment: Sulphadiazine or streptomycin for a week. Bathe the ulcers with salt or potassium permanganate solution.

Outlook: No after effects. No chronic stage.

Special Sections

CHILDREN'S SECTION

Childhood is not a disease, but it is a very different condition from adulthood. An adult who slept as much as a baby would be suspected of having encephalitis lethargica, or some dread disorder of the heart if his pulse rate approached that of a 2-year-old. Some conditions, such as eczema, have special characteristics in infancy; some, for instance rickets or croup, are barely known outside childhood; some, such as osteoarthritis, do not attack children at all.

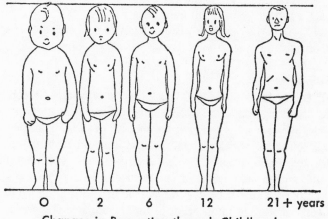

| 0 | 2 | 6 | 12 | 21 + years |

Changes in Proportion through Childhood

First Year

FEEDING DIFFICULTIES

Hiccups
Normal in a young baby after a good feeding. Do nothing.

Wind

All babies swallow some air with their foods. This is minimized and comes up most easily if baby is nursed as nearly upright as possible, African style, or lying on top of his mother (more difficult with a bottle). The baby should be held against the shoulder and his back gently rubbed halfway through and at the end of his feeding to allow the wind to escape.

Excessive flow of milk in a breast-fed baby should be controlled by two fingers, above and below the nipple; on the other hand, baby should not be allowed to suck after he has obtained all the milk.

In bottle-fed babies, usually the nipple is too small, and that causes baby to suck air. Before each feeding it should be tested; the milk should drip rapidly out if the bottle is held vertically. Do not, of course, hold the bottle horizontally while feeding, or baby will get a mixture of air and milk from it.

Prolonged crying, from any cause, leads to air being gulped into the stomach.

Vomiting

All babies bring some milk back, active wiry types the most. Some comes up with excessive wind (see above); some flows out because baby's head is too low; see that his head is slightly higher than his feet after meals. Some babies bring up their food as a pleasurable habit; usually they are bottle-feeders, and thickening the milk with a teaspoonful of cereal checks the trouble.

Vomiting will never be due to breast milk's not suiting the baby, and very rarely due to an artificial food (properly prepared) not suiting him.

Unexplained vomiting in a baby that has not vomited before, to any extent, may be due to an infection coming on. If a baby suddenly starts bringing up a whole meal at once, report it to the doctor immediately.

Insatiable Appetite

Baby apparently hungry after big meals, say 8 oz.: start weaning to solid food and/or supplements by cup and spoon.

Poor Weight Gain

(Less than 4 oz. per week.)

If baby is happy, lively, sleeps well, and looks well, there is no need to keep weighing him. If he seems dissatisfied and is perhaps constipated, check that he is putting on at least 6 oz. a week (after the first).

Reasons for Inadequate Gains

Insufficient food. Offer more, thicken milk, start weaning to solids. In a very small baby, under 3 months, increase the number of feedings.

Too much of the food brought up: see Vomiting, above.

Excessive sweating: fewer clothes and covers needed.

Loose stools: see Diarrhea below.

Loneliness: young babies, some more than others, need their mother's company and interest to make life and feeding seem worthwhile.

An infection: a cold?

Overfeeding: Too Fat

There is no such thing in the first three months; after that, a very fat baby should be weaned to purées, etc., rather than cereal.

Constipation

Irregularity is not constipation—only inconvenient. Breast-fed babies can go 2 or 3 days without having a movement, and still, since the movement is soft, not be constipated. No treatment.

Hard or infrequent movements in bottle-fed babies call for changing to brown sugar in the formula, adding an extra teaspoonful to each feeding, and if necessary giving up to 4 teaspoonfuls of prune juice or purée daily.

In the weaning, set up the fruit and vegetable, prunes also. Constipation is less common at this age.

Diarrhea

Breast-fed: Unlikely to be true diarrhea unless there is loss of weight and baby looks ill.

Soft, loose stools, as many as 5–6 a day, sometimes expelled with explosive force, and in the first 2 months sometimes green or containing visible curds, are *normal.*

Orange juice occasionally causes diarrhea: in this case use ascorbic acid tablets instead.

Bottle-fed: Sudden diarrhea in a baby whose movements have been normal before, particularly if they are now green, loose, and offensive, suggests gastroenteritis.   [A: S]

Treatment: Send for doctor promptly. Meanwhile stop milk, etc., and substitute of this mixture:

>   warm boiled water—1 pint.
>   sugar or glucose—1 level tablespoonful.
>   salt—¼ teaspoonful.

Give him a few ounces every 2 or 3 hours if he wants it: he may be thirsty. Doctor will advise from here. *Insidious onset* [S] may mean dietetic errors, usually too much sugar or fat in the formula, but occasionally due to orange juice or vegetables and fruit.

Doctor's advice necessary, since diarrhea causes rapid loss of weight. *Associated with disorder elsewhere* [S], e.g. ear trouble, cold, other infection coming on.

During an attack of diarrhea, the skin around the rectum needs protection with a diaper cream.

Refusal of Food: Weaning Difficulty

Causes

Starting too late. Best to begin at three months, and have baby accustomed to cup and spoon as well as bottle or breast by 6 months.

Overkeen, overanxious mother. Babies do not feel hungry if they are pressed. Be nonchalant.

Dislike of food offered. Try something else.

Too hot. Lukewarm is preferred.

Thirsty. Offer a drink first (water).

Too tired. Let him have a sleep instead.

Uncomfortable. Check diaper, etc.

Too bored. Let him help himself. Clean up later.

Not so hungry. Let baby's own appetite determine the amount: it normally becomes less towards the end of the first year.

He may be ill, or have a sore gum from teething.

Reluctance to Give up Bottle

Weaning should be begun early and be a gradual process.

Varying aspects of the problem of the baby who clings to the bottle:

(1) A bedtime bottle is a harmless pleasure and comfort. Let baby go on with it until he wants to give it up. Make his other meals as interesting as possible.

(2) Too much milk is bad nutritionally after 9 months, so if he fusses for a bottle every meal, give water, not milk, or progressively smaller amounts, so that his appetite is not satisfied by bottle alone.

(3) What he really wants is love and babying: give him plenty.

Three Months' Colic, Evening Colic [Ch: S, 6–6/12]

Identification: Attacks of crying lasting 2–20 minutes, then starting up again, usually from around 6 till 10 or 11 P.M., commonly starting at around 3 months, but sometimes when baby is only a few weeks old.

Cause: Much doubt.

Treatment: Two are suggested:

(1) Give baby more and smaller feedings for a while, say twice as many, half the volume, working back to normal. The idea is that some babies' digestive apparatus cannot cope with the 3-month size quantities given 4-hourly.

(2) Dicyclamine hydrochloride: 1 teaspoonful at 5:30, from doctor.

Outlook: He will outgrow it in a month or two anyway.

CRYING

Five or ten minutes fussing several times a day is normal, good exercise, since baby puts everything, arms and legs included, into it, and nothing to worry over. More than this is intolerable to you and your household and bad for baby, since crying makes him gulp in air and distend his stomach, and may make him sick, and the psychological effect of long periods of unhappiness in babyhood may be far-reaching.

Causes and Management

Hunger: Not enough milk? If he cries shortly after a feeding and the bottle is empty, offer more: always enough for there to be some left over.

If breast fed, have a test-weighing.

Withholding night feeding in the first 8–10 weeks. Some babies need it.

Feeding schedule too rigid.

Weaning to more solid foods needs starting or stepping up.

Note: Feed baby if he cries from hunger, but do not let him panic you. It will do him no harm to wait at least as long as a diner who has ordered a soufflé in a first-class restaurant.

Thirst: Especially in hot weather, or if he has been sick recently.

Wind: This is not a universal reason for crying, and is unlikely to be the cause more than 15 minutes after a feeding. However, any baby crying for long swallows air, which may come up. Lay baby face down on your knee or against your shoulder; rub his back.

Discomfort: Too hot; too cold; diaper wet or soiled: check and change. Many babies cry while evacuating, perhaps useful to raise the abdominal pressure.

Sun in the eyes: It may creep around the carriage without your realizing.

Three months' colic, evening colic (above).

Boredom
Loneliness } from 3 months on.

Try: A change of scene, particularly bringing him where he can see, hear, and feel your companionship; cuddling, rocking, carrying around on your shoulder; talking or singing to him; toys.

Tired and struggling against sleep. Make him comfortable, draw the curtains. Leave him in peace for 15 minutes.

Fright: Sudden noise; insecurely held; after 6 months, the sight of strangers.

Mother feeling tense: Baby catches mother's emotions. Get someone to take over for an hour or two, while you restore your serenity.

Pain, e.g., tooth, ear ⎤ Sharp or persistent crying that is
Illness   ⎬ not abated by picking baby up.
He has vomited   ⎦ Inform doctor.

Babies do not cry without reason—but some cry more for less!

SLEEPING PROBLEMS

Average requirements:

> 0–6 months 12–22 hours
> 6 months 18 hours
> 12 months 14–16 hours
> Wide individual variation

Difficulties

Crying on being left to go to sleep: the "testing cry." Leave baby alone for 15 minutes: he will have gone to sleep if it was that type of cry.

Blocked nose: Clear out with cotton. Do not put him on his back to sleep. Discomforts, such as gas, pain, and wet diaper, and all the reasons for crying (above) which apply equally to wakefulness. Cold can be avoided by using a sleeping bag, and hunger dealt with by a feeding at the time, and extra cereal in the evening feeding for another night. Baby aspirin tablet will help a child in pain from teething, etc.

Disturbed: Young babies are never awakened by noises to which they are accustomed, but sharing the parents' room may be disturbing. A separate room is desirable by 6 months.

Standing up instead of lying down in his cot: Let him wear a sleeping bag; let him stand up until sleep catches him. Covers on later.

Waking and crying sharply: Nightmare! Comfort him. Vomiting: check for this, clean him up if necessary, and put him back to sleep on his side.

Movement passed: check for this and change him if necessary.

Early waking: Feed a small baby; leave toys at hand for older infant.

Bad habit: Start and keep to a reasonable sleep routine, with a peaceful time just before bed.

Note: A happy day with fresh air, exercise, loving to look back on, and a warm bath in the evening help to induce sleep at night.

BABY'S SKIN

Babies' skin does not need constant or complicated care for health or beauty. It is a tough, adaptable coat designed to protect, not hamper, the possessor.

Three Conditions not to Worry over
Peeling
All babies' faces, hands, and feet peel in the first few weeks; some, particularly babies who were overdue, peel all over.
Treatment: Ignore.
Spots on the Face
Minute, white or yellowish spots, particularly on the nose: they are glands that have not opened up yet. Normal.
Treatment: Ignore.
Occasional acne-like spots, so-called *"milk rash"* (there is no such condition) occur in all babies.
Treatment: Ignore; they will go away by themselves.
Mauve or blue lower parts of arms and legs.
   Normal for the newborn. Pink in a few days.
Treatment: Ignore unless it continues for more than a week, or the blueness affects other parts.
   Swelling and blueness of an arm that has got uncovered while baby is sleeping disappears in an hour or two, and does no harm (but see Cold injury).

Birthmarks, Nevi
"Stork Bites"
   Reddened patches on the skin of the forehead, upper lip, or back of head and neck. Very common.
Treatment: Ignore. Those on the face disappear in a few months; those at the back are hidden by hair.
Port Wine Mark
   Flat purple stains in same area as stork bites, and on the limbs. Do not disappear, but grow in proportion to the rest of the skin.
Treatment: Cosmetics disguise the marks well. Skin grafting gives good results in suitable cases.

Nothing to worry about for years yet, however.

Strawberry Marks

Soft, raised, red and rounded areas, sometimes bluish, appearing in the first few weeks, enlarging for a month or two, and then remaining the same until, in most cases, they gradually disappear. *Treatment:* Wait until child is 7 years old, by which time the mark will probably have disappeared.

Mole, Pigmented Nevus

Brown or black, flat or raised, sometimes hairy. Very common. *Treatment:* Surgical removal if disfiguring or in the way; otherwise no need for any.

Diaper Rash   [A: N or 2, S]

All babies have this sometime or other, and fair skins suffer most.

Causes

Warmth and wetness, only: Folds of the skin most affected. Plastic pants aggravate the condition. Infection can settle in, later. *Treatment:* Leave diaper area exposed whenever possible; leave off plastic pants anyway, and do not dress baby so that he is too hot. Powder thinly but thoroughly. If infected: Roccal lotion.

Acid bowel movements: Bubbly stools are often acid and are caused by too much fat or sugar in the diet. The area affected most is that in contact with the burning movement.

Treatment: Adjust diet. Petroleum jelly or zinc oxide paste.

Ammonia: The smell of it is most marked in the early morning. Areas most affected are those in contact with the urine.

Treatment: Frequent changing. Petroleum jelly or zinc oxide paste. Rinse diapers in water to which has been added sodium bicarbonate, 1 teaspoonful per pint. With ammoniacal urine rash, a diaper ointment and lotion, prescribed by doctor, are useful.

Prevention

Petroleum jelly applied three times a day, and no other particular care, prevents most diaper rash, but rinsing out of detergent or soap from diapers is a wise precaution.

Heat Rash   [A: 48]

Profuse, tiny, red raised spots, some with minute blisters, mainly on parts most heavily clothed, such as the trunk. The sweat pores become obstructed by the damp, hot, macerated skin.

Treatment: Fewer clothes and covers. Light dusting all over with talc.

Cotton, not wool, next the skin.

Disappears in a day or two.

Moist Skin Around the Navel [A: S]

If this area does not dry up when the stump of cord has separated, inform doctor, who will prescribe antiseptic powder or lotion. Do not put on a binder, which will only overheat baby.

Scaly Scalp, "Cradle Cap" [Ch: N, X]

Very common, especially over the fontanelle where mothers may not wash the scalp so vigorously.

Treatment: Daily washing of the scalp with shampoo containing salicylic acid. Soaking the scalp with olive oil overnight may help a resistant case.

Eczema [Ch: S; A: X]

A special reaction of the skin to internal or external irritation, in sensitive individuals.

Identification

In the first three months: redness and peeling only.

3 months to 2 years (the commonest time is 6 months to 2 years, when the teeth are coming through): closely set tiny blisters on a hot red skin, or tiny cracks oozing serum.

Site: Cheeks, forehead and scalp mainly; or bends of arms and legs and other folds mainly.

Much itching, so the child is fretful and scratches and may not sleep.

Causes: Basically a matter of constitution, but set off or made worse by:

Externally: On the face: food, dribbling, too much sun or wind; on the trunk and limbs: friction from scratchy clothing or covers, or inadequate rinsing out of detergents. Overheating.

Internally: Sensitivity to foods, such as egg white, egg yolk, fruit juices, milk proteins.

Treatment: Keep baby cool. Silk or cotton next the skin. Keep the fingernails short to prevent scratching. Avoid soap and water: use emulsifying ointment instead.

Dry eczema: no applications.

Wet and weeping: cream or lotion through doctor.

A sedative may be needed at night.

Take doctor's advice on diet, in case of sensitivity.

Outlook: Most cases improve by age 3, and all are easier to manage then. No scars are left, in fact the skin is likely to be particularly clear and soft.

Not an infection. Not contagious, so there is no need to restrict meetings with other children.

Asthma and hay fever, also allergic conditions, sometimes arise in children who have had eczema, especially the type in the folds, flexural eczema.

MISCELLANEOUS TROUBLES

Thumb-sucking [Ch: N]

All babies do some sucking apart from feeding times, some more than others; it may be hand, fingers, forearm, or a blanket that is sucked, but most commonly it is the thumb. It can even begin before birth, and is usually at its peak from 18 to 21 months. All direct attempts to check it (bitter substances, splints, gloves, nagging) are worse than useless.

But does it, after all, matter so much? What is the reason for it? It could mean hunger—but fat babies suck their thumbs, too —not enough sucking at eating time, boredom, or the need for comfort . . . Why not just for pleasure?

Management: Do nothing direct, but give him the chance for more food and longer sucking, go slow over weaning, and pile on the mothering; for the older baby, see that he has plenty of interest to do with his hands.

Rocking, Bumping, Head Banging [Ch: N, 6–6/12]

All these rhythmical activities are harmless. They commonly arise at about seven months and go on for two or three months, then less often until the child is about four.

Treatment: Ignore. However, since there could be an element of insecurity, be lavish in mothering. A baby who rocks his crib is best moved into a bed which is too big to rock around the room.

Similar habits which cannot and should not receive any treatment, because if ignored they will disappear: ear pulling, lip biting, tongue sucking, tooth grinding (this last can also occur in severely ill or defective children).

Masturbation in the first year is also in this category, although there may be some itching or irritation of the area.

Swollen Breasts

These may occur in boy or girl babies in the first few days, due to breast-stimulating substances that have passed from mother to baby in the blood before birth. Do nothing: the trouble subsides in a week or two.

Jaundice

A slightly yellow tinge to the skin is common in normal babies, but especially premature ones, in the first few days of life. It is due to the liver having not yet developed completely, and usually the color disappears in a few days, though it may last a week or two. No treatment necessary.

More severe jaundice, perhaps due to Rh incompatibility, should be reported to doctor.

Cross-Eye

Under the age of three months, all babies go cross-eyed from time to time, because they have not yet learned to focus. If, however, the turning in of the eyes is continuous, or goes on after four months, get advice.

Sneezing

Babies sneeze easily, often because a little dust or normal nasal discharge tickles the nose. It does not necessarily indicate a cold.

Snuffles

Many babies from two to twelve weeks have a clear discharge from the nose. If nothing else is amiss, it is not a cold, but merely an extra profuse secretion of mucus, the materials which cleanse and lubricate the nose. The nose naturally runs after crying, because there is a duct from eye to nose, inside.

Grunting and Snoring

Normal in a young baby, nothing to do with a cold or mucus. He has not yet learned to control his soft palate.

Bowleg

Under the age of two, most babies' legs show an outward curve and an inward twist at the lower end. This is an aftermath of the way the limbs are arranged to fit in the womb, and disappears gradually on walking.

Bulky diapers between the legs make the condition more noticeable.

Flat Feet

A fatty pad normally occupies the arch of the foot until the child is two or three years old, when it gradually disappears. In any case, flat feet rarely cause trouble in children, and should be ignored.

Flattening of Head

A flat, bald patch on the back or, less often, the side of the head comes usually from lying on that part a great deal, and gets better spontaneously when baby spends more time sitting up. There is no point in trying to make a baby give up sleeping in his favorite position, but in the first few weeks, he may be trained to sleep on his abdomen, and so avoid this effect.

Some babies are born with asymmetrical heads; these, too, usually cure themselves, and anyway cannot be helped.

Cold Injury [A: U]

Medical name: Hypothermia.

The dangers of chilling for new babies have been fully recognized only in the last few years.

Identification: Lethargy; unwillingness to suck; pink, swollen legs, feet, hands, and arms; skin very cold to touch; temperature below normal.

Treatment: A dangerous condition if not dealt with promptly, properly, and preferably in a hospital. Re-warming must be very gradual indeed.

Prevention: Day and night nursery temperatures in the first few weeks should be around 65°; 35° is the danger point.

Convulsions [A: U]

Identification: Eyes fixed or rolling upward; arms, legs, or whole body twitch convulsively.

Usually due to a high fever at the onset of an infection.

Treatment: Call doctor. Give baby a warm bath (104°F.), then put him to rest in warm, quiet, dark room, until the doctor comes.

Frightening to parents, but not fatal.

Rupture at Navel [Ch: N]

Medical name: Umbilical hernia.

Due to the incomplete closure of the place in the abdominal wall where the cord entered.

Identification: Lump, pea-sized to that of a big plum, at the navel, especially noticeable when baby cries.

Treatment: None necessary nor helpful. This condition corrects itself in time. There is no danger of strangulation with this rupture. Some pediatricians still like to put a belt round the abdomen.

Rupture in Groin [Ch: S]

Medical name: Inguinal hernia.

A minor error of development, much commoner in boys than girls.

Identification: A lump in the scrotum or groin, which is more noticeable when baby cries. May be one or both sides.

Treatment: Report to doctor. Early operation is usually recommended because of the possibility of a strangulated hernia.

Hydrocele

A collection of fluid in the scrotum which may accompany or be mistaken for a rupture. Usually gets better by itself: do nothing for a few years.

Common.

Circumcision

The cutting off of the foreskin that covers the head of the penis. Done for religious reasons among the Hebrews, but not now considered absolutely necessary or desirable otherwise, unless there has been inflammation of the area or the urinary flow is obstructed.

Normally the foreskin cannot be pulled back in a young baby because it has not developed fully; it is therefore better to leave it alone.

Red Urine

Commonly due to eating beets, red sweets or cough drops. A pink spot, especially on the diaper of a boy baby, is likely to be due to uric acid crystals in the urine making a minute scratch on their way out: no significance.

Blood in the urine is always a matter for the doctor. Moderate amounts give the urine a smoky appearance; it takes considerable bleeding to produce frankly bloodstained urine.   [A: S]

WHEN TO CALL THE DOCTOR FOR BABY

If a baby is happy, eating his food, gaining weight, and sleeping at night, all is well with him, and such trifles as losing his appetite for one meal, or vomiting once, crying for half-an-hour, or a slight snuffle should not worry you nor cause you to call the doctor.

You should, however, seek advice without hesitation—even if it turns out to be a matter of reassurance only—in the following circumstances:

Baby *behaving oddly:*

Listless.

Drowsy.

Irritable.

Baby *looking odd: Pale, blue, yellow.*

Convulsions.

Screaming and cannot be comforted—apparently in pain. Legs may be drawn up, fists clenched tight.

Diarrhea, more than several loose movements in an infant whose stools have previously been formed.

Vomiting, if persistent.
Soft spot in head sunken.
Cough.
Loss of appetite for more than one or two feedings.
Injury to head, if baby not normal and happy within 15 minutes.
Blood in urine, stools, or vomit.

IMMUNIZATION OF BABIES

Vaccination against smallpox works; diphtheria as a clinical problem no longer exists in Britain, Canada, or the U.S.; yet both these are killing diseases, as virulent as ever, present in the world today. Immunization is the foundation of the remarkable health of the nation and the safety of her children, and complacency and neglect can only lead to disaster.

The basic program of immunization is carried out in infancy.

RECOMMENDED TIMETABLE

Age Approximately	Immunization Against	Method
2 months	Diphtheria–Tetanus–Whooping Cough	Injection
3 months	Diphtheria–Tetanus–Whooping Cough	Injection
4 months	Diphtheria–Tetanus–Whooping Cough	Injection
2 months	Poliomyelitis	By mouth
3 months	Poliomyelitis	By mouth
4 months	Poliomyelitis	By mouth
15 months	Diphtheria–Tetanus–Whooping Cough	Injection
	Poliomyelitis	By mouth
16 months	Smallpox	Scratch
5 years	Diphtheria–Tetanus–Whooping Cough	Injection
	Poliomyelitis	By mouth

His immunization record should be kept for reference if the child is ill or injured.

Reasons to postpone or omit immunization:

Presence of an infection.

Eczema, other signs of allergy.

Recurrent chest infections.

Convulsions.

Measles: Live vaccine recommended.

Typhoid, etc.: For travelers abroad mainly.

Reactions to immunizing program:

Poliomyelitis—none.

Diphtheria–tetanus–whooping cough: Within three to four hours, passing off the next day: sore arm, crossness, fever, loss of appetite. High fever, headache, stiff neck, or rash should be reported to doctor.

Vaccination: 3rd to 10th days: soreness, itching, and slight swelling at the site, crossness, loss of appetite, and fever.

High fever, headache, stiff neck, rash, or marked swelling should be reported to doctor.

Ages 1–13

Runny Nose

A cold (below).

Early stages of an infectious fever. [48]

Allergy, including hay fever.

Discharge clear and watery. [S]

Sinus infection. [S]

Discharge thick and yellow, more long-lasting than the thick stage of a cold.

Something in the nostril.

Discharge thick and yellow, on one side only. [S]

Do not attempt to remove any foreign object yourself.

Mouth-Breathing   [Ch: N or S]

Obstruction: for instance a cold. Adenoids are not usually a cause of mouth-breathing, but are worth checking for.

Habit: often after having a cold, or run of colds.

Lips too small and/or teeth too projecting for mouth to be closed without continuous effort. Thumb sucking after 5 years may be a factor.

In infant: normally the upper lip is bowed upwards instead of being straight, until some time in the second year; in some this infantile shape persists.

Treatment: Eliminate physical difficulties such as protruding teeth or obstruction. Otherwise: *IGNORE.* Comment makes for unhappiness without improvement.

Children who mouth-breathe (except for genuine imbeciles with lolling tongues) are no less intelligent than nose-breathers, and need treating accordingly.

Enlarged Glands in the Neck   [Ch: S]

So common as to be almost the normal situation from 4–8 years, while school immunity is being built up.

Throat infection.

Infected place on scalp or skin.

Infectious mononucleosis.

German measles.

Tuberculosis. Now *rare.*

COUGHS, COLDS, AND COMMON RESPIRATORY INFECTIONS

Coughs and colds and their allies—sore throat, tonsillitis, earache, bronchitis, and wheeziness—are the plague of childhood and the despair of parents. The conscientious mother asks herself whether it is all her fault that the child succumbs to these troubles, if, for instance, there is something he lacks, or his diet is wrong, the tonsils to blame. Other people's children never seem to have as many colds, but their robustness is more apparent than real: we simply do not see them when they are indoors, snuffling.

It is to answer and allay these widespread parental anxieties that we shall spend time considering what are among the mildest disorders.

Coughs and Colds [A: N, I, W; Ch: N or S, W]

Identification: Running, snuffling, and blocked nose; cough; not feeling very well.

Measles [S]: Can start in a similar way, before the rash comes out, with runny nose, cough, sore eyes, and whininess. Has your child been in contact with a case?

Whooping cough [S]: May also start like a cold, with irritating cough but no whoop, and runny nose. Any contacts?

Allergic conditions [S]: Bouts of violent sneezing, and sore, red, and itching eyes should bring these to mind.

These three possibilities will become more obvious after 48 hours, and if you suspect them, then consult your doctor.

Treatment: Copious hot drinks, the luxury of one or two cough drops, and a restful time indoors for a day or two. This is the occasion to discourage lively pursuits and bring out boxed games and quiet, simple pastimes. Sympathy without pandering.

Antibiotics, cough syrups, nasal decongestants, and other medicines are seldom any help, and each has its dangers and disadvantages. Use them only if your doctor specifically advises it in your child's case.

Outlook: Most ordinary, acute colds get better in about 7 days. Some, however, drag on for weeks with runny, stuffed nose, and mouth-breathing or barking cough, especially at night. Medicines do not usually help this type either, but neither short-lived nor protracted colds cause lasting harm.

Management and Prevention

All children get colds, boys slightly more than girls, winter far more than summer. They occur to a certain extent in babies, but the peak in evidence is between the ages of 3 or 4 and 8, the earlier age applying to those with brothers and sisters at school. After 8, regardless of treatment or otherwise, there is a sudden, definite drop in the number of colds and this welcome change continues into, and through, adult life.

It is right and reasonable as a parent to expect, and accept as a nuisance, but normal, a run of colds in your child, lasting 2 or 3 years, around the time he starts social mixing and school. It is, however, a phase that will pass, and meanwhile it brings a benefit to the child: at the period when colds are most frequent, he is grappling with his first real contacts with the uncushioned world outside his home. A cold means staying safely close to mother for a few days and tasting again, temporarily, some of the comforts of being "babied."

Another aspect that may cause anxiety is that your child may look peaky and less fit than he used to. It is natural for a chubby, rosy toddler, outdoors so much of the day, to become drawn out into a skinny, comparatively pale, schoolchild: a normal, developmental stage.

What should be done for the child who has had a run of colds, to build up his strength and prevent, as far as possible, further troubles?

A sensible healthy regime will stand him in good stead throughout his childhood and be to his ultimate benefit, even if it has no specific effect on the nose and throat. Points include: a good mixed diet, with restriction of candy, cake, and cookies; regular rest and bedtimes; adequate sleep and outdoor exercise; stimulations and interests to avoid the depressing effects of boredom; well-ventilated quarters; and light, warm clothing, never more than three layers.

Measures that do not have any proven effect on frequency of, or resistance to, coughs and colds: mineral tonics, extra vitamins; ultraviolet lamps; antihistamine drugs; removal of tonsils, unless there has been recurrent frank tonsillitis. Isolation, except for very young babies, is not usually practicable nor sensible.

Tonsils and Adenoids

These are glandular structures concerned with the defense of the body against infection entering by nose or mouth. The tonsils can be seen at each side of the back of the throat, but the adenoids in the back spaces of the nose are invisible except with special instruments. Enlargement of the latter can cause obstruction to breathing, or block the tubes from the ear to the mouth.

Removal of the tonsils and adenoids is essentially an operation of Western civilization. Most of the operations are asked for by parents; it is important therefore to consider the justification.

Good reasons for removal of tonsils and adenoids:

Repeated attacks of tonsillitis, say 4 times in a year.

There is, however, a tendency for ordinary sore throats to become less frequent after the age of 8, and those in the other prevalent age group, 15–35, are seldom severe enough for tonsillectomy to be performed.

Repeated attacks of middle ear infection.

Persistent obstruction of the nose, definitely shown to be due to enlarged adenoids.

Inadequate reasons:

Enlarged tonsils: they can be perfectly healthy, and will become smaller by the time the child is 12.

Recurrent coughs and colds. There is equal improvement if the tonsils are not removed, after the age of 7 or 8.

"Adenoidal face": Mouth-breathing, vacant look, protruding teeth, and often also protruding shoulder-blades constitute a physical type, not connected with enlarged adenoids (nor are these children any less intelligent than others: some have an IQ well above average).

Acute Middle Ear Infection   [A: S, B, An, 1–6]

Medical name: Acute otitis media.

(See Ear Section.) Very common.

Additional Notes for Children

Identification: Earache, with or without a discharge, usually following or accompanying a cold or sore throat. Fever, from 99°–103°F. Sometimes there is vomiting or diarrhea at the onset, and no specific complaint of the ear; and on the other hand babies often rub or pull their ears without having any disorder in them.

Treatment: (See Ear Section: Otitis media).

Outlook: Pain usually better in 2–4 days, but the ear drum takes 7–14 days to return to normal (your doctor can examine it), if there has been no discharge, or about 21 days if there was some discharge.

In either case, usually there is complete recovery with no residual deafness or chronic inflammation.

Prevention: 75% of cases occur in those under 10, and the peak ages, 4, 5, and 6, correspond with those for coughs and colds. Similar management and parental outlook are needed.

Acute Sore Throat, including Tonsillitis   [A: S, IR, An, 1]

Very common, particularly from 4–8 years, and also from 15–35 years. Unlike coughs, colds, and earache, sore throats occur equally at all times of year.

Identification: Sore throat (red, swollen, and possibly with white spots on the tonsils), tongue furred. Abdominal pain, sometimes with vomiting or diarrhea, may accompany or replace pain in the throat. Fever usually 100°–102°F., but there is wide variation from feeling only slightly ill to high fever and misery.

Types

Streptococcal: There may be a rash of small red spots on face, trunk, and thighs, and a faintly sweet-smelling breath. This type of sore throat is important, as it can be associated with rheumatic fever and kidney disorders.

Virus type: Also common. Does not respond so well to penicillin.
Part of influenza, measles, etc.

Mononucleosis

Treatment: First two types: probably antibiotics through doctor. Aspirin, hot drinks, rest in bed or chair or sofa (depending on child's feelings), warm well-ventilated room.

Outlook: Comfortable in 48 hours, well within 5 or 6 days usually. Attacks may recur, or merge into a mild continuous *CHRONIC TONSILLITIS*. There is a natural enlargement of the tonsils from about 4 years which settles between 8 and 10 years, and at the same time a susceptibility to tonsillitis and sore throat subsides in most children.

Prevention: General health measures, as for coughs and colds (above).

See also Tonsils and Adenoids (above).

Headache
(See Head Section.)
Headache of convenience, typically connected with school.
Onset of feverish illness [S]: if associated with pain and stiffness in bending head forward, inform doctor immediately, because of the possibility of meningitis.
Migraine [S]: recurrent, associated with abdominal pain and vomiting. Children tend to outgrow this.

Anxiety.

Sinusitis (below).

Eyestrain is not now considered to be a factor.

Sinusitis   [A Ch: S]

Infection of the air cavities in the facial bones adjoining the nose, always involved to a certain degree, in a cold. The sinuses in the cheek bones, so troublesome in adults, do not develop until a child is 4 years old, and those in the forehead not until he is 6.

Acute sinusitis is not as common as *chronic sinusitis* in children, typically with *recurrent bronchitis* (sino-bronchitis).

Identification: Child keeps catching colds, and these go down on to the chest. Blocked or running nose. Cough brought on by changes in position, e.g. lying down, getting up, running.

Mucus and pus from the infected sinuses run down the back of the throat, setting up an irritation. Face ache and headache.

Treatment: Acute stages: as of coughs and colds or acute chest infections.

Chronic condition: general: extra good diet, extra rest, extra fresh air, avoidance of colds. Vacation, but no swimming. Cool bedroom.

Doctor may advise special treatment.

Croup   [A: S or U, l, 1]

The spread of a cold to the larynx, causing swelling of the vocal cords, plus a nervous spasm of the laryngeal muscles, combining to produce difficulty in breathing. Sometimes due to allergy.

Age: 6 months to 3 years most commonly.

Identification: Attack of noisy and difficult breathing, particularly on drawing breath in; shrill, barking cough; in severe case child may be struggling for breath, blue, and frightened.

Usually had only a mild cold, cough, and fever in the day or may have gone to bed apparently well.

Treatment: Sit him up; calm him down by singing, talking soothingly, reading a story; hot drink. Steaming kettle in the room. Warm room. (*Severe cases:* urgent call for doctor.)

Later: Treatment for infection as advised by doctor. For the next few nights have the child's bedroom especially warm, and keep a vaporizer at hand. Make the last meal of the day half-an-hour earlier than usual. Give an extra pillow.

Outlook: The attack of breathing difficulty is unlikely to last more than half-an-hour at a time, but there may be several bouts in one night, and the tendency to them is likely to go on for 2 or 3 nights.

The susceptibility to the infections that underlie croup diminishes around 7 years, but the croup reaction becomes less common after 5 years.

The Chesty Child

Frequent colds that always develop into a cough. This trouble is usually outgrown at 8 or 9 years. Meanwhile, it may be due to several causes, and needs appropriate management.

Ordinary cough and cold, the infection remaining in the upper air passages.

Wheezy chest.

Acute chest infection, bronchitis or pneumonia.

Sinusitis, sinobronchitis.

Croup.

Note:

Teething is not a cause of chest troubles, but the lowered resistance of a child in pain from erupting teeth may make him more susceptible to infection.

Acute Chest Infections   [A: S, 2]

Acute bronchitis, pneumonia: these two conditions overlap, the former comprising infection mainly in the tubes, the latter in the tissue of the lungs; both are important, both present the same picture of symptoms and signs, and they require the same care. Therefore we shall consider both forms of acute chest infection together, and leave to your doctor the precise diagnosis.

Nearly always following a cold or such infections as measles or whooping cough.

Age: Especially in the first year and from 4–8 years.

Sex: Boys very slightly predominate.

Identification: Short, hacking, painful cough, becoming looser and more comfortable with sputum. Flushed face; fever 100°–105°F.;

rapid breathing (nostrils may work with each breath); drowsiness; irritability. Wheezy sounds may be heard.

Treatment: Antibiotics usually, through doctor. Aspirin, dose according to age, at night. Cough medicine if prescribed.

General: Simple diet with plentiful fluids, warm room, and not more than two layers of blankets. In bed while child wants to be there, or couch or armchair otherwise.

Breathing exercises.

Outlook: Modern drugs have made these infections far less dangerous, though no less frequent than formerly. An acute attack usually lasts about a week, and the child is back to normal in a fortnight.

The tendency to these attacks becomes much less after age 8, but in some children there may be infection in the sinuses, causing recurrent bronchitis. This can be investigated and dealt with. (Chronic bronchitis is *rare* in childhood.)

Particular vigilance needed in babies with acute chest infections.

The Wheezy Child   [A: S, RI, 1; Ch: S, X]

Sensitive chest, asthma, bronchial asthma are labels variously applied to wheezing in the chest, a frequent symptom in childhood, and also in old people.

Wheezing in a child, so common that 20% of all 10-year-olds have had at least one bout of it, does *not* imply a lifelong illness, and so the term asthma is best not used; call it wheezy or sensitive chest instead.

What is a wheeze? The combination of whistling sounds made by the breath if the airways are temporarily narrowed by muscular spasm of their walls, swelling of the tube linings, mucus inside them, or glands pressing from the outside.

Identification of wheezy attack: Breathlessness with particular difficulty in breathing out; noisy breathing; tight feeling in the chest; cough; slight fever.

Wheeziness commonly follows a cold or other infection involving the nose and throat, but sometimes is preceded by a runny nose with a clear uninfected discharge.

Between acute attacks, which commonly last 2–3 days, the child will have a tendency to cough whenever he runs, and to wheeze

occasionally without a discernible cause being necessarily present.
Causes of Wheezing
Infection, as from a cold spreading downwards. Not all children
with colds wheeze, so other factors must also operate.
Heredity: A constitutional predisposition of the chest to react
this way.
Allergy: A condition of hypersensitiveness to certain materials,
usually proteins, definitely inherited. Asthma, eczema, hives, migraine, or food sensitivity in parents or other relatives makes the
allergic type of wheezy chest likelier, and it is common for a
wheezy child to have had *infantile eczema* earlier, and the signs
may still be visible in the flexures of his knees and elbows. Allergic
wheezers are those whose noses run a watery discharge which is
not a cold.
Emotion: Any upset: quarrel, parents' disagreement, reprimand,
or excitement before a trip or party; or longer-lasting stress, such
as worry over school work, jealousy of a new baby, parental in-
difference *or* oversolicitude, may bring on an attack. These children
are usually bright and intelligent, but given to introspection and
bottling up their feelings.
Treatment
Of attack: Common sense; warmth; quiet; rest, but not necessarily
in bed; medicines as prescribed, likely to be antispasmodics, antibiotics, and sedatives, as individually required.
Between times: Treat as normally as possible, erring on the side
of risk. Do not restrict outdoor play, school games, swimming,
camping. A slight wheeze, without fever, is no reason to keep him
away from school. These children need a great deal of love, but
not mollycoddling, overclothing, nor fussing. A calm, happy home
can help much.
Breathing exercises.
Prevention: Infections cannot be avoided, but some immunity
develops during the first 3 or 4 years at school. Nor can the hereditary tendencies be changed.

Emotional serenity can be cultivated: do not say which day, for
instance, the vacation trip is to start, nor quarrel in front of the
child. Try to iron out school difficulties if you can.

Special sensitivity can sometimes be pinpointed by skin tests (arranged through doctor), and you may observe for yourself that certain foods or circumstances initiate an attack. Many wheezy children are sensitive to house dust, animal hairs, feathers, or pollens. Their bedrooms are best uncluttered, with foam rubber pillow and mattress, no eiderdown, and chintz curtains.

Family pets should not be sacrificed because of the emotional upset, but they should not be replaced.

Outlook: Short term: individual attacks of wheeziness seldom last more than 3 or 4 days, but they may recur.

Long term: Good. Common wheeziness, as a reaction to infection, is usually outgrown by 11 or 12. The allergic type lasts longer, but is usually gone by 15 to 17 years, or very much less trouble.

The small minority whose wheezing attacks continue into adult asthma can be much helped by modern medicines.

Do not think of wheezing children in terms of cure, but of living through an awkward age.

TEETH: A PARENT'S RESPONSIBILITY

Milk teeth, 20.

Wide variation in when they come through. Very rarely, one is present at birth. Sometimes they do not start to arrive for 10 or 11 months. No need to worry unless none has appeared by the first birthday.

Permanent Teeth, 32.

Wisdom teeth: aged 17–22 years.

All others by 12 years.

Discoloration

Yellowish: a normal variation of color; inadequate brushing, especially after eating orange. Yellow in patches or lines, becoming brown, affecting milk teeth: tetracycline taken in early life, or by mother during pregnancy. No treatment.

Green milk teeth, following severe neonatal jaundice. No treatment.

Brown or dark lines or patches: decay. See below.

Decay, Dental Caries

Disturbingly prevalent.

Identification: Toothache, discoloration, pain on eating hot, cold, or sweet things, or nothing.

Treatment: By dentist. Extraction of milk teeth should be avoided, because it leads to overcrowding of the permanent teeth.

Prevention: Cleanliness, brushing at least twice daily, after every meal if possible. Use of florides—consult your dentist.

Restraint in candy and cookie eating; chocolate is least harmful, toffee the worst. Best time is at the end of a meal when there is plenty of saliva to wash away the remains. Finish meals with fruit if you can.

Have overcrowded teeth dealt with.

Have regular dental checks, say, twice a year.

Avoid sweetened pacifiers for babies.

Irregular Teeth, Protruding Teeth

Treatment: By dentist specializing in orthodontics.

Causes: Modern jaws too small; milk teeth staying in too long (another reason to visit dentist regularly), or extractions at an early age; congenital troubles.

Thumb sucking is rarely a cause of the teeth sticking out.

Injury

Immediate attention by dentist essential, even for a small chip.

Toothache

Probably due to decay. Dental treatment as soon as possible. Meanwhile, aspirin according to age; paint iodine or clove oil on gum, hot water bottle.

Sensitivity to heat, cold, and sugar: a forerunner of decay, due to damaged enamel. Dental treatment.

Teething

Not a cause of bronchitis, diarrhea, inflammation of the ear, colds, or fever.

Pain (including ear pain due to ear and teeth sharing the same nerve) and excessive dribbling can be directly due to teething.

Teething powders, jellies, or rings to chew should not be given, but baby aspirin may help at night.

SHOULDERS AND LIMBS

Round Shoulders
Causes
Fatigue: homework at the end of the day.
Illness, anemia.
Lack of self-confidence because of too much criticism or difficulties at school.
Self-consciously tall adolescent, especially a girl.
Lateral curvature of spine, an insidious fault in development, making one shoulder high and the shoulder blade prominent [S].
    Usually gives no trouble except for the appearance.
Near-sightedness or other error of refraction [S].
Bone diseases, such as rickets or tuberculosis. *Rare*. (See also Back Section: Round shoulders.)

Bow Leg and Knock-Knees
(See Lower Extremities Section.)
    Bow leg is normal up to 1 year but may be made more obvious by a thick bulk of diapers between the legs, after the child has begun to walk.
    By around 3 years the normal bowing has changed to a normal condition of knock-knees, i.e. more than 1 inch between the ankle bones if the knees are together. This disappears usually by 7 years, occasionally not until 9 years. Excessive bowing and knock-knees used to be due to soft bones caused by Vitamin D lack, *rickets*.
    Knock-knees persisting after 9 years of age, or causing leg pain, should be treated: shoes built up on inner edge, exercises, operation.

Joint Pains
Injury: one joint only affected.
Recurrent limb pains: muscles, not joints, hurt.
Rolling-in ankles, and slight flat foot cause leg pain.

Juvenile rheumatoid arthritis. Still's disease: sore throat, high fever, pale pink spots, painful swollen joints which persist.
Rheumatic fever (below).
Bone infection, osteomyelitis, may cause pain on moving joints.
Purpura: joint pains, swelling of eyelids and hands. Rash on legs maybe.
Poliomyelitis, onset of: sore throat, stiff neck, limb pain before paralysis.
Acute leukemia: pain and swelling in joints, ill and weak.
Sensitivity reaction to penicillin or certain foods: joints affected, hives.

Rheumatic Fever [A: S, 6, X]

Becoming more common, but less severe, partly due to better feeding, housing, and medicines.
Age: 5–15 years, peak.
Identification: Sore throat or tonsillitis (maybe too mild to be remembered), followed 10–20 days later by: fever, aching joints, first one and then another, each being completely normal afterwards. Abdominal pain, rash sometimes.
Chorea, St. Vitus' Dance may occur as part of acute rheumatism: constant uncontrolled movements of hands, arms, feet, and face.
Treatment: Rest, penicillin. *IN THE HOSPITAL.*
Outlook: Recovery from acute illness usual, but heart may be affected.

VOMITING

A frequent symptom in children, far less significant than in an adult. (See First Year Section.)
Common Causes
Indiscretions of diet:
Too much.
Indigestible: too sweet or fatty; unripe; grassy; rich; much dried fruit.
Contaminated: babies are ignorant, children careless, of hygiene.
Onset of any infection, especially tonsillitis, ear infections.
Periodic vomiting, allied to migraine.
Fear, excitement: school, for instance.

Travel sickness, from 6 months onwards.
Food poisoning.
Allergy: sensitivity to certain foods.
Acute appendicitis, with abdominal pain often in the night.
Meningitis: child ill: headache, stiff neck.

INFECTIOUS DISEASES

Chicken Pox [A: S or N, I, C, 2]
Medical name: Varicella

Highly infectious: affects most children by the time they are 10. Mild. Peak in evidence in autumn and winter. Caused by a virus closely related to that of shingles.

Incubation: 12–20, usually 14 days.

Infectivity: 24 hours before rash appears until 7 days after. Not necessary for every scab to separate.

Spread: Droplet from respiratory tract.

Identification: Rash usually first sign: comes in crops, starting as dark pink, flat spots, becoming blistered in a few hours, then pustular; then scabs. Starts in scalp and mouth, and spreads to back of trunk; limbs and face last and least affected. Very irritating. Fever 100°–102°F. Slightly runny nose, but the child does not feel ill.

Treatment: Rest during feverish stage. Any maneuver to avoid scratching: talcum powder, keeping cool. Loose clothes.

Outlook: Complete recovery in 2 weeks. Scars from pustules that became infected fade slowly.

Diphtheria [A: U]

Rare in Britain and the U.S. because of routine immunization. Dangerous.

Incubation: 2–5 days.

Infectivity: Until laboratory tests clear.

Spread: Droplet from respiratory tract.

Identification: Pains in limbs, no appetite, foul breath, sore throat, swollen neck glands. Child obviously ill.

Treatment: Doctor, maybe hospital.

Prevention: Immunization is extremely effective and should be done in the first year and again before starting school.

Infectious Diseases of Childhood

Illness	Usual incubation period	Prevention	Isolation	Back to school or normal life
Chicken pox	14 days	Avoid contact	7 days after rash appears	8 days
Diphtheria	2–5 days	Immunization	Until laboratory tests clear	14 days, but see column before
German measles	17 days	Avoid contact Gamma globulin (Inoculation soon)	7 days after rash appears	7 days
Measles	10 days	Immunization Gamma globulin	10 days after rash appears	14 days
Mumps	17–18 days	Avoid contact	Until swelling down	8 days
Poliomyelitis	1–3 weeks	Immunization	7–21 days after onset	3 weeks or up to 6 months
Roseola	–	–	–	7 days
Whooping cough	7–10 days	Immunization	5 weeks	6 weeks
Feverish cold	3 days	Vaccine for some types	2–3 days	1 week
Common cold	–	–	–	3 days
Scarlet fever	3–7 days	Avoid contact; throat culture	1 week	1 week

Smallpox [A: U, C]
Medical name: Variola.
Very rare.
Incubation: 10–14 days.
Infectivity: 2 days before rash until the last scab has fallen off.
Spread: Droplet from respiratory tract, contact with the scabs.
Identification: Headache, backache, prostration; later rash, especially on face, similar to that of chicken pox but worse. Fever.
Treatment: Hospital.
Prevention: Vaccination. Protects for 5 years.

German Measles [A: S, C, I, 1]
Medical name: Rubella.
A mild disease, caused by a virus, important only because if an expectant mother contracts it during the first three months of pregnancy, her unborn child may be affected, and eye, ear, mental, or other defects result.
Incubation: 10–21, usually 17 days.
Infectivity: 7 days from appearance of rash.
Spread: Droplet from respiratory tract.
Identification: Mild fever, mild catarrhal symptoms, rash of small, flat, pink spots, most profuse on the body, lasting 1–2 days only. Glands at back of neck may become tender and swollen.
Treatment: None special. Usually better in 4 days.
Prevention: Important in early pregnancy: gamma globulin is given to pregnant contacts. Inoculation may soon be generally available. *Girls should be given every chance of acquiring this illness before marriage.*

Measles [A: S, C, 2]
Medical name: Morbilli.
Highly infectious, catching mainly 1–6-year olds. Epidemics in the winter and spring in U.S. Caused by a virus.
Incubation: 7–21, usually 10 days.
Infectivity: 4 days before until 10 days after the rash appears.
Identification: 4 or 5 days before the main illness: fever, up to 103°F., runny nose, vomiting maybe, feeling ill.
Main symptoms: sore, red eyes and dislike of light; apparent bad

cold; miserable outlook; barking cough; blotchy rash, dark red, beginning behind the ears, then spreading over chest, body, and limbs.

Treatment: None affects the virus, but antibiotics may be given to suppress secondary, bacterial infection.

General care: in bed for the first week. Darkened room, eye washes (1 teaspoon salt to 1 pint of tepid water), and no reading, if eyes uncomfortable. Measles should not be regarded lightly, because although most cases resolve rapidly and uneventfully there is a possibility of complications.

Outlook: Rash fades, and skin peels, in 3–5 days. Simultaneously, temperature falls and the patient soon feels himself.

Complications to watch for: cough becoming worse, breathing faster; bronchitis; earache or discharge; infection of the middle ear; *rarely* severe headache, vomiting, drowsiness: encephalitis.

Prevention

Temporary immunity is provided by mother to baby for about 3 months, and gamma globulin gives temporary immunity to a delicate child who has been exposed.

Long-lasting, active immunity is given by inoculation.

Mumps [A: S, C, An, 2]

Medical name: Epidemic parotitis

A virus disease, affecting mainly children of 5 to 15, and attacking various glands, but particularly those that produce saliva.

Incubation: 12–28, usually 17–18 days.

Infectivity: 1 day before illness is obvious to 7 days after all swelling has disappeared.

Spread: Droplet from respiratory tract.

Identification: Sometimes slight fever and sore throat 24 hours before main symptoms: swelling of gland in front of ear on one side, followed usually by the other in 4–5 days. Painful to open mouth.

Other manifestations, not necessarily present: enlarged, tender testicle (orchitis), commoner after puberty; abdominal pain due to inflammation of the ovary (oöphoritis) may occur, but far less commonly, in girls.

Treatment: None specific. Hot water bottle, analgesics for the pain. Fluid foods.

Outlook: Usually a mild disease, leaving no ill effects, but occasionally if the testicle has been involved, fertility may be impaired, and occasionally deafness on one side is a sequel.

It is good if boys get mumps before puberty: do not keep them away from infection.

Poliomyelitis   [A: S, B, C, 2–6/12]

Once this disease frightened all parents, particularly when referred to by its other name, *infantile paralysis:* inaccurate doubly because it does not usually affect infants, and only a minority of cases incur paralysis.

Nowadays, since the universal availability of an oral vaccine, the danger of contracting this disease is becoming less and less likely.

It is caused by a group of viruses; it usually affects children of 5 to 9 years, but is not uncommon in young adults. Epidemics occur in late summer and autumn.

Incubation: 1–3 weeks.

Infectivity: Probably a day or two before symptoms appear until the temperature is normal, or 7 days, whichever is the longer. Some authorities prefer 14 days, or even 21 days, to elapse.

Spread: Droplet from respiratory tract, and probably contamination from patients' bowel movements, possibly fly-borne.

Identification: Fever, headache, vomiting, sore throat, stiff neck, pain in neck and back, sometimes diarrhea. Usually this is all that happens: in paralytic cases pain and tenderness develop in the muscles in 12–72 hours, and then paralysis.

Treatment: In the doctor's hands. Strict bed rest in acute phase, and isolation.

Outlook: Recovery continues for at least 6 months in paralytic cases, and after that other muscles take over much of the work of the affected ones, so improvement can go on indefinitely.

Prevention: Oral vaccine; in childhood.

Provocation poliomyelitis

An injection for any reason into a muscle when a person chances to be incubating polio may bring on paralysis of that muscle.

Roseola Infantum   [A: S, I]

Commoner in America than Britain, and important only because it may be confused with other infections. Affects children under 3 years old, usually under 12 months.

Identification: Sudden fever lasting 3–4 days; this departs and the rash (like German measles) then appears.

Treatment: None.

Scarlet Fever [A: S, C, I]

Rarely diagnosed nowadays, partly because there has been a marked decrease in its violence and a marked advance in the efficacy of treatment in the last 50 years, and partly because, although it is not essentially different from *acute sore throat* caused by streptococci, the label scarlet fever causes difficulties with school and other authorities.

Incubation: 2–5 days.

Infectivity: Until laboratory tests negative or doctor agrees.

Spread: Droplet from respiratory tract.

Identification: Sore throat and/or abdominal pain; fever; flushed cheeks; transient rash of tiny red spots on a flushed base, limbs, neck, and trunk, coming on in 1–4 days; vomiting at onset commonly; furred tongue.

Treatment: As for Acute sore throat.

Outlook: Complete recovery in a week usually, but complications to watch for are: earache due to middle ear infection, inflamed neck glands and, a fortnight later, rheumatic fever or acute nephritis. Unlikely, but important.

Whooping Cough [A: S, IC, 6]

Medical name: Pertussis.

Commonest at ages 1–4, and *to be avoided under 12 months,* if in any way possible, and taken seriously in the first few weeks.

Incubation: 7–10 days.

Infectivity: 4 days before the illness appears at all, until 28 days after.

Spread: Droplet from respiratory tract.

Identification

"Cold" stage: runny nose, watery not thick; sneezing; hacking cough, becoming worse; slight fever. 4–5 days.

Paroxysmal stage: bouts of coughing, often bringing on vomiting; face goes blue and eyes bloodshot.

The *whoop,* a mechanism for drawing the breath in quickly after the cough has caught the sufferer unawares (unlike other coughs), occurs only in older children, never in babies; it is *not necessary* for a diagnosis of whooping cough. Usually 2 weeks. Getting better takes another fortnight usually.

Treatment: Ampicillin through doctor, in the early stages.

General: Rest, if not actually bed, in first two stages. Non-irritating diet, i.e. no crumbly biscuits, apple peels, or crisp toast, but frequent small milky meals. Replace food lost by vomiting, directly; it will usually be retained. Fresh air: outdoors when weather warm. Breathing exercises.

Outlook: The cough may go on for 8 weeks, and the typical whoop may be heard whenever the child has a cough or cold for years afterward. This is not whooping cough again, but merely that the child has learned the trick of drawing the breath in that way.

Important that doctor should check, perhaps with X-ray, at end of illness to make sure that there is no residual blockage of the small air tubes in the lungs.

Prevention: Immunity from mother to baby slight and unreliable, so it is important that babies should be inoculated in their first few months.

Immunization is very effective.

OTHER CHILDHOOD PROBLEMS

Fat Children

(See Obesity in General Section.)

Fatness matters. It is a mistake to admire as "healthy" a child who is overweight.

It causes misery at school, because the child is teased; he usually gives a poor performance at games; and no clothes fit him properly. It causes misery in the unself-confident self-consciousness of adolescence. It may lead to coronary disease in adult life, and painful feet and knock-knees before that.

Causes

Too much or the wrong type of food. Sugary and starchy foods are unfortunately cheap, easy, and popular.

Too little exercise. Buses to school, car at home, sedentary pleasures like T.V.

Sadness or insecurity, leading to eating as a solace. Boredom.

Hereditary factors, but even if parents are big, this may be due mainly to their family eating habits.

Treatment

Provide plenty of happy occupations apart from eating. Deal with any anxieties. Encourage exercise.

Step up: (1) Fruit, but not bananas.

(2) Vegetables, but not potatoes, peas, baked and butter beans.

(3) Proteins, but not sausages or sardines.

Cut down: milk (not more than 1 pint daily); bread and butter (not more than 3 slices a day).

Cut out: snacks, sweets, cakes, pastries, fried foods, cookies.

Treats: dried or raw fruits when others are having sweets; sugar-free jams and sodas; canned fruits.

Praise. Encouragement. Example.

It is sufficient for a growing child's weight to remain stationary: he will become slimmer and taller.

Outlook: In many children a fat stage passes, though perhaps not until adolescence, even without treatment, and if treatment involves misery and nagging, it will do more psychological harm than physical good.

However, if parents and child both want the obesity reduced, very satisfactory results can be obtained in 2 or 3 months. Care is required indefinitely.

Thin Children

It is far more healthy to be below average weight than above it.

Causes and Treatment

Skinny type: if full of energy and bounding health: just be glad. Common.

Overactive. Output of energy outruns calorie intake. Tired and listless at end of day.

Nursery school, to provide sedentary occupations. Midday rest.

Poor appetite, due to too much urging. Ignore for a while.

Defective assimilation of fats: do not push cream, milk, butter, eggs, but step up carbohydrates, especially extra sugar or glucose.

Chronic illness. Medical check.

Adolescent girl's loss of appetite: anorexia nervosa.

Poor Appetite: Food Refusal

(See First Year Section.)

Very common at all ages with a crescendo period from 2 to 4 years.

Causes

Natural variation, from individual to individual, day to day, and meal to meal.

There is a normal falling-off in appetite after the first 6 months of tremendous weight gain.

Not allowing 1-year-old to feed himself, when his independence is developing strongly.

Food dawdling, normal and natural up to 2½, can be mistaken for poor appetite. Do not hurry the child, but take plates away after reasonable period.

Too much piled on plate: discouraging to a small person. Where possible, the child should be allowed to help himself. You decide what is to be available; he chooses the quantity.

Appetite already satisfied.

Milk (give not more than 1 pint a day).

Snacks and sweets.

Lack of fresh air and exercise. Overheated room.

Anxiety, insecurity, any unhappiness.

Illness: temporary effect.

Attempts to force food: The commonest cause, but no healthy child ever starved because he was not made to eat.

Management: Sounds easy but calls for much willpower and devotion by parents:

Ignore the child's appetite. Take no interest in what he eats or does not, neither praise nor punish; but do not feed between meals, and remove plates after the mealtime is over. Complete refusal—

or rather, leaving the whole lot (for you will not have asked him to eat)—should be treated in exactly the same way.

From 1 year up there is no need to feed the child.

Sleep Problems
Refusal to go to bed.
Delay in getting off to sleep.
Waking and calling parents.
    In evening and night.
    In early morning.
Causes and their avoidance
Faulty habit: A child that, perhaps from 6 months, has been used to being cuddled and perhaps brought downstairs if he calls will naturally try to perpetuate this state of affairs.

The habit takes about two weeks to correct. The child must understand that he is to call only if he is ill.

Too exciting a period before bedtime: Avoid romping games or Westerns on television at this time.

Attention-seeking: Due to jealousy or need for more interest from parents during the day. Extra affection before bedtime, firmness after.

Fear of dark, or other anxiety: Fix a light that he can turn on (better than a flickering, possibly dangerous, night light). Sharing room with brother, sister, baby, or pet.

Disturbed: Reasonable quietness is necessary—more for an older child than a baby, although they are less considered.

Summer evenings, light and noisy, call for later bedtimes.

Too tired
Not tired enough } try altering the bedtime.

Too hot, too cold. Nose blocked. Not well.

Parental anxiety: The biggest factor, and unnecessary. Do not go in to see if your child has gone to sleep any more than you would repeatedly check if he is breathing, a similarly natural function. A child who has the opportunity of rest in bed is not harmed by lack of sleep: if he complains that he cannot get to sleep, offer him a reward if he can stay awake all night. There is as wide a variation in sleep requirement as in appetite: wiry children need less than placid, stolid types. Toys and books at the bedside will occupy the early waker; the only harm he does is in disturbing his parents if bored.

Never offer rewards for going to sleep. Do provide fresh air and exercise in the day.

Nightmares, night terrors: Common at 4–10 years. The child wakes screaming, panic-stricken. Cause may be much excitement (e.g. going to a circus), anxiety as from school, too large a last meal, the onset of an infection, occasionally pinworms.

Comfort the child and tuck him in again; if frequent, seek cause for anxiety.

Restless sleep: Tossing, talking, tooth grinding. Ignore.

Sleepwalking: Similar causation to nightmares: the child is acting out his dream. Do not regard as anything special, but shut bottom of bedroom window. Accidents are rare.

Twitching, Grimacing
Habit spasm.

Chorea, St. Vitus' dance.

Autism.

Mild epilepsy.

With breath-holding attack.

TICS, HABIT SPASMS

Age: Commonly around 6, boys especially.

Identification: Repetitive movements, such as blinking, grimacing, shrugging, sniffing, often perpetuated from a simple habit like rubbing an eye which was once sore. Can stop the movements temporarily if asked (cannot do this in *chorea*).

Causes and treatment: Caused, in a nervous type of child, often with nervous parents, by some tension. Find cause of this and deal with it. Otherwise ignore.

Outlook: Tic usually disappears after a few months. Sometimes replaced by another one.

Irritating, but not harmful.

Breath-holding Attacks
Closely related to temper tantrums, 1–3 years, almost unknown after 4.

Identification: 2 or 3 loud cries, then holds breath for 5–20 seconds, turns blue, may fall down and, after a few moments' confusion, recovers.

(If he holds his breath a second or two longer, he has a convulsion, like epilepsy—*rarely*.)

Causes: Pain, from a fall, for instance; sudden fright; thwarting, or anger in a child who is also given to temper tantrums.

Treatment and prevention: Minimal fuss. Sometimes a slap at the beginning of an attack may make the child cry, and cut the spasm short, but anyway the attacks become less frequent and finally there are none. Try to avoid predisposing and precipitating causes.

See doctor anyway, however, because often children who have these attacks are *anemic*. See the doctor also if you have any doubt about the possibility of epilepsy (below). *Unlikely*.

Epilepsy, Fits, Convulsions [A: S, 1/7; Ch: S, X]
(See also General Section.)

Causes

Hereditary disposition—relatives may have fits; brain disorder such as birth injury; conditions which trigger off an attack in the susceptible, e.g., high fever, whooping cough.

Identification

Two types.

Petit mal: Frequent, momentary losses of consciousness, with break in what child was saying, or doing, pallor, and eyes turning up.

Grand mal: First, child looks bewildered and turns to mother; becomes unconscious and falls; goes stiff with arched back, blue; twitches. Recovers, and sleeps.

Treatment: Immediate: only see that he does not hurt himself. Later: advice and medicine from doctor. Help child to live as normal a life as possible.

Outlook: Many become entirely free from attacks. All are helped by treatment.

Bed-wetting

Medical name: Enuresis.

There is great variation in the age at which control is acquired. Average: dry by day between 2 and 3 years, dry at night between 3 and 4½ years, but wet nights up till 5½ years are well within normal limits.

Types: Primary: the child has never been dry.

Secondary: A return to wetness after a period of dryness.

Causes of Primary Enuresis

A slow developer in this area. May run in the family. Patience is the best treatment.

Small bladder, particularly in boys, whose bladders are smaller anyway.

Training the child to "wait" longer by day helps the bladder to hold more.

Rarely, malformation may be a cause.

Causes of Secondary Enuresis

Emotional: jealousy, excessive strictness, bullying at school, going to the hospital.

Relapse because of illness such as measles, etc.

Infection of urinary tract.

Treatment: None before 6½–7 years. Have physical causes excluded.

Make child feel secure and loved. Do not punish for wetness, but reward for dryness.

Buzzers and drugs are sometimes helpful. Take doctor's advice for your particular child's problem.

ABDOMINAL PAIN

All children have this at some time.

Causes

Gastroenteritis: A common infection. Nausea, vomiting, diarrhea, slight fever. [A: 48]

Unsuitable food: Too rich; too much; unripe.

No fever. [A: 48]

Constipation or laxative: no fever. [Ch]

Tonsillitis or other infection of nose, ear, or throat.

Perhaps due to enlargement of glands in the abdomen.

Fever. [A: S]

Acute appendicitis: Pain at first central, then on right.

Slight fever. [A: U]

Urinary or kidney infection. [A Ch: S]
Lead poisoning from sucking toys or paint: headache, constipation. And other uncommon causes.

These seven causes account for around 10% of the abdominal pains of childhood. The rest are due to *emotional causes:*

Abdominal Pain of Convenience   [A: 48, 1/7]
"Monday morning tummy."
Identification: Comes on only before some activity the child wishes to avoid, e.g. school on certain days; he recovers when the crucial time is past. No vomiting. No fever.

Abdominal Migraine: Periodic Syndrome   [A: 48, B, 1/7–1]
(At one time incorrectly called acidosis.)
Identification: Recurring "bilious attacks," with fever, furred tongue, headache, abdominal pain, pale or normal movements, vomiting for a day usually. Breath may smell fruity after much vomiting.

Predisposition may be indicated by history of similar attacks or of migraine in parents or motion sickness. Overexcitable, easily tired children, with extra-anxious parents, commonly.

Treatment: Of attack: bed, sips of glucose in water. Absence of fussing. Sedative may be prescribed.

Between times: Do not worry; there is no disease, only emotional unrest. Try to find and remedy this, calmly.

Extra rest may help: nursery school may provide this for overenergetic preschooler. Early bedtimes. Drink with glucose in it last thing, helps some. No point in restricting fatty foods, milk, etc.

Outlook: Individual attack passes in two to three days, with rapid return to normal.

Tendency to attacks is outgrown in a year or two, though occasionally migraine may take their place.

Recurrent Pains—Non-specific
Cause often never discovered. Some due to tension.
Abdominal pains: Commonest.
Identification: Center of abdomen. No vomiting, diarrhea, or

fever. Can be extremely severe. Brought on by fear and anxiety, e.g. before school.

Treatment: Explain how normal stomach and intestine movements of squeezing and relaxing to churn and pass the food along may become too energetic and thus painful, if the person is worried or excited.

Deal with any anxieties.

So-called Growing pains: Non-specific muscle pains in growing children.

Identification: Pain in calves or thighs usually, coming on after exertion or in the evening or night. Nothing to do with growth or rheumatism. Ankles may turn out if feet are slightly flat.

Treatment: Reassure child, no harm in continuing games. Foot exercises may help.

Head pains: In the forehead, any time of day, not associated with vomiting.

Recurrent Fever

Emotional tensions may produce recurrent fever, similar to recurrent pains. No other symptoms. Ignore: do not keep child in bed.

DEAFNESS

Common: 10% of children.

Important: untreated, can impair intellectual and social development and, in infancy, learning to speak.

Some deafness is present from birth and is permanent; the commonest types are intermittent, due to infection of the middle ear, or colds blocking the tube from ear to mouth.

Identification: In infancy: missing normal milestones, e.g. startle reflex in first two months at sudden noise, turning head to listen at three months, recognizing own name at eight months, understanding various words and trying to imitate mother from 9–12 months. Learning to speak at 2 years. Cooing and other baby noises which are not imitative occur in deaf as in other babies.

Older child: may be obvious, but some are self-taught lip readers; these get in hot water at school for turning around to look at whoever in the class is talking, and they have difficulty with dictations because they cannot simultaneously lip-read and write.

Treatment: Tests by doctor; lip reading lessons; speech training; special nursery or other school if necessary.

At home: talk to the child a lot, close to his ear; give him plenty of social life, as he will suffer emotionally if allowed to feel cut off.

Outlook and prevention: Very few children are completely deaf, and their remaining "islands of hearing" can be made useful. They tolerate hearing aids well, the earlier the better.

Earache and discharge should never be neglected, as they can cause deafness. Expectant mothers must avoid German measles.

SPEECH DIFFICULTIES

Delay in Learning to Speak
Causes: NEVER DUE TO LAZINESS. NEVER DUE TO TONGUE-TIE.

Normal variation: far the commonest. Einstein, for instance, did not speak until he was four. Often runs in families, for instance, the Darwins. There is often a hold-up while another skill, e.g. walking, is being acquired.

Lack of opportunities to learn: Separation from mother, or too much isolation in carriage, playpen, etc.

Mother who accurately interprets every grunt may remove stimulus to talk normally.

Deafness. [S]

In both ears: No speech.

Partial: Particular difficulty in saying *g, l,* and *r,* which he cannot see being spoken.

High tone deafness: Child can hear low frequency clicks, whispers, radio, car engines, but not normal voice tones.

Twins: No one knows why they should speak later.

Boys also tend to speak later than girls.

Mental backwardness, *only if other milestones in development are also delayed.* Understanding words, shown by pointing out cat, bus, etc., in a picture if asked, or by obeying requests, indicates normal intelligence. [S] Spastics, due to muscular or other difficulty. [S]

Treatment: Doctor's advice if you suspect physical disorder. See that your child has plenty of chance to hear speech and be listened to in his first three years, but do not anxiously force him.

Inability to speak causes much frustration, even temper tantrums.

Indistinct Speech, Lisping
Causes
Nasal, due to a cold temporarily, or, if longer, adenoids or chronic catarrh. [S]

Faulty use of tongue, especially for *s*.

Partial deafness. [S]
High tone deafness. [S] } (see above).

Imitation of someone with a speech disorder.

Physical defect: cleft palate, awkwardly shaped jaws, spastics.

Treatment: Most indistinct speech, unless there is a physical basis, rights itself. After the age of 4, however, and before school starts, advice should be sought about speech training.

Stuttering
Commoner in boys, commonly running in families, usually begins between two and six years. Normal or above average intelligence.

Emotional upset often associated.

Two stages:

(1) Excessive repetition of syllables, often unconscious.
    Treatment: Ignore. Relieve any tensions. The phase will probably pass.

(2) Child agonizingly aware of his disorder; in his effort, muscles of larynx, throat, and chest, even fists, go into tight spasm. Speech blocked.
    Treatment: Speech therapist, through doctor, at once.
    Otherwise as (1), however difficult.

GROWING UP

The drawn out miracle of childhood changes character. Chemical forces that transform grub into butterfly, schoolchild into mature man or woman, surge up. For the child it is bewildering. His body, his emotions, his sense of values, even, suddenly are different. He has difficulty in managing them. It is as though, on a carefree bike ride, the bicycle without warning became a motor bike, powerful but untried—and it is impossible to dismount from. The pace of present day life and the pressures of the school and college system increase the problems with which the teenager must grapple.

Parents, going through an all time low in popularity, must yet protect, support, guide, and comfort their child until at last he can, with some degree of confidence, take on, himself, the responsibility of himself.

Puberty and *adolescence* are both terms applied to the processes of growing up. Puberty covers the physical maturing to the point where reproduction is possible; adolescence is the more subtle all-over transition to adulthood. Until age 9, the average girl lags an inch or so, a pound or two, behind the average boy, developmentally. The middle years of childhood, 7–11, are the period of slowest growth, but between 10 and 12 the girls begin to forge ahead, with a growth spurt of maybe three inches in a year, mental maturation, and the acquisition of the physical attributes of woman. Boys of the same age mark time. At 13 a girl is three-quarters woman, a boy a grubby schoolboy as before. No wonder sub-teen dances are a flop!

Then, while the girls' growth gradually comes to a standstill, the boys, having given them a two-year start, begin. An increase in height of up to six inches in twelve months is one facet of the fantastic drama of growth, which brings the boys ahead once and for all, when childhood is left behind at around 18.

PROBLEMS OF PUBERTY

Normal Changes

Girls	Boys
Begin at 11 (7–15 years are normal limits).	Begin at 13 (11–15 years normal limits).
Breast development.	Increase in height and weight.
Body hair.	Enlargement of penis, testes and scrotum.
Altered shape of body, due to broadening of hips and fat deposition over thighs, breasts, hips, buttocks.	Hair at base of penis. Shoulders broaden.
Periods begin (usual age 13).	Voice changes due to growth of larynx.
Internally ovaries and uterus enlarge and change shape.	Hair in armpits and on upper lip.
Increase in bodily height and weight.	Wet dreams (seminal emissions and erotic dreams; about age 14).
Growth ceases at 16.	Internally, prostate gland enlarges.
	Growth ceases at 17¾.

The order in which the changes occur is subject to normal variation, depending on whether, for instance, breast area or body hair region is the more sensitive to the hormones that set off development.

Management

Factual instruction required from home/school/family doctor about:

The phases of life and development.

Reproduction: the parts of the body concerned and how they work.

Menstruation: its purpose, importance, and hygiene.

General health rules, including moral aspects.

Most girls need extra iron [S]: Conveniently in tablets, during the years 15–18. Have doctor check for incipient anemia.

Precocious Development   [Ch: S]

I.e. before the age of 10.

Commoner in girls, and in fat children (though their appearance may suggest delay in boys, because the organs hardly show in rolls of fat). Muscular boys tend to develop early.

Causes and Treatment

(1) *Constitutional,* often running in the family. Commonest cause. No treatment, but boarding school could be embarrassing, and the child must be guarded psychologically from being treated as though she were older than she is, and having too much expected of her. Also since pregnancy is possible, she must be supervised like an adolescent.

(2) *Rare:* Due to disorders in the brain or certain tumors in the brain or abdomen.

Delayed Development   [A Ch: S]

Girls

Menstruation not occurring by 18 years.

Causes and Treatment

Malnutrition. Commonest. May be due to food fads, slimming, anorexia nervosa.

Diet with plenty of protein, fresh air, exercise, extra iron and avoidance of fatigue.

No gland treatment.

Constitutional, from childhood illness or heredity.

No special treatment.

Hormone lack: can be confirmed by laboratory test.

Complete absence of breast and body hair development.

Hormone treatment through doctor.

Boys

Constitutional, including long-lasting illnesses in childhood. Time, healthy life needed.

Hormone lack. The testes, etc., remain child size.

Hormone treatment, with gaps to see if the natural hormones are taking over.

Eunuchoidism: condition from birth, of absent or very small testes. Extra long arms and legs. Hormone treatment indefinitely.

Undescended Testes   [Ch: S]

In most boys the testes are present in the scrotal sac at birth, but in some they remain in their before-birth position in the abdomen. Sometimes they come down but retract when touched; sometimes they may be seen halfway, in the groin. Any of the conditions can occur on both sides or one only.

Usually undescended testes come down spontaneously some time before puberty.

Treatment: Operation. Usually advised at 8 years.

Swelling in the Neck: Puberty Goiter   [Ch: S, 6]

Enlargement of the thyroid gland, in the front of the neck. It is one of the hormone producing glands very busy during puberty, and its enlargement is almost normal.

Treatment: Medicines through doctor.

Outlook: Usually subsides with the active phase of puberty.

Obesity of Puberty: "Puppy Fat"   [Ch: S, X]

Not uncommon.

When growth is proceeding at a phenomenal rate and organs such as heart and muscles are increasing in solid size, as happens for a year or so at puberty, there is need for an enormous intake of food, more than at any other time of life, even pregnancy. The appetite matches the need.

Snag: appetite and consumption may continue past the relatively short period of need, particularly in girls in whom it is over sooner. The result is excessive fatness, often accompanied by lethargy and feeling the cold.

The "puppy fat" of puberty is *not* due to glandular disorder except very rarely. Nor is it gluttony: the appetite is genuine, though "set" wrong.

Treatment: In some cases, without treatment, the excessive fatness disappears in a year or two, but no reliance can be placed on nature, and so restriction of diet should be instituted and the habit broken of eating more than is now necessary.

Parents' attitude is the key to success. Appetite depressants are sometimes prescribed. (See Obesity.)

Abnormal Breast Development

Undue enlargement. Embarrassing. Well designed brassières, loose fitting garments, and, in extreme cases, cosmetic operation will help.

Underdevelopment. Usually a part of generally delayed puberty (above).

May be also due to being a thin type.

Asymmetrical development. One breast smaller than the other. Special underwear prevents embarrassment in this and in under-development.

Enlarged Breasts in Boys [Ch: N, 1 year]

Swelling of the breasts occurs in one in three boys at puberty, due to sensitivity to the circulating sex hormones.

A small tender nodule in the breast area is the usual condition. (The appearance of having the female breasts in fat boys is just due to fat.)

Treatment: None. The condition disappears in 12–18 months.

Discomfort Associated with Periods

It is natural for the body, and the girl, to take time to adjust to this new, though normal and healthy, recurring event. Menstruation can be expected to be irregular in occurrence and duration for the first year, but should not, now or at any time, require any special restriction of activity. Bathing, hairwashing, and school games should proceed as usual.

Discomfort, if it arises, should be dealt with.

Premenstrual tension [S]: Irritability, depression; tender, enlarged breasts; swollen abdomen; headache; backache.

Worsening of acne, asthma, or nose and sinus trouble.

Period pain [S] (See Women's Section.)

Excessive Flow and Irregularity of Periods [Ch: S]

Delay in the normal adjustment of glands and ovaries concerned in producing menstruation is often associated with a generally run-down state.

Treatment: Attention to diet, which needs to be full and protein-ous, plenty of sleep, avoidance of fatigue, fresh air and stimulating exercise. Gland extracts and hormones may be prescribed by doctor.

Iron tablets may be needed to make up for blood loss.

Skin Disorders

The skin, the mirror of personality, mood, and physical state, inevitably participates in the mysterious upheavals of puberty.

Its very texture changes, becoming thicker, coarser, more prominently pitted with pores, oilier. More sweat is poured out, and for the first time the apocrine glands, distributed in the armpits, around the breasts, and the genital area, come into action. Their reaction gives rise to a distinctive bodily odor, and the ordinary sweat in other parts, such as the feet, also becomes stronger-smelling, to the youngster's embarrassment. The character and distribution of the hair is modified.

So marked are the changes that some infections, such as ringworm of the scalp, cannot survive this alteration in environment and disappear. But other disorders are swept in on the tide, and in the super-self-consciousness of adolescence, any skin trouble is seen more than life-size, and must therefore be treated with sympathetic seriousness.

Excessive Oiliness, Sweating or Odor [Ch: S, 6/12]

An exaggeration of the normal conditions.

Treatment

Scrupulous cleanliness.

Antiseptic lotion (hexachlorophene) in the bath for body odor.

Soaking daily in potassium permanganate solution and special dusting powder may be used on the feet.

Outlook: These troubles pass in a year or two.

Some skin troubles are commoner in adolescence than at any other period. They are considered elsewhere. Acne: isolated pustules and boils; pityriasis; dandruff; eczema; warts; athlete's foot; psoriasis; ringworm of the groin; chilblains; cold blue legs; Raynaud's disease.

Lassitude [Ch: 6/12]

Lassitude, languor, fatigue, laziness—call it what you will; it is a characteristic of adolescence, not all the time, but in all growers-up part of the time.

Physically, it can make the youngster sluggish to wake up, heavy-eyed all day; psychologically it can mean nothing's worth the effort. Stuffing indoors all day with a book, but perhaps not even reading it, too inert even to pick up his clothes from the floor, he can drive a busy parent to distraction. It is a help to understand.

Causes

Glandular upheaval: energies directed to development.

Growth spurt: energies and nutrition absorbed in increasing size.

Fatness: makes any physical activity literally more burdensome.

Revolt against authority, to demonstrate independence, e.g. not washing or tidying to show revolt against parents, avoiding school games as a stand against school authority.

Fatigue of excitement and anxiety about self, sex, career, God, the world.

Late nights, part of the struggle towards independence.

Self-consciousness and desire for privacy, causing the teenager to shut himself in his room, instead of being active and sociable.

Boredom with outgrown childish occupations.

Anemia, neglected colds, or other sub-health, particularly since, although the adolescent spends time brooding over his appearance and health, he seldom takes any practical steps about it or tells either parents or doctor.

Treatment: Early nights; lots of sleep. Food with plenty of protein (meat, fish, eggs, cheese). Stimulation: new interests, not too much time with family, exercise. Better organization of available time.

Outlook: Six months to a year sees this phase past.

Fear of Growing Up

Identification: Excessive school spirit and interest in children's games; hearty, boisterous boys; tom-boyish girls; mother's darlings of either sex; unduly devoted stay-at-homes.

Idol worship of singers, T.V. personalities, etc., is a sign of fear of emotional maturity, preference for "letting go" only from a safe, anonymous position in a crowd.

Treatment: Expanding experience, contemporary friendships and frank discussions; getting away from home, but certainty of love there.

Active occupations; sports; social or other work—all beneficial at this stage.

Loss of Appetite [Ch: S, 6]
Medical name: Anorexia nervosa
    Usually girls.
Identification: Severe appetite loss, and loss of weight.
Depressed, anxious, and often slow and apathetic.
May follow slimming in a formerly fat girl. Periods may cease or not begin.
Treatment
    Good loving, good living, encouragement. Tranquilizing medicine, via doctor.

Conflict between Instinct to Progress and Desire to Retreat to Safety
    Emotional tension during adolescence (and later) is a healthy stimulus to effort, but some will not accept the challenge, and instead react in various ways.
Morbid anxiety, frustration, and feeling fed up. [S] Everyone is to blame but himself. More humor and lightheartedness are needed, mixed with not too much sympathy.
Refusal of effort [S]: Slipping into lethargy and "don't care," or more active withdrawal into religious or other bypaths, with a loss of former ambitions, interests, enthusiasms, and pleasures.
Touchiness: Seeing slights that are not intended, and feeling that people are noticing and talking about him. This usually means the child has an unfulfilled wish to be noticed! Taking a more active, prominent part in school and home affairs helps to give these youngsters the confidence they lack.
Phobias [S]: Anxiety or near-panic in restaurants, trains, theaters, or crowds. Indicative of school or general behavior standards being set too high, often by parents' ambitions. Phobias are usually transient.
Melancholia [SU]: True melancholia, in which self is blamed, not other people, and all thought and activity are slowed down, is rare

in adolescents. Characteristic is early morning waking, when the feelings are at their worst, with gradual improvement during the day. This pattern requires specialist advice without delay: see the doctor.

Hysterical symptoms: Headaches, abdominal pains, even paralysis, unusual breathing, lack of sensation in some skin areas, loss of voice or sight, or other disorders that are often dramatic but not due to disease. This is the body coming to the rescue of the mind, and getting the youngster excused from whatever he fears by providing an apparent illness.

Only a doctor can disentangle hysterical from serious symptoms: to the sufferer they seem equally real.

"Nervous breakdown" [SU] with definitely strange behavior and talk can also occur in adolescents.

Treatment: In many cases a sympathetic listener, outside the family, is all that is needed.

Aggression and Delinquency   [Ch: S]

Five times commoner in boys. Peak age: last days at school.

All adolescents need to express their natural aggression: the drive that gets them on, and their need for activity, competition—and mastery of some subject or skill. Signs that there is not sufficient outlet are: persistent pilfering, larceny, truancy, bullying, hooliganism and gang warfare; excessive aggression.

Treatment: Punishment (not excessive). Forgiveness. Outlets for self-expression.

Understanding: delinquent children often come from broken or unhappy homes, where love, security, and parental example are faulty; it is up to the parents to remedy this. Stealing, by young people, is said to be an attempt to steal love; it may be significant if he steals from the same person every time. A gang is a substitute for home affection, and much delinquent behavior is performed out of bravado, to win praise and admiration from his fellows that he feels the lack of at home, work, or school.

Neither material poverty nor intellectual limitation need make a home poor emotionally, nor do these attributes guarantee happiness or security for a child. Outside advice is vital to get the position in perspective.

Smoking and Alcohol [Ch: S]

Smoking is provedly harmful, predisposing as it does to lung cancer, coronary thrombosis etc; alcohol is also often deleterious to health. Yet some 15-year-old boys smoke, and the consumption of alcohol among the young is going up.

Causes

As delinquency: lack of inner security.

Curiosity.

Imitation of parent, teacher, or hero.

Empty intellectual or emotional life, coupled with desire to feel and look adult.

Advertising, though fantastically large sums are spent on it, does not apparently increase the over-all consumption of tobacco (though it may popularize certain brands) because in Sweden and Czechoslovakia where such advertising is banned, smoking is just as rife.

Management: Bolster confidence, and restore security if lacking. Example, and frank discussion of the dangers and disadvantages of tobacco and alcohol may help.

Promiscuity, Venereal Disease, and Illegitimacy

There is a great increase in sexually contracted illness, particularly disquieting among children of school age, in all walks of life. V.D. is discussed elsewhere but the causative factors that apply particularly to young people are dealt with here:

Inadequate parental responsibility: Broken homes account for a high proportion: 75% of the girls, 50% of the boys at one V.D. clinic. Other parents, though not separated, may fail to give the necessary *example, guidance,* and *moderate discipline.*

School: Failure of tradition, of adjusting to earlier maturing of adolescents, and of teaching how to use leisure.

Higher education and work: Better, more interested relationship required between those who have just left the shelter of school, and tutors or employers.

Changes in moral values and social habits generally.

Decline in religion: Both the beliefs and as a family-uniting practice.

Alcohol.

Preventive measures are obviously dependent on the causation.

MEN ONLY

The male genital system is intimately associated with the urinary system, so that difficulties in the one cannot help but affect the other: infection of the urine may involve the testes; enlargement of the prostate gland may obstruct the outflow of urine. Normally when the shared apparatus is in sexual use, its other function is blocked.

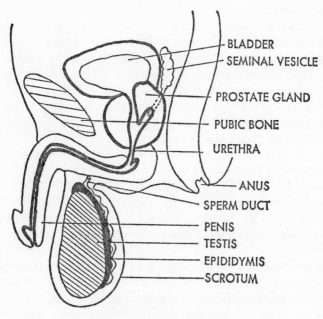

BLADDER
SEMINAL VESICLE
PROSTATE GLAND
PUBIC BONE
URETHRA
ANUS
SPERM DUCT
PENIS
TESTIS
EPIDIDYMIS
SCROTUM

Male Genital System: the sperm duct enters the
urethra in its prostatic position

The testes, the organs which produce the sperm or male seed, are covered only by the twin scrotal sac. The prostate gland at the neck of the bladder is essential to reproductive ability in some way not fully elucidated yet, but it makes its presence felt in the senior years when it becomes bigger.

THE PENIS AND SCROTUM

Pain in the Penis

This occurs not only with trouble in the penis itself or the urethra, the pipe carrying urine from the bladder down the penis, but may also be due to disorder of the kidney, bladder, or prostate gland—or even the appendix.

Causes

Pain felt only while passing water: inflammation, narrowing or stone in urethra; prostate disorder, inflammation, growth or stone; acute inflammation of the bladder.

Pain immediately after passing water: inflammation, stone or growth in the bladder; stone or inflammation in the ureter, the pipe from kidney to bladder; inflammation, growth or stone in the prostate gland; growth in rectum; inflamed piles or anal fissure of back passage.

Pain unconnected with passing water: inflammation, inside or outside, of the penis itself (there may be pain on erection); kidney colic, but pain in the loin is then more striking; leukemia; inflammation low in the abdomen as from appendicitis.

Warts of the Penis

Medical name: Penile papillomata.

Identification: Moist warty outgrowth with offensive watery discharge.

Treatment: Diathermy, through doctor. Particular attention to cleanliness.

Outlook: Easily cured, but neglected over many years, could lead to cancer.

Sore on the Penis

Ulcers of the end of the penis secondary to inflammation under the foreskin, either simple due to inadequate hygiene, or in those with diabetes or gout.

Daily cleansing with salt solution (1 teaspoonful salt to 1 pint water).

Circumcision after.

Chancre, one hard red patch which breaks down to form an oozing ulcer.
Soft sore, several running sores with enlarged glands in the groin.
Both of these are associated with sexual connection.
See Venereal disease.

Cancer of the Penis
Not common.
Identification: Mild irritation and discharge from foreskin, becoming blood-stained and foul. No pain. Or a pimple that does not heal, may appear on the penis. Glands in groin may be enlarged.
Treatment: See doctor; radium is particularly successful for this kind of cancer.

Herpes
Blisters, which may break down, on a red inflamed base; painful.
One-sided: Shingles.
Both sides, and especially if it has happened before: simple or catarrhal sores.
Treat as cold sore.

ERECTION DIFFICULTIES

Weak or Absent Erection
Run down from ill health; advancing years and lack of confidence combined; diabetes; alcohol; drugs such as morphine; disease of nerves in the spinal cord—but most commonly: *nervous upset.*
Sheaths used for contraceptive purposes may inhibit erection, particularly in middle age.

Inability to Obtain Erection at the Right Time
Strong erections occur inopportunely, and there are emissions in sleep, but there is nothing doing at the vital moment, or else too soon, so that the penis is flaccid before insertion is complete. Common in the first few weeks of marriage. Psychological: give it time and stop worrying.

Crooked Erection

Medical name: Chordee.

Usually accompanied by pain: due to inflammation, often gonorrheal, of urethra, in which case there will also be a discharge. Treatment is by tablets. In men over 40, sometimes a type of inelastic scar tissue forms along one side of the penis, possibly due to a long-past injury. The pain gradually disappears, and the condition may improve in a few years without treatment.

Priapism [S]

Erections that are unrelated to sexual function and may be painful. Common in the elderly, associated with enlarged prostate, gouty or other local inflammation, piles, or with no obvious physical cause.

Other Causes

Children: Tight foreskin, worms, inflammation of penis, circumcision.

Young adult: Gonorrhea, back injury, alcohol and certain drugs and poisons, e.g. strychnine; convalescence from acute illness; epilepsy; leukemia, an early sign.

Persistent priapism, in which the organ remains painfully erect, is usually due to a clot forming in the prostatic veins. Anticoagulant drugs from a doctor can help.

Swelling of the Scrotum

Causes

Hydrocele [S]: A collection of watery fluid in the tissue surrounding the testicle.

Translucent: lights up if a flashlight is shone through it.

Hematocele [S]: Blood and fluid surrounding the testis, the result of an injury. Not translucent.

Varicocele [S]: A collection of varicose veins in the scrotum. Feels like a "bag of worms."

Spermatocele [S]: Above and behind the testis. Consists of seminal fluid. Faintly translucent.

Cysts [S] of the epididymis (head of the testicle). Translucent.

The above conditions are all harmless but should be investigated by a doctor to make sure what they are and to be dealt with if they cause discomfort.

Hernia [S or U]: An inguinal hernia may come right into the scrotal sac and even become as big as a football. May slide back into abdomen on lying down, or may be too big, or gummed down, or strangulation (sudden pain, and tense tenderness) may supervene.

Tumor [S U]: Heavy swelling. Loss of normal characteristic sensation of testis. Other conditions may produce these effects, but it is important to make sure, especially in a young adult.

Epididymitis [S]: Inflammation of the head of the testis, usually from urinary infection. A large, irregular, tender swelling.

Mumps of the testis [S]: Acutely painful swelling coming on suddenly during an attack of the mumps.

Twisting of the testicle [U]: Sudden pain, vomiting, collapse.

Testis swollen and tender. Can be untwisted by *immediate* operation.

Twisting of a small part called the hydatid of Morgagni causes the same symptoms, but less severe.

THE PROSTATE

Enlarged Prostate Gland
Simple [Ch: S]

The enlargement of this gland, which surrounds the urethra (pipe from bladder to exterior), may cause very slight symptoms or none, or it may give rise to trouble.

Age: 50+.

Identification: Increased frequency in passing water, at first at night only (around 2–3 A.M.), later day and night; difficulty in starting to urinate (straining is useless—one may have to wait patiently for a full minute); urgency, a feeling that one cannot wait to pass urine; slow, weak stream; dribbling at end of act; occasionally a drop of blood at beginning or end of passing water; increased sexual interest, then diminished ability.

Treatment: Usually operation, sometimes a minor type. Convalescence varies with operation.

Outlook: Post-operatively: fresh vigorous strength and comfort.

In mild cases without operation, no worsening of the condition is likely after 10 years.

Cancerous [Ch: S]

Only a small proportion of enlarged prostates are cancerous. *Age:* 45+.

Identification: As in simple enlargement, but may come on in a matter of weeks rather than many months; pain in lower abdomen, or between legs; pain in the back, or like sciatica, legs also.

Treatment: Hormone treatment. Rarely operative.

Inflammation of the Prostate Gland

Medical name: Prostatitis.

Any age.

ACUTE [A: S, B, 6]

Apart from gonococcal prostatitis (see Venereal disease), the infection usually comes via the blood, from some other part of the body.

Identification: Ill, shivery, temperature up to 102°F., flu-like aches all over, especially in the back; heavy feeling between the legs; discomfort on sitting; discomfort on passing water; discomfort with bowel movement.

Treatment: Bed and antibiotics for several days. Copious bland drinks. No alcohol or intercourse for six weeks.

Outlook: Normal in six weeks, but it is important to follow your doctor's directions patiently and meticulously, or this trouble may recur.

CHRONIC [Ch: S, R, 6]

Infection usually from elsewhere in the body: boils, throat, etc.

Identification: Vague and variable symptoms: dull ache between legs, in rectum, or low in the back, like lumbago. Recurring attacks of slight fever. Sexual difficulties.

Treatment: Antibiotics for six weeks, as prescribed; skilled techniques, such as prostatic massage, through doctor.

SEXUAL PROBLEMS

Impotence [Ch: S]

Inability to perform the sexual act, but not necessarily implying sterility, the incapacity to produce children.

Causes

Mainly as for erection difficulties.

Extreme obesity.

Fetishism, the ability to be aroused sexually only in certain speci-
fied circumstances, a psychological aberration.

Artificial insemination using the husband's semen is sometimes
of use when the impotence is not amenable to treatment.

Infertility and Sterility   [Ch: S]

Difficulty in having children. Either husband or wife, or a combination of slight weaknesses in both, may be responsible.

Causes in the Man

Impotence, physical or psychological.

Reduced number of sperm in the seminal fluid, or less active than
normal (doctor can test for this).

Undescended testicles.

Testicles injured, on both sides, by mumps in youth, or occasionally by other virus infection.

Aftereffects of sports or other injury.

Lowered general health.

Varicocele.

Blockage of ducts carrying sperm from testicles: after rupture
operations on both sides, occasionally, or infection, particularly
gonorrhea.

Prostate disorders, especially tuberculous infection.

Swellings in the scrotum pressing on the testicles.

Treatment: Special, e.g. operative, or psychological where indicated. Hormones help in a few cases.

General: Physical discipline: cut down food (if fat), alcohol,
tobacco.

Do not have too frequent intercourse when it is likely that the
wife is in an infertile period, i.e. just before, during, or after her
menstrual period.

Sperm counts are a diagnostic aid and a check on progress.

WOMEN'S SECTION

Woman is the stronger sex: she lives on average six years longer than the male, and her lead is lengthening. The two main scourges of the West today, coronary disease and lung cancer, attack women far less frequently. Right from the start, women have the edge on men: they may hand on, but very rarely indeed suffer from, such hereditary disorders as colorblindness and hemophilia. Women have better resistance to exposure, as in an open boat or Alpine snows, and better resistance to most diseases than men.

Nevertheless they are ill more often than men, partly because of their complex and ever changing reproductive system.

THE BREAST

Pain in the Breast
Causes and Types
Normal increase in tension, felt as tingling discomfort, fullness, or prickling. Occurs at puberty, before periods, in early pregnancy, and for the first few months on taking oral contraceptive pills.

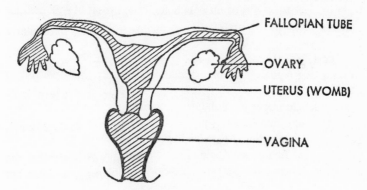

Section of Female Reproductive Organs
Front View

Intermittent pain at the time of the menopause and during the 10 years preceding it. Not as a rule significant. [S]

Breast may feel lumpy: fibroadenosis.

During breast feeding: first few days, normally much tension; cracked nipple; abscess. [S]

Cysts, may be felt as rounded lumps. [S]

Tumor, harmless or cancerous. It is *rare* for pain to be a prominent feature in cancer of the breast, however, and if at all, it occurs on one side only. [S]

Causes outside the breast: indigestion; heart pain; shingles.

Lump in the Breast   [Ch: SU]

Single Lump

Fibroadenosis, often associated with discomfort, usually at age 40–55.

Cyst, rounded ¼ to 2 inches across. Any age.

Harmless tumor.

Cancer. Pain unusual.

Abscess during breast feeding. Much pain.

Several Lumps

Fibroadenosis.

Multiple cysts.

Tumors, harmless or cancerous. Unlikely.

Deformities of the ribs or abscess behind the breast may sometimes simulate lump in the breast.

Enlarged Breasts

Normal in pregnancy or breast-feeding. Firm brassière with deep band needed.

Undue development at puberty. Supporting brassière, or plastic surgery in extreme cases.

Sagging breasts: after breast-feeding, in middle age, or due to fat. Hormone medicines may help. Plastic surgery in severe cases.

See also Lump in the breast (above).

Small Breasts

Treatment: Hormone medicines may help those between 20 and 30 whose breasts have not fully developed, but in the over-40's such treatment is ineffective because the breasts are naturally undergoing involution by then. Corsetière will help cosmetically.

One breast smaller than the other: an aberration of development to be dealt with as Small Breasts, above.

Discharge from Nipple
Normal: clear fluid or milk during pregnancy, or breast-feeding.
Clear fluid as above, in either sex, at birth or puberty.
Breast may also be red and swollen and tender. Due to hormones. Will settle down by itself.
Clear fluid at other periods due to cyst.
Bloodstained: tumor either innocent or cancerous.
Greenish or blackish: Either as above, or more likely, fibroadenosis.
Pus: Breast abscess during breast-feeding, or tuberculous (*rare*).

Indrawing of the Nipple [Ch]
Occurring at puberty: an aberration of development which may hinder breast-feeding.
Treatment: Draw out the nipple with finger and thumb daily for three weeks. Glass nipple shield worn under brassière also helps.
Occurring in middle-aged or elderly: may indicate a tumor of the breast. See doctor. [S U]

Fibroadenosis [Ch: SU]
(Formerly called chronic mastitis.)
   May occur at any time after puberty, but most commonly from 40 to 55, in women either childless, or who have not breast-fed.
Identification: Pain or discomfort in one breast, sometimes both, especially before periods, or after using the arm; breast substance may feel lumpy; occasionally discharge, not blood-stained, but often green or blackish, from the nipple.
Treatment: Usually none is necessary, but doctor must check in case of tumor. Firm brassière is helpful.
Outlook: These changes are part of the normal changes in the breast tissues at the beginning and more particularly towards the close of the childbearing period of life. No cause for worry.

Cysts and Harmless Breast Tumors [Ch: SU]
Common, particularly after 40.

Identification: Lump or lumps in the breast; pain or discomfort; discharge, sometimes bloodstained from nipple.
Treatment: Doctor must check that there is no cancer. Treatment may be small, safe operation, or none may be needed.

Cancer of the Breast [Ch: SU]

A cancer that can be treated very effectively, particularly if it is noticed early.
Identification: Points to watch for particularly from 40 onwards: lump in the breast; discharge, bloodstained or otherwise, from the nipple; pulled-in nipple on one side (unless it has always been like this); dimpled skin of breast, resembling orange peel; itching irritation round the nipple; pain (unusual).

Any of these symptoms is likely to have a simple explanation, but it is essential to go to your doctor to make sure.

PERIODS

Normal Periods

The ovaries are, between them, responsible for producing an ovum or egg on the average once in every 28 days. The egg travels down the tube to the womb, whose lining is now thick and velvety. If the egg is fertilized, it embeds itself in this soft, deep tissue to develop; if not, the lining breaks down and is discarded. The flow of blood thus brought about is called menstruation.

Time Factors
Begin: 10–16 years
End: 45–50 years
Time between periods (cycle) 3–5 weeks.
Length of period 2–7 days.
Normal symptoms: Some of which may occur at one time or another, none severely: fatigue, lack of concentration, irritability, headache, feeling of heaviness, backache, abdominal ache, fullness and tenderness of breasts, constipation then relative looseness, shadows under the eyes, spots on the face, varicose veins if present become temporarily bigger.
Normal Management

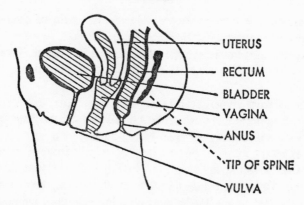

UTERUS

RECTUM

BLADDER

VAGINA

ANUS

TIP OF SPINE

VULVA

Section of Female Reproduction Organs
Side View

External protection is recommended for young girls. Internal tampons are harmless in married and older girls.

No need to stop games, baths, or hairwashing.

No need for anything special except, if necessary, aspirin.

Douching at the end of a period is NOT desirable. The vagina is self-cleansing.

Premenstrual Tension   [Ch: R]

Most women feel slightly different psychologically and physically for a few days before each period, and relief when it starts. A few, particularly between 30 and 45, have the symptoms described under normal periods (above) accentuated to the point of misery, and lasting for as long as 10 days. Often goes with restless energy and overanxiety.

Treatment: Reorganization so that a midday rest is possible every day.

Drink less, and cut out salt the 7–10 days before a period, to prevent overaccumulation of fluid. Tablets, via doctor, may help in addition.

Period Pain   [Ch: S]

Medical name: Dysmenorrhea.

Two types.

Primary

Directly due to menstruation: essentially a first-day-of-the-period pain.

Secondary

Arising from some organ other than the uterus, may come on in the days preceding period and be relieved by the flow, or less commonly be equally severe before, during, and just after the period.

PRIMARY DYSMENORRHEA

Some discomfort occurs in 50% of all women, and especially at 18–24 years, but really incapacitating pain is becoming less common.

Identification: Lasts up to 12 hours from just before flow starts, spasmodic pain mainly below navel, and sometimes down *front* of legs. May be pale, sweating, sick.

Does not usually arise in the first three years of having periods.

Treatment and outlook: Usually gone by 24 years, and nearly always after childbirth; meanwhile, check anxieties, diet (good?), general health, sufficient exercise daily.

During pain: aspirin or similar drug, hot water bottle if very severe, otherwise a walk.

It is unwise to ask for more drastic treatment or stronger drugs for an event that recurs each month.

Dysmenorrhea with large clots occurs only with excessive flow. See below.

SECONDARY DYSMENORRHEA

(1) *Congestion in the area of the womb* becoming more noticeable before period starts: usually due to anxiety, domestic responsibilities weighing too heavily, sedentary life, occasionally chronic infection inside.

Identification: Dull vague ache front and back.

Treatment: Correct nervous tensions if any. Try cold baths between periods to tone up circulation.

See also Premenstrual tension (above).

(2) *Intestinal pain associated with periods.* Very common.

Identification: Pain in lower left corner of abdomen up to a week before period, and relieved by it. Constipation before period, looser movements during it. Tenderness on left side.

Same pain and constipation occasionally occur without a period. Basic trouble is the disturbance of the bowel.

Treatment: via doctor: Ironing out of anxieties, perhaps a sedative; nonirritating diet; avoid fierce purgatives, but senna, agar, or paraffin may help.

See also Premenstrual Tension (above).

Low Backache, before or during periods, or dating from pregnancy, is *rarely* due to internal female organs.

Between-Period Pain

Occurs from time to time in many women, perhaps due to increased tension in the ovary at this time, when an egg is released.

Identification: Discomfort lower in abdomen either in the middle or at one side, lasting about 12 hours, midway between periods; maybe a little bleeding.

Treatment: None usually needed.

Scanty, Infrequent, or Absent Periods   [Ch]

Causes

Normal [N]

Childhood: see doctor if periods have not started by 16 years.

Adolescence: stoppages lasting 2–12 months in the first 2 years after periods start are normal.

Pregnancy.

Lactation. Milk production suppresses the periods, and if they return it is a sign that the supply is falling off—*not* that the periods put off the milk.

Menopause. Periods may stop for 2–3 months and then start again. Not likely to be due to this before 40.

Abnormal [S]

Nervous shock or emotional upset: job; love affair; marriage; separation; death.

Too vigorous dieting in someone already slim.

Obesity.

Any acute illness (temporarily).

Certain medicines.

Diabetes, or thyroid disorder.

Periods that are scanty and infrequent, but not entirely absent, are usually a normal type. People vary greatly.

MISCELLANEOUS

Vaginal Discharge

(Not including bloodstained discharges.)

Causes

Normal, not enough to produce more than an occasional stain on the underwear.

Normally increased: at the time, midway between periods, when an egg is released; the day or two before a period; pregnancy.

Undue increase in the natural reaction:

Puberty, the few years before and after the periods start. Gets better by itself.

Frequent douching.

Standing for long periods, prolapse, convalescence, sedentary occupations: all causes of congestion below.

Erosion of the cervix.

In all the above cases the discharge is never offensive, never causes itching or irritation, and although creamy-white at first, when dry makes a brownish-yellow stain, and the discharge comes gradually, not suddenly. Not in any way connected with cancer or venereal disease.

Inflammatory discharges:

Foreign body accidentally left inside: tampon, contraceptive device.

Douche too strong or hot.

Special sensitivity to a drug, e.g. penicillin, liver extract.

Infection of vulva and vagina with various organisms.

Infection of the cervix: gonorrhea, or after childbirth, or infected erosion.

Inflammation of the womb.

Tumor, harmless or other types.

Color varies from cream to yellow or green. All but the second and third conditions may produce an offensive discharge. Any of these

discharges may cause irritation and reddening but only two organisms (T. vaginalis and C. albicans) cause itching.
Treatment: As cause, above.

Painful or Difficult Intercourse [Ch: S]
Causes
Inexperience, especially of both parties. Usually 3–4 weeks are sufficient to overcome the initial difficulties, but it may be more than a year before the wife *regularly* finds full satisfaction in intercourse. A bruised feeling is normal after the first attempt at intercourse, and it may be best to wait 2–3 days before having another go.
Vaginismus: Spasmodic tightening of the muscles surrounding the vaginal entrance, usually due to anxiety such as fear of pregnancy or absence of desire, but sometimes due to tenderness in the area, or too gentle and considerate a husband. Very common.
Entry to vagina too dry, because glands not doing their job of lubricating, due to the same causes of vaginismus, or hot bath just before. Lubricants help.
Failure by husband to produce or maintain stiff, erect penis (see Men Only Section).
Thick or tough hymen, the skin that partly covers the vaginal entrance in a virgin.
Stitches after childbirth, or scarring from operation for prolapse, for instance.
Painful conditions in the area: infections of vulva, or vaginal glands; piles or anal fissure; disorders of the colon or cervix; misplaced womb.
Contraceptives, particularly a diaphragm.
Enormous fatness.
Treatment: Must vary with the cause: righting of physical disorders; sex education and practice; gentle dilatation of the vagina if it is tight. Your doctor can help; talk it over with him.

"Honeymoon Cystitis" [A: 48]
Identification: Discomfort and frequency in passing urine, tenderness of urinary passage, in first few days of marriage.
Treatment: Have a few days' rest from intercourse. The trouble is bruising of the urinary passage, not infection.

Excessive or Abnormal Bleeding   [A Ch: U or S]

Causes

Normal period intervals, but bleeding heavy or for extra long: fibroids; misplaced womb; psychological upsets such as overwork, anxiety, marital disharmony; growing up, first two years of periods.

Regular but too frequent: inflammation anywhere in the genital tract or nearby organs in abdomen; emotional upsets as above. Both types are often associated, with the latter group of causes, mostly.

Irregular or continuous bleeding: trouble associated with a pregnancy (probably not recognized yet); pessaries and intra-uterine contraceptive devices, sometimes; tumor, either harmless or important; metropathia.

An acute illness, say influenza, may bring a period on before its time; so may excessive exercise.

Mistake: bleeding from urinary or rectal passages, for instance from piles or a caruncle.

Treatment: The cause must, of course, be dealt with by doctor, urgently if heavy bleeding is occurring at the time. General measures: rest in bed during heavy bleeding, but active exercise between times. Any causes for worry should be dealt with; the harassed young mother should break the physical and nervous tension by an hour or two of sleep or rest in the middle of the day.

Note:

High blood pressure and heart disease are not now considered to be causes of excessive bleeding, and anemia is more likely to be an effect of the blood loss rather than a cause.

Bleeding after the Menopause   [A Ch: S, U]

Always calls for advice from doctor.

Causes

Menopause not really complete. There should have been a clear year without periods or age be over 55 years.

Tumor, harmless or cancerous. *Important.*

Infection of vagina or uterus.

Bleeding from rectum, mistaken for vaginal bleeding (piles, etc.).

Rubbing by a pessary.

Blood disorders (*rare*).
Medicines containing estrogen.

Metropathia Hemorrhagica [Ch: S, 6]
Usually in the few years before the menopause, not invariably.
Identification: Irregular bleeding, sometimes preceded by missed period.
Bleeding is always painless, lasts 2–8 weeks.
Treatment: Doctor necessary.

See also general treatment for excessive or abnormal bleeding (above).

Fibroids [Ch: S, 2]
Medical name: Fibromyomata.
Common, harmless tumors of the womb, usually several, and may grow enormous.
Age: 35–45 years, most commonly women that have not had children.
Identification: Increasing loss at periods which are regular but may be prolonged: "flooding" on second and third days; sensation of weight in pelvis; frequency of passing water in the day; varicose veins may be worse; anemia.
Treatment: Operation, if causing excessive bleeding.

Polyp of the Womb [Ch: S, 1]
Harmless pea-sized lumps in the womb.
Identification: Excessive bleeding at periods, discharge between periods, or after the menopause. Occasional abdominal pain.
Treatment: Curettage (doctor).

Cancer of the Genital Tract [Ch: SU]
Not as common as formerly, far more effectively treated, and far more easily detected.
Main warnings: All of these can have perfectly simple explanations, but it is wise to be on the safe side after 40, and report: irregular bleeding or discharge, abdominal swelling.
"Pap" smear: A method of checking against certain cancers, named

after a Dr. Papanicalaou, who introduced it. A scraping of the cells inside the vagina is examined microscopically, and normal and abnormal can be distinguished.

Other methods of early diagnosis used by doctors are with new optical instruments, and curetting.

Prolapse [Ch: S]

A common and awkward condition in which the vagina, and sometimes the womb also, protrudes through the vaginal entrance between the legs.

Causes

Childbirth, because of weakening of the supporting ligaments and muscles, often after an easy labor. But it may also occur in those who have not had a child.

Weakening of supports due to advancing years in older women. Family tendency.

Factors Which Make Prolapse Worse

Chronic cough; heavy lifting; straining on the toilet; extra physical work (e.g. nursing sick relative); early pregnancy; small polyp or fibroid in the womb.

Identification: ALL SYMPTOMS IMMEDIATELY AND COM-PLETELY RELIEVED BY LYING DOWN. Feeling of fullness in vagina, or of "something coming out"; dragging or "bearing down" sensations; frequent passing of water, at first only in the daytime, later at night also; difficulty in passing water, made worse by straining; escape of urine on laughing, etc.; difficulty in completing bowel movement; discharge; low backache—never felt in bed or on getting up.

Treatment: By doctor. Pessary temporarily. Operation.

Outlook: Operation very satisfactory, and safe.

Chronic Cervicitis [Ch: S]

Chronic mild infection of the lining of the neck of the womb, usually so slight as to produce no symptoms.

Identification: Discharge of mucus and pus: low backache only slightly relieved by rest; aching in pelvis and legs; bleeding and discomfort after intercourse occasionally; period pain; excessive periods; irritable bladder. All symptoms tend to be worse before the periods.

Treatment: Varies according to severity of condition. Cauterization and minor surgical procedures.

Chronic infection of the lining of the womb gives similar symptoms and needs a doctor's care.

Erosion of the Cervix [Ch: S]

A change in the type of cell lining the neck of the womb, not necessarily ulcerated.

Identification: May be no symptoms; or discharge, perhaps blood-stained; or bleeding after intercourse or bowel movements; backache; vague discomfort.

Treatment: Cauterization by doctor.

Low Backache in Women [Ch: S]

(See also Back Section.)

There is no doubt that:

Low backache is commoner in women than men.

It is always worse before a period.

It often dates from pregnancy.

This has led to the idea that the trouble lies with the genital organs, but it is more likely due to the weaker muscles and ligaments that women have, and their stretching, etc., during pregnancy, followed by extra physical work, plus lack of sleep, and anxiety, which always underline any physical disability.

Causes in the Genital Tract

(Never localized in one spot, always in the middle or equally on both sides.)

Prolapse or bad position of the womb: may cause backache by dragging on the ligaments. *Immediately better on lying down.*

Swelling in abdomen: anything from a baby to cancer may strain the supporting back muscles or press on the nerves, in which case the pain sometimes goes down the leg.

Before periods, so common as to be normal. More marked in premenstrual tension.

Causes Elsewhere

Muscle and ligament disorders (fibrositis, strains, rheumatism): always worse before periods or during pregnancy, sometimes worse in bed. Pain tends to be in a circumscribed area and the place tender.

Bone and joint troubles. Pain and tenderness in one area, sometimes going down the back of the leg. Worse after rest, easing with movement.

Kidney pain.

Rectal trouble.

Treatment: According to cause. In cases without a clear cut cause, life should be reorganized to include definite rest periods.

The Menopause

The change of life, when the periods cease (the menopause) is the counterpart to adolescence; its effects are comparable, and as natural. It may pass without noticeable disturbance, or there may be discomforts, but the end of the change is invariably the beginning of a better life, when dignity, tolerance, serenity, and assurance combine with a period of usually untroubled physical health.

Age: The menopause may occur at any time from 39 to 59, but the average age is around 47. Symptoms may spread over 1 to 5 years, if present at all.

Identification: "Hot flushes," comparable to the easy blushing of the 16-year-old: reddening of face and neck, accompanied by sweating, and followed by a cold shiver, brought on by nervousness, and a hot atmosphere but sometimes occur in bed at night. Headaches, dizzy spells. Moodiness, including depression and crying without much reason, inability to concentrate, grumpiness, loneliness. Variability in appetite, usually an increase. Dyspepsia, flatulence, constipation. Irregular periods, sometimes flooding, sometimes scanty.

None of these disturbances may occur at all, or some may be noticed, not all, and not all the time, but as capriciously as the weather: one day may be fine, the next stormy.

Treatment

General: Have a medical check to eliminate any physical troubles. Avoid middle-aged spread by care over diet. To avoid precipitating a hot flush, do not take alcohol, coffee, seasoned dishes, or very hot baths, and do not go into a hot atmosphere.

Medical: Your doctor may prescribe a sedative, or a hormone replacement may be indicated.

Avoid self-pity and long discussions of your symptoms: the change is a natural and healthful transition period. For completer understanding, ask your doctor's advice.

Fallacies

The menopause does not produce white hair or other signs of aging. It does not produce a middle-aged spread unless you eat more, but there is a tendency for the figure to thicken at the waist and shoulders proportionately and for the breasts to become smaller. There is no loss of femininity, although the facial hair may become slightly more noticeable.

It does not mean the end of sexual desire or intercourse. There may be a temporary diminution in desire, but afterwards sexual life can be very satisfactory, untrammeled by fear of pregnancy.

Fertility is not increased at the change; in fact, it is diminished, but because the periods may be irregular, there can be no reliance on the rhythm method, and two to three months without a period do not mean that a pregnancy is impossible.

Contraception

Although either husband or wife may employ family planning precautions, the question is obviously of more intimate concern to the woman, and is therefore dealt with in this section.

Method

Rhythm method: Restriction of intercourse to those times in the monthly cycle when there is little chance of there being an ovum present which could be fertilized. Only applicable, and then not with absolute certainty, when the cycle is very regular. The "safe" time is the seven days before the period, the four days of the flow (medically suitable but esthetically unacceptable to many couples), and the three days following.

Daily taking of the rectal temperature may assist in working out the safe period, but is unreliable, as temperature varies for many reasons.

Interrupted intercourse: Psychologically harmful.

Sponge: Soaked in vinegar or spermicidal solution placed in vagina: easily dislodged, and ineffective.

Male sheath: Relatively efficient, especially if used with a spermicidal jelly. Some diminution of pleasure, and may be difficult for older man.

Douching after intercourse: Has to be absolutely immediate and is useful only if some other method has gone wrong, e.g. sheath broken.

Chemical contraceptives: Pastes, jellies, or suppositories. Effective only if used in conjunction with some other method.

Diaphragm: A rubber device which shuts off the entrance to the womb. Needs expert fitting in the first instance. Usually effective, especially if used with a chemical also.

Intra-uterine device: Appliances fitted inside the womb, for a year at a time. Particularly useful in countries where cheap, reliable, long-term control is required; but many hundreds are in use in this country—with no ill-effects, although some authorities fear that they could damage the lining of the womb.

"The Pill": Oral contraceptives act by preventing the production of an egg, and the bleeding that occurs in women on a course of the pill is not a true period. The pill is taken for 21 days and then stopped for seven days, and this must go on indefinitely. Many millions of women have used these pills for long periods, and no harm has resulted, nor have they been unable to have children when they wanted. Mild troubles sometimes associated with the pill are increase of weight, nausea, and breast discomfort, usually only in the first three months. A few cases have been reported of liver troubles, and clotting in the veins (thrombophlebitis) in women on the pill.

GLOSSARY OF MEDICAL TERMS

For further information, or for terms not listed here, see the Index.

Abdomen, -inal Part of the body between the chest and the pelvis, containing the digestive organs.

Abortion Miscarriage: expulsion of immature baby from the womb before the 28th week of pregnancy.

Abscess A collection of pus.

Accommodation Of the eye: adjustment for seeing at different distances.

Acidosis Disturbance of the acid-base balance of the body: term formerly used for abdominal migraine in children.

Acute Sudden, sharp, often severe; of an illness, not lasting long.

Addison's disease Rare disorder characterized by weakness, pigmentation of the skin and inside the mouth, and vomiting attacks.

Adhesion Abnormal growing together of tissues, usually after inflammation or injury.

Adolescence, -ent Period between puberty and adult state, around 13 to 18 years.

Adenoids Lymphoid tissue, like that of the tonsil, at the back of the nose and throat.

Adenoma A tumor of glandular tissue. Not malignant.

Adenomatosis Multiple overgrowth of glandular tissue.

Allergen A substance which induces allergic symptoms.

Allergy Sensitivity to certain substances which do not affect most other people.

Alopecia Loss of hair, baldness.

Amenorrhea Absence of menstrual periods.

Analgesic Drug to reduce sensitivity to pain.

Anemia A condition in which the blood contains less hemoglobin than normal, and/or fewer red corpuscles.

Aneurysm A weak, bulging place in an artery, often the aorta, the main pipe from the heart, or a brain artery. Symptoms are those of pressure on the surrounding organs.

Angina Literally a choking sensation: *Angina pectoris,* pain and oppression about the heart region; *Angina cruris,* pain in the calf due to obstructed arteries.

Antibiotic A substance which inhibits the multiplication of, or kills some living organisms, especially bacteria, but in some cases viruses or fungi. Many different antibiotics are now used in medicine.

Antibody A protein substance produced by the body, and circulating in the blood, normally concerned with defense against disease-causing agents and with immunity.

Anticoagulant A substance which prevents or delays the clotting of the blood.

Antihistamine A substance which counteracts the effects of histamine in the body: often used in treating allergic conditions.

Antiseptic An agent that destroys, or prevents the growth of, micro-organisms.

Anus The waste outlet of the digestive tract.

Aorta The main trunk of the arterial system, arising from the left ventricle of the heart, curving downwards and descending through the chest into the abdomen.

Apoplexy Stroke or seizure.

Appendicitis Inflammation of the vermiform appendix.

Appendix, vermiform appendix A fingerlike process projecting from the caecum, the first part of the large intestine.

Arteriosclerosis Thickening, hardening, and loss of elasticity of the arterial walls.

Arthritis Inflammation of a joint.

Arthrosis Disorder of a joint, possibly degenerative.

Asthma Bouts of breathing difficulty accompanied by wheezing.

Atabrine Drug, now nearly superseded, used in treating malaria, often producing a yellow staining of the skin: not jaundice.

Bacillus, -i, -ary A type of bacteria all of which are rod-shaped; commonly a cause of one kind of dysentery.

Bacterium, -a, -al Micro-organisms, some of which are the cause of disease, including spherical types, like streptococci and others which are rod-shaped and spiral.

Bile A product of the liver which helps in the digestion of fats.

Bile duct Pipe conveying bile to the duodenum, from the liver.

Biliary colic Pain due to the passage of gallstones along the ducts.

Bilious attack A disordered condition of the liver, but the term is sometimes used loosely to refer to an attack of vomiting from any cause, particularly in a child.

Blepharitis Inflammation of the edges of the eyelids, involving the hair follicles.

Bronchitis Inflammation of the bronchi: the large tubes into which the windpipe divides.

Bunion Inflammation and enlargement round the big toe joint.

Calcium An element whose presence in the body in adequate amounts is essential for bone and tooth development, clotting of the blood, lactation, and other functions.

Callus A thickened, hardened area of the skin.

Cancer An abnormal growth of some of the body cells.

Carbuncle A giant boil, discharging pus through several openings.

Cardiac To do with the heart.

Carminative A medicine to remove gas from the stomach and intestine.

Carpal To do with the wrist.

Cartilage Gristle, constituting part of the skeleton. There are two discs of cartilage inside the knee joint.

Caruncle Any small, fleshy eminence, normal or abnormal. Most common is an urethral caruncle, a small, painful growth at the urethral opening of a female.

Cataract Cloudiness of the lens of the eye.

Catarrh Literally, a flowing down: popularly applied to a persistent blocking or runniness of the nose.

Cathartic A fierce purgative.

Cerebrum, -al The largest part of the brain, comprising areas which control movements, others which receive sensation, and the seat of the higher intellectual functions.

Cervix, -ical The neck; the narrow entrance of the womb.

Chancre A sore that is the first sign of some venereal diseases.

Chiropodist A person qualified to treat minor foot troubles.

Chronic Long drawn out, as opposed to acute.

Circumcision Removal, by cutting round, of the end of the foreskin.

Cirrhosis A chronic liver disorder, with changes in structure.

Colic Painful spasms of any hollow organ, e.g. gallstone colic in the

Colic (*cont'd*)
bile ducts, intestinal colic in the intestine.

Colitis Inflammation of the colon.

Colon The 4–6 feet of large intestine between the small (narrower) intestine and the rectum, or last part, leading to the outlet.

Coma Abnormal deep stupor, resulting from illness or injury.

Conception Fertilization: joining of egg-cell and seed.

Concussion, cerebral concussion Injury to the brain, usually from a fall or blow, causing unconsciousness.

Conductive Of deafness: the fault lying in the transmission of the sound vibrations through the parts of the ear.

Congenital Present at birth.

Conjunctivitis Inflammation of the membrane covering the eye and lining the eyelids.

Constipation Sluggish or infrequent action of the bowels, with hard stools.

Constitution Physical make-up and propensities.

Contagious Readily transmissible from one person to another, possibly indirectly as well as by personal contact: infectious.

Contraceptive Something used to prevent pregnancy.

Convalescence, -ent Period of recovery after illness or operation; literally, becoming strong.

Convulsion Bout of muscular spasms: fit.

Corticosteroid A steroid substance produced by the adrenal gland as a hormone; there are several which are used as medicines.

Debility Physical weakness.

Decongestant Drops or inhalant to clear the nose by making its lining shrink.

Deformity Abnormal shape or distortion of any part of the body.

Delirium Wandering of the mind, and incoherence.

Depilatory A substance used to remove hair.

Dermatitis Inflammation of the skin.

Diabetes, -ic *Diabetes mellitus:* a disorder of the body's dealing with carbohydrates, resulting in excessive sugar in the blood, in turn causing sugar in the urine. *Diabetes insipidus:* a condition in which large volumes of watery urine are passed.

Diagnosis Identification or recognition of a disease or disorder.

Diaphragm A muscular sheet dividing chest from abdomen, important for breathing.

Diathermy Treatment by high frequency current to produce heat in some part of the body.

Dilate Expand.

Disc A round, flat structure, particularly the gristly pads between the vertebrae.

Discharge (noun or verb) An abnormal oozing out or flowing away of material.

Dislocation Displacement of a bone, putting it out of joint.

Distension Being blown out, or swollen up.

Diuretic A substance that increases the production of urine.

Duodenum The part of the small intestine that joins on to the stomach.

Dysentery Various intestinal disorders involving pain and diarrhea.

Dysmenorrhea Painful or difficult menstrual periods.

Dyspepsia Poor digestion: a symptom, not a disease in itself.

Dyspnea Difficulty in breathing.

Eczema Inflammation of the skin, more a symptom than a disease.

Edema Swelling because the tissues contain excessive amounts of fluid.

Enema Injection of fluid into the rectum and colon through the anus, either to wash them out or to introduce a drug.

Enteritis Inflammation of the intestine.

Epilepsy A convulsive disorder.

Enuresis Bed-wetting.

Eruption A breaking out—*on* the skin, or *of* the teeth.

Esophagus Gullet, swallowing tube from mouth to stomach.

Excrescence An outgrowth from the surface.

Expectorate Cough up and get rid of mucus or other material from the throat or lungs.

Expectorant A medicine that eases expectoration.

Exudate Fluid oozing out, abnormal.

Felon Whitlow: inflammation with pus in the last joint of a finger.

Fibroid, fibroma Benign tumor of connective tissue, especially of the womb.

Fibrositis Inflammation of connective tissue anywhere in the body, causing pain, but not serious.

Fissure A cleft or slit. *Anal fissure:* a narrow ulcer of the anus.

Fistula An abnormal passage, often near the anus, as a form of abscess.

Flatulence, -ent Excessive gas in the stomach or intestine.

Follicle Small sac in the skin from which a hair arises.

Gastric To do with the stomach.

Gastritis Inflammation of the stomach.

Gastroenteritis Inflammation of the stomach and bowels.

Genital To do with the organs of reproduction.

Goiter Swelling of the thyroid gland.

Graves' disease A disorder of the thyroid gland, with goiter and bulging eyes.

Growth Normal increase in stature; abnormal increase in some tissue forming a swelling or tumor, harmless or malignant, sometimes called a new growth.

Heartburn Burning sensation behind the breast bone associated with dyspepsia.

Hemoglobin The iron-containing red pigment of the blood which is the vehicle for oxygen for the tissues.

Hemophilia A rare hereditary disease in which the blood fails to clot.

Hemorrhage Bleeding.

Hemorrhoids Piles, enlarged veins around the back passage.

Hernia Rupture, protrusion out of its normal site, of an organ or part of it, especially of a loop of intestine.

Hives Itching rash, resembling that produced by stinging nettles; urticaria.

Hormone A chemical substance secreted by an endocrine gland which, circulating in the blood, stimulates or inhibits the activity of other glands.

Hypertension High blood pressure.

Hyperthyroidism Overactivity of the thyroid gland.

Hypothyroidism Underactivity of the thyroid gland.

Idiopathic Of a disease; without recognizable cause.

Immunity Condition of being resistant to injury, particularly from bacteria.

Immunization Making a person resistant to infection by a certain organism, usually by inoculation or vaccination, with dead or attenuated organisms.

Incontinence Inability to control escape of urine or stools; lack of sexual restraint.

Infection Invasion of the body of a micro-organism or virus, causing illness.

Infectious Readily transmitted from person to person, with or without contact: contagious.

Infertility Difficulty, but not proven absolute inability in having a child.

Inflammation Defensive reaction of the tissues to injury or irritation, chemical, bacterial, or mechanical.

Influenza An acute infectious illness with fever, and respiratory or gastro-intestinal symptoms: grippe.

Insidious Of the mode of onset of an illness: gradual, almost imperceptible.

Involuntary Not under the control of the will.

Jaundice Yellowness of skin and whites of the eyes from the presence of bile pigment: various causes.

Kyphosis Humpback, or exaggeration of the normal slight backward bulge of the spine.

Lactation The function of producing milk.

Larynx The organ of voice, a gristly box at the top of the wind pipe, noticeable as the Adam's apple.

Laryngitis Inflammation of the larynx.

Leukemia Cancer of the blood.

Lumbago Pain or aching low in the back: Latin *lumbus,* loin.

Malaise Discomfort; uneasy, ill feeling.

Malaria A common tropical disease spread by mosquitoes, characterized by fever, chills, and a tendency to relapse.

Manipulation Treatment in which the parts are moved by handling by the operator.

Massage Methodical rubbing, kneading, and pressing on the bare skin as treatment.

Membrane Thin, soft, pliable covering of internal structures, analogous to the skin outside.

Meningitis Inflammation of the coverings of the brain or spinal cord.

Menopause The change of life when the monthly periods cease permanently.

Micturition The passing of urine.

Mitral stenosis Narrowing of the hole from the left atrium to the left ventricle of the heart, due to deformity of the mitral valve.

Mucus, -ous A viscid fluid secreted by the membranes lining the nose and respiratory system, the mouth and digestive tract, etc.

Myalgia Pain or tenderness in the muscles.

Nasal To do with the nose.

Neonate, -al Newborn infant.

Nephritis Inflammation of the kidney: Bright's disease.

Neurosis, -otic A psychological disorder.

Nevus Birthmark.

Node A knob, especially of lymphoid tissue: a lymph gland.

Nodule, -ar A small knob or knot.

Obesity Fatness, corpulence.

Obstruction Blocking of a passage in the body, thus interfering with its function, for instance, intestinal obstruction.

Osteoarthritis, osteoarthrosis A chronic disorder involving the joints.

Otitis Inflammation of the ear.

Ovary Gland in women that produces the ova or egg cells.

Ovarian cyst Cyst of the ovary, single or multiple, producing obvious swelling of the abdomen: harmless or cancerous.

Ovum, -a A female reproductive cell, egg cell.

Palpitation Sensation in the chest.

Pancreas Gland attached to the duodenum; it produces insulin and one of the digestive juices.

Parasite An organism that lives at the expense of a host.

Paroxysm A bout or periodic attack of symptoms, e.g. pain or cough.

Pelvis Basin of bone containing the lower abdominal organs.

Pellagra Disorder due to deficiency of niacin, part of the vitamin B complex.

Penicillin One of a group of antibiotics, made by molds, which inhibit the growth of certain disease-producing organisms.

Peptic To do with digestion.

Peptic ulcer Ulcer in the stomach, duodenum or esophagus.

Perceptive Of deafness: the fault lying in the receiving part of the hearing apparatus in the inner ear.

Peritonitis Inflammation of the membranes covering the abdominal organs: serious.

Physiotherapy Treatment by massage, electricity, and mechanical means: physical therapy.

Piles See **Hemorrhoids.**

Placenta The flat, spongy disc in the womb by which the developing baby gets its nourishment: afterbirth.

Pleurisy Inflammation of the membrane covering the lung.

Pneumonia Inflammation of the lungs, usually acute.

Poliomyelitis Inflammation of the gray matter of the spinal cord by a virus.

Polyp A tumor on a stalk, commonly in the nose, womb, or rectum.

Precancerous Tending to lead on to cancer if untreated.

Precipitate To trigger off or hasten the appearance of an illness or symptom.

Precordial In the area over the heart.

Premature Of a baby: born before

fully developed, or before the full term of pregnancy has been completed.

Prolapse Protrusion or downward displacement from its normal position of an organ or part of one.

Prostate A gland concerned with the sexual functions in the male, wrapped round the urethra where it leaves the bladder.

Puberty Period in life when sex organs mature and become capable of functioning: around 12–15 years in girls, 13–16 in boys in temperate climates.

Pulsating Throbbing or beating in rhythm with the pulse.

Pulse Rhythmical thrust felt over an artery, as it expands in time with the heart beat; the radial artery in the wrist and the carotid in the neck are commonly used to examine the pulse.

Purgative A medicine to cause the bowels to act: cathartic.

Pus Product of inflammation, liquid to creamy in consistency, usually yellowish.

Pustule Pimple filled with pus.

Pyelitis Inflammation of a part of the kidney, its pelvis.

Raynaud's disease Disorder of the circulation, especially of the fingers.

Rectum, -al Last, lowest part of the large intestine.

Reflex An automatic, involuntary response to a stimulus, e.g blinking if something is waved near the eyes.

Refraction, error of Condition in which the eye does not focus perfectly due to a fault in the shape of the eyeball or of the lens of the eye.

Regurgitation Coming back of food or drink to the mouth.

Respiration, -atory Breathing.

Rhesus factor A substance found in the red blood cells of the rhesus monkey and about 85% of hu-

Rhesus (*cont'd*)
mans, the remaining 15% being termed Rh negative.

Rhinitis Inflammation of the lining of the nose.

Rhinorrhea Watery running of the nose.

Rupture See **Hernia**.

Salmonella A genus of bacteria some of which cause food poisoning.

Sciatica Pain low in the back and running down the back of the thigh.

Scoliosis Lateral curvature of the spine.

Sebum Fatty secretion of the glands of the skin.

Sedative A calming agent, maybe a medicine.

Semen Fluid which contains the sperm or seed.

Senile To do with growing older.

Serum The watery portion of the blood left from clotting. Serum from an immune animal is sometimes used to treat an infection.

Shingles Herpes zoster: illness due to a virus, with blistering rash along the course of a nerve.

Spasm An involuntary, sudden movement, or a feeling of pain or other sensation due to it.

Sperm Male germ cell, that which fertilizes the ovum.

Spermicidal Causing the death of sperm.

Sphygmomanometer Instrument for measuring the blood pressure.

Sputum Material produced from throat and breath passages.

Staphyloccus, -i Genus of bacteria commonly causing illness, including one form of food poisoning.

Sterile Unable to reproduce; or free from living micro-organisms.

Steroids Group of organic compounds including sex hormones, Vitamin D, bile acids, and adrenal hormone.

Stertorous Of breathing, loud and labored.

Streptococcus, -i A genus of bacteria, some of which are dangerous disease-producers. Commonly present in sore throat.

Streptomycin An antibiotic used in tuberculosis, among other conditions.

Stress Mental or physical strain.

Stroke Sudden, severe attack: seizure; usually due to cerebral disaster, clot or bleeding of an artery in the brain.

Suppository Medicine in semi-solid vehicle for putting into the rectum or vagina.

Symptom An untoward change in the body which may indicate disease.

Syndrome A group of symptoms running together.

Tendon Strap of connective tissue joining a muscle to a bone.

Thrombophlebitis Inflammation and clotting in a vein.

Thyroid Endocrine gland in the neck that controls the speed of various bodily processes.

Tic Habit spasm: muscular twitch usually in face, neck, or shoulder.

Tonsil Small lump of lymphoid tissue in the back of the mouth: one on each side.

Tranquilizer A drug that acts on the emotional state and calms and makes more amenable those who are disturbed or overactive.

Tuberculosis A disease caused by a bacillus, usually affecting the respiratory system.

Tumor A swelling or enlargement or new growth of any kind.

Ulcer An open sore on the skin or a membrane.

Umbilicus Navel.

Urethra Pipe for urine from the bladder to the outside.

Urinalysis Chemical and other examination of the urine.

Urinate Pass water.

Uterus, -ine Womb.

Vaccination Inoculation to produce immunity, especially against smallpox.

Vagina Passage from womb to outside.

Varicose Of a vein, tortuous and dilated.

Venereal disease Disease acquired through sexual connection.

Vertebra, -al One of the 33 small bones of the spine.

Vertigo Giddiness, disorientation in space.

Vesicle Blister.

Virus, -al Disease-producing agent smaller than the bacteria.

Vitamins Accessory food substances necessary in minute amounts for full health.

Weal Roundish, red or white swelling in the skin, itching: seen in hives.

INDEX